CHILDREN IN THE WHITE HOUSE

CHILDREN

IN THE

WHITE HOUSE

Christine Sadler

G. P. Putnam's Sons
New York

Contents

❧❧❧❧❧❧❧❧

Contents

CONTENTS

THE JOHNSON SISTERS
Two Dark-eyed Charmers

CHILDREN IN THE WHITE HOUSE

Foreword

❧→⟫→⟫⟪←⟪←

In all, 176 children have lived in the White House. Only five of our Presidents—Polk, Pierce, Buchanan, McKinley, and Harding—lived in a childless White House. Three other Presidents—Washington, Madison, and Jackson—had no children of their own but attained fatherhood status by marriage and adoption.

Washington was an attentive father to his wife's two children and, as President, a proud and loving grandfather to Nellie and "Little Wash" Custis, whom he adopted "to rear as my own" at the death of their father. He found time also to counsel their two sisters, who visited in the executive mansions in both New York and Philadelphia but are not included among the 176.

Madison had a handsome although wayward stepson, who called him Father but who added financial and personal embarrassments to the former President's later years by serving terms in debtor prisons. This son caused his mother, the beautiful Dolley, many a heartache and money worry.

Jackson adopted one of his wife's many nephews and reared several other boys. Three children were born in the White House during his years there, and he walked the floor with them when they were teething or had colic. He deeded a young slave to one of them and liked no job better than that of a baby-sitter. One of the most festive Christmas parties ever given in the old mansion was for the "children of President Jackson's household": six youngsters, four of whom

called him Uncle Jackson, two of whom knew him as Grandfather.

The number 176 is somewhat arbitrary. It excludes two of
the Custis children but does include President Eisenhower's
four grandchildren, even though their father maintained his
own home nearby and took trouble to see that 1600 Pennsylvania Avenue never was their real address. But they were in
and out of the White House so often, had so much fun there—
at birthday parties and Saturday afternoon movies—it truly
seemed more accurate to include them.

It excludes, among others, John Quincy Adams, who was
abroad all the time his father was President, and his brother
Charles, who was the first but unfortunately not the last of
the Presidential sons to hasten his death by drink and who
might not have been welcome. The first child to live in the
present White House was Charles' little daughter Susanna,
whose grandmother, Abigail, brought "the mite in a black
dress" on to Washington with her after stopping in New
York to see Charles—then near death—en route to the new
capital city.

Franklin D. Roosevelt's thirteen grandchildren, all there
were at the time, stayed in the White House for his fourth
inaugural, but only three of them—daughter Anna's children
—actually lived there and so are included in the 176. By the
same rule, none of William Henry Harrison's ten children is
included because not one of them was in Washington during
his thirty days as President, although two grandsons were.
And, naturally, the second family of seven sired by John Tyler
are not included in the number, because all were born after
his Presidency.

This book, although it focuses on the 176 children before
mentioned, does not limit itself to them because one of its
aims is to tell about the Presidents as fathers without particularly rating them as such. That meant writing about all their

children, as well as about many of their grandchildren.

This book was written for pleasure and with the hope that it makes White House family life as interesting to others as I found it to be. It follows a traditional and chronological pattern and, insofar as I know, puts all the Presidential children in one volume for the first time.

It seems to me that the Presidents who had to cope with children while endeavoring to run the country had the happiest administrations despite their added problems. Theodore Roosevelt, that most devoted of fathers, assuredly had his problems with daughter Alice, but think what his terms would have lacked in glamour without her.

There is no rule by which to measure what the White House "does" to children or by which to determine whether a President's children obtain more sadness than gladness from his tenure in the highest office. It is obvious, however, that tenure in the White House sets the children apart and marks them forever. Some react one way, and some another; but by and large they seem to have become basically the same people they would have been in any event.

Taft "accepted" the Presidency not because he wanted it but because of what he thought it would mean to the future of his children and their children. Van Buren's sons and later Tyler's neglected their own careers to work for their fathers'. Margaret Truman refused to be changed by the White House years and went on with her singing, promising herself only that she would not become engaged during her father's Presidency because during that time she could not be sure who liked her better than her position.

Recent occupants think that because of TV and expanded communications they have it harder than earlier occupants, but Nellie Custis had a rigid schedule, too. John Adams, the Vice President, commented that Nellie's sister Martha, not a regular member of the Presidential household, had much

more color in her cheeks because Nellie had to attend so
many parties and sing for Congressmen. Nellie herself could
not wait to return to peaceful Mount Vernon and get out of
cities, but she longed for those cities again when her own
children needed educating.

Garfield's son had to wait a week to talk to his Presidential
father about a budding romance which changed his ideas
about education. Franklin D. Roosevelt's sons had to make
appointments to discuss personal matters with their father.

The happiness of White House children is not ensured by
national law. Monroe's oldest daughter, wishing to be separated from her family, died alone in Paris. Wilson's daughter
Margaret went to India to find the peace which was impossible for her in America. The first divorce in a Presidentially
connected family was that of Martha Washington's oldest and
most beautiful granddaughter; the first suicide was that of
John Quincy Adams' son. White House children are not immune to tragedy any more than other children are. Both their
joys and their sorrows, however, seem heightened by having
lived in the President's house.

In addition to credits given in the book, my special thanks
for aid in research go to Mrs. B. K. Nehru and the Honorable
Francis B. Sayre for material about Margaret Wilson's life in
India; to Margaret Patterson and Mrs. Herbert P. Richards
for new material about and pictures of Andrew Johnson's
family; to Margaret Klapthor of the Smithsonian Institution
and James Ketchum, the White House curator, for answering
innumerable queries; to Katharine McCook Knox for gener-
ously sharing much source material; to Virginia Dickins and
the curator of Monticello for help with Jefferson's grandchildren; to the office of Senator Ross Bass for keeping me
supplied with Library of Congress reference books; and to
Richard L. Coe and Ruth Cowan Nash for patiently reading
my raw chapters.

The Custis Children

ALTHOUGH it became fashionable to think of George Washington as a childless President, and to quote the Englishman who said, "Providence denied him children that a nation might call him Father," he in reality established a long and splendid record as father and grandfather. Few if any among our Presidents lavished more attention and advice on their offspring, or worried more about school grades of their young, than he did.

He became a father at the age of twenty-six when he married the rich and charming widow named Martha Custis, who had two small children: John (Jacky or Jack) Parke Custis and Martha (Little Patt or Patsy) Parke Custis. Jacky and Little Patt were four and three years of age when he brought them to live on his rolling acres at Mount Vernon, Virginia, beside the Potomac River. He never called them stepchildren, but "the children." They called him Father.

As Jacky once wrote him, "He best deserves the name of father who acts the part of one. I first was taught to call you by that name. . . . Your goodness (if others had not told me) would always have prevented me from knowing I had lost a parent. I shall always look upon you in this light."

Matching miniatures by Charles Willson Peale show that

Jacky grew into a handsome young man and Little Patt into a lovely young girl who deserved the title of "dark princess" which the servants gave her.

Little Patt was delicate from birth, however. She was a victim of epilepsy, and died of it and tuberculosis before she was seventeen. Washington wept at her death. Because of her he had scheduled many a visit to the health springs of Virginia.

Mrs. Washington was perhaps an overly protective mother and her husband bowed to her wishes in not sending Jacky away to school as soon as he would have a son of his own. The children had tutors, but he believed in the discipline of school. A most practical man, he had scant regard for many Southern schools of the day and would have preferred a Northern school for Jacky. Yet he sent him to the well-recommended Rev. Jonathan Boucher's school for boys at nearby Annapolis, Maryland.

The young Reverend Boucher paid little attention to Washington's letter stressing that he wanted Jacky fitted for "more useful purposes than being a horse racer" and as for accounting, which Washington wished his son to learn, that was for the servants. You could hire that done! The future Father of his country sent the neophyte minister a scathing letter outlining his views that anyone with accounts to keep should know how to keep them.

But by then Jacky had become engaged to sixteen-year-old Eleanor Calvert of the famous Lord Baltimore family. When this news came, Washington rushed to Annapolis and, with the help of young Eleanor, convinced the seventeen-year-old lad that before marriage he needed at least two years in "a strict Northern school."

He then personally escorted Jacky to old King's College in New York City and saw him comfortably settled in, and had the pleasure of a letter from the boy saying he had learned more in two months there than in the two years before. Also, the school's president wrote that Jacky was an excellent student.

After Little Patt's death, however, Jacky did not wish to return and before he was nineteen he and Eleanor married. Mrs. Washington took the newlyweds with her when she went to join her husband at Cambridge, Massachusetts, for the first winter encampment of the Revolutionary War. Jacky was an aide to his father that winter, but he saw little action during the Revolution because both his wife and mother thought that he, as the last of his family, should have a son to succeed him as heir to a considerable fortune before he exposed himself to too many bullets.

He did serve in Virginia's General Assembly, though, and tried to be a good citizen. And his only son was not born until after he had fathered three daughters: Elizabeth, the Betsey of Washington's diaries who later called herself by the then more stylish name of Eliza; Martha, named for her grandmother; and Eleanor, the Nelly of Washington's eight years as President and beyond. Then came George Washington (Little Wash) Parke Custis, the long-awaited son, the pet of the Washingtons for many a year.

Little Wash was only a few months old when General Washington and his victory-bound troops stopped briefly at Mount Vernon—the general's first trip home in seven years—on their way to Yorktown, where the British finally surrendered. Jacky went on with them and contracted camp fever on the battlefield. The general left the scene of victory to be with him when he died at the nearby home of an aunt.

Immediately Washington "adopted to rear as my own" the two youngest children. He adopted them in the sentimental sense and not the legal one, however, and all four children remained with their mother, who married Dr. David Stuart and had many more children, until the Washingtons returned home after the last war prisoners were released and treaties made in 1784. They were delighted that Nelly, almost six, and Little Wash, three and a half, were awaiting them at Mount Vernon.

Washington relished being a grandfather and as he trod his acres planning repairs and improvements his lively and diminutive namesake trudged right behind him. The lad had an amusing new nickname by then. Someone had teased him about not being large enough for a whole wash and said, "You're only one little tub." And Tub his doting grandmother often called him. "Tub is the same clever fellow you left him," she wrote a relative.

Grandpapa ordered him a horse and wrote the man who sent it: "The Horse for little Washington came safe. He finds beauty in every part and, tho' shy at first, he begins now to ride with a degree of boldness which will soon do honor to his horsemanship." "Your young friend is in high health, as full of spirits as an eggshell is of meat," he wrote the Reverend William Gordon.

To his friend G. W. Fairfax he wrote a little later: "The two youngest children of Mr. Custis live with me: the oldest a girl of six years, the other a boy little turned of four. They are both promising children, but the latter is a remarkably fine one and my intention is to give him a liberal education, the rudiments of which shall, if I live, be in my own family."

When the aged Lafayette made his return visit to America in President Monroe's administration he told the by-then forty-three-year-old Tub, a member of his welcoming committee, that he had seen him first on the portico at Mount Vernon. "A very little gentleman with a feather in his hat holding fast to one finger of the good general's remarkable hand, which —so great that hand!—was all, my dear sir, you could well do at the time."

Sister Nelly would have more space in the history books when Grandpapa became President, but Tub ruled the hearts of the Washingtons for many years. "Grandmama always spoiled him," Nelly would claim later. "He was the pride of her heart."

Both were delightful children to look at and have around. Tub was an ingratiating and active lad with blondish wispy hair, gray eyes and the contented smile of a pet. He never needed to vie for attention. Nelly was far less passive.

She was exuberant and given to extremes. She had pretty brown eyes and a mass of dark curls which she detested having combed. Tub had superb good manners, received compliments and pats on the head from all the general's visitors. Nelly, on the other hand, was in constant hot water. Grandmama often accused her of having been born "without a center of gravity." She learned to get the general's attention by holding the last button on his long vest and telling him an engaging story.

Both were precocious but Nelly was the better student. She surprised everybody by learning to "spell perfect," an unusual accomplishment for a girl of her day.

Grandmama, something of an artist on the spinet, was determined Nelly should be an accomplished musician. She made her practice four to five hours daily and was not above thumping knuckles when notes went sour. Next to having her curls combed, Nelly resented the practice hours. Tub said later his earliest memory of his pretty sister was of her "practising and crying, and then practising some more."

Grandpapa sympathized with Nelly at the aging spinet when she longed to be out romping and paid the almost unheard-of sum of $1,000 to get her a grand new harpsichord. It and stacks of music, much of it copied by Grandmama, are at Mount Vernon today.

Nelly was ten and Tub was eight when Grandpapa became President in April, 1789. They rode up the Eastern Seaboard in the carriage with Grandmama to New York, the first capital, about a month later—their departure from Mount Vernon accompanied by many tears and great excitement.

The journey was a pageant of church bells, bonfires, lavish meals and speeches. Gaily uniformed militia troops relayed them from city to city. By the time they reached Philadelphia, Grandmama reported, "The children were very little of being sick" from all the hullabaloo. "Little Wash," she wrote in a letter, "was lost in a maze at the great parade made for us all the way we came."

Grandpapa met them in Elizabeth, New Jersey, took them across the Hudson on the same fine barge designed for his own entry into the city. Cannon boomed as they passed the Battery. Their new home on Cherry Street was "five windows wide, three stories tall" and its raised front stoop had steps up both sides. It was furnished all new for the first First Family in mahogany furniture with scarlet upholstery and drapery.

A townhouse in a bustling city and flush with the street bore no resemblance to the acres of Mount Vernon. Tub and Nelly had some adjusting to do, and Nelly "lost her center of gravity" anew as she flew from window to window to watch the amazing traffic.

As the first children to live in a President's house, Tub and Nelly had the run of three homes, two in New York and one in Philadelphia when it became the second capital city. Nelly was kept on a tighter schedule than Tub, who concerned himself with everything that was going on. He watched while Nelly had her painting lessons and sat in when the President had portraits painted. He visited with the Presidential secretaries, who lived on the upper floor, and especially appreciated David Humphrey's poetry recitations. (Humphrey was quite a versifier. The other secretaries did not care for his readings, but Tub loved them.)

Tub spied on grown-up parties, too, and in his *Recollections* told how happy everybody was when the First Family moved from Cherry Street to a higher ceilinged mansion with French doors and a great view of the Hudson.

The children went to church with the Washingtons every Sunday and on Saturday—barring a real crisis—Grandpapa took them for a ride around Manhattan Island, a dashing distance of fourteen miles.

The Presidential carriage was a treat to behold. Cream-colored and "shaped like a hemisphere," it was painted with cupids and panels depicting the four seasons and was sped over the cobblestones by six matching bays. Outriders on white chargers, plus mounted escorts in uniform, added to the eighteenth-century spectacle, and at times, the President's better-horsed friends saddled their own fine steeds and went along for the rides.

The life around him was much too interesting for Tub to do well in school, and Grandpapa was too busy to realize this until they moved to Philadelphia. Then he was assigned to Nelly's tutor for the hour before breakfast while she attended Grandmama. Being with Grandmama while she readied herself for the day and again for the hour before she went to bed was routine for Nelly. Some of her friends left accounts of how she left their parties to read and sing for Grandmama at night.

Friends of Nelly and Little Wash always were welcome at the President's house. The President, very fond of dancing, loved to watch Nelly and her friends dance, but learned he must remain out of sight or all dancing stopped. This grieved him and Nelly, too. She could not understand why tongues became tied and feet stopped when Grandpapa showed up. She became a true mimic of some of his more pompous friends and delighted him with her takeoffs. "Many people who knew him well never heard him laugh out loud," Nelly said, "but he frequently did."

The President took the children with him to the theater, one of his favorite forms of entertainment, in both capital cities. They loved it when at his entrance the orchestra played "The President's March"—or "Hail Columbia."

In addition to music and painting, Nelly learned French and Italian. She wrote a friend of getting up at 4:45 A.M. to master a long Italian lesson before Grandmama needed her. Her musical talents were a source of pride to both Washingtons and she frequently sang at state dinners. In a letter declining an invitation to tea she wrote she had to sing "for a large company of Congressmen, who like to hear music although they know not one note from another."

During Washington's first term in office the first First Lady wrote, "My grandchildren are very much grown. Nelly is a woman in size and Washington begins to be a sturdy boy."

Grandpapa, slowly becoming aware that his namesake had too much diversion and not enough discipline, put him in the "College of Philadelphia" at age ten—hoping he would acquire good study habits. It did not take the President long, however, to realize that the school was lax in both discipline and study habits.

He considered sending the lad to a "good Northern school" such as Andover, but—knowing his wife would object (or at least thinking so)—he let him continue where he was for two more bad years. Then, in 1796, his wife concurring, he sent Little Wash to the "College of New Jersey" at Princeton, where "order, regularity and a proper regard for morals" were stressed.

Always, though, Little Wash learned more from being with Grandpapa than he did from books or other teachers.

Historian Murray H. Nelligan, who went into Little Wash's unfortunate school days rather deeply, thought today's educators would be appalled by the too-strict, then too-lax routines set for the lad. His immaturity, compared to Grandpapa's age, was immense and his youth was always stressed at discipline times. Unvarying acceptance of his instructors' views also was expected. There was no room, he said, for the boy to formulate opinions of his own. He would defend his position for a while, then give way and become indifferent.

With his turn of mind, which ran to embellishments, he appeared to follow Grandpapa's statements too literally. He would brag to Grandpapa about having written so many letters and when Grandpapa cautioned him not to take too much time from studies, he took everybody off his letter list. He wrote of his friends and when Grandpapa cautioned against making friends too easily he became monastic.

"That the older man was usually right made their arguments all the more stultifying," Nelligan said. Little Wash was much loved, but the man whom he loved most really despaired of him during his adolescence.

However busy he was the President always found some time for Little Wash, and for all three of his wife's granddaughters, for that matter. He took his namesake with him when he went to lay the cornerstone of the permanent Capitol in the new Federal City named Washington. Eliza, the oldest granddaughter, was there, too. It was an impressive ceremony followed by a barbecue and Eliza never forgot how happy Grandpapa seemed that day.

Eliza and her sister Martha visited the Presidential family both in New York and Philadelphia. In the latter city the President took all the children to watch a balloon ascension and to Rickett's Equestrian Circus. Vice-President John Adams, noting the bloom on the cheeks of young Martha—first of the grandchildren to marry—wrote his wife how radiantly healthy she was and ventured the thought that she had seen much more of the out-of-doors than Nelly ever had.

Nelly, lively, lovable and accomplished, was noted for both beauty and sweetness. A foreign visitor wrote, "She plays the piano, she sings, designs better than the usual woman of America or even of Europe" and as for her beauty, "that is perfect." When the Presidential family and Congress resided briefly in Germantown, due to typhus in the capital, she learned to ride horseback. Her grandmother virtually grew up on a pony, but Nelly's schedule had never before included it.

Nelly wrote her friend, Elizabeth Bordley, with whom she would correspond for more than 50 years, "I have learned to ride on horseback and am very delighted with it, believe me. . . . I have spent ten days most agreeably teaching our pretty green pet to sing 'Pauvre Madelon' . . . a master piece of thorough base (in music spelled bass, but I thought base would give you a better idea of his harmonious voice). . . . I forgot to tell you the name of my nag. It is Rozinante. . . ." She signed the letter, "Myself, harum scarum sans souci."

When Eliza, the most beautiful daughter, became eighteen she wrote Grandpapa for his picture as a birthday present, and "as readily as if he had no burdens of state he promptly sent it and indulged himself in a long letter on love and marriage."

"Love is a mighty pretty thing," he wrote her, "but like all other delicious things it is cloying when the first transports of passion begin to subside, which it assuredly will do. . . . Love is too dainty a food to live on *alone,* and ought not to be considered farther than as a necessary ingredient for that matrimonial happiness which results from a combination of causes." Then he advised her not to look for perfect felicity before she consented to wed. "There is no truth more certain than that all our enjoyments fall short of our expectations. . . ." he warned her.

In 1795, when the First Lady's namesake granddaughter married Thomas Peter and went to live in the new Federal City, the First Lady—amazed at how rapidly time was passing —made Nelly go spend the winter with her own mother, sisters and stepsisters and brothers so she would get to know them better.

"I have gone through the greatest trial I ever experienced —parting with my beloved grandmother," Nelly wrote Miss Bordley.

Grandmama sent her some attire for her first ball and wrote: "I think your chemise will look much better with a handkerchief than without. Ask your cousin to assist in dressing you when you go to the ball. I wish you to look as neat as possible, and let all your things be of one piece. My love to you and I wish you may have as much pleasure as you expect." Then she warned, "Going to these places one always expects more pleasure than they realize after the matter is over."

Before her birthday she wrote Miss Bordley, "Tomorrow I will be 17 and now will be Miss Custis. From today, I have decided, I am to be called Eleanor, as Nelly is so extremely homely in my opinion." In another letter, replying to the nationwide rumors that she and Charles Carroll (of *The* Carrolls) were in love, she asked her friend to believe no rumors of a romance except from her own self. This time she signed her name E. P. Custis and below it wrote "alias Deborah Bridget Muckleweaver Tackabout, à votre service."

She wrote Grandmama about the ball and revealed her intention to remain a spinster. The President, no doubt intrigued at the thought of effervescent Nelly as an old maid, wrote her not to be too sure about that and gave her some advice on how to spot real love when it came her way:

"Men and women feel the same inclinations to each other *now*," he assured her, "as they have always done and will continue to do until there is a new order of things. . . . In the composition of the human frame there is a good deal of inflammable matter, however dormant it may lie for a time. . . . When the fire is beginning to kindle and your heart growing warm propound these questions to it: Who is this invader? Have I competent knowledge of him? Is he a man of good character, a man of sense? For, be assured, a sensible woman can never be happy with a fool. . . ."

Nelly was a beautiful eighteen and Little Wash, still a struggling student at Princeton, was sixteen when Grandpapa's eight years in office ended and the family—except for the student—headed homeward. It took several days to pack and Washington became so irked at his wife's and Nelly's constant reminders not to forget some of their treasures he wrote Tobias Lear:

"On the one hand I am called upon to remember the Parrot, on the other to remember the dog. For my own part, I should not pine if both were forgot." The parrot belonged to his wife, the dog to Nelly. They made the journey home in the carriage while the tired ex-President rode happily alone in the phaeton.

The journey to Mount Vernon was tedious and tiring, took seven days, and even vibrant Nelly was wilted by it. Reaching the new Federal City, the family dined in midafternoon with Eliza and husband and proceeded on past the present White House, then under construction, to the home of Martha and Thomas Peter in Georgetown, where they spent the night.

Nelly hastened to write Elizabeth Bordley her joy at being home again, "When I look at this noble river and all the beautiful prospects around, I pity all those who live in cities—for surely the country life is the most rational and happy of any. I can hardly realize Grandpapa is no longer in office. . . . If it is a dream I hope never to awaken from it."

Nelly was to change her mind about country life before she died—but that was after Mount Vernon was no longer home to her. Little Wash evidently wished he were home, too. His grades showed no improvement. After writing Grandpapa how perfect he was in Roman history and French, he flunked some midyear exams—and received no comfort from home. In fact, Grandpapa, in a peeve that was unlike him, wrote the president of the college a letter which would influence (unjustly, some think) historians' estimates of the boy far into the future.

"From his infancy," he wrote, "I have discovered [in him] an almost unconquerable disposition to indolence in everything that did not tend to his amusements. . . ."

After that, for reasons never fully known, the lad's days at Princeton ended most abruptly. "Mr. George W. Custis having been guilty of various acts of meanness [sic] and irregularity, and having endeavored in various ways to lessen the authority and influence of the faculty was suspended and ordered to leave the college," read the faculty minutes.

Little Wash, age sixteen, was disgraced in the eyes of Grandpapa and the fact that five years later students would burn Nassau Hall in protest against "oppression" at Princeton was no help to him at all! The daughter of Little Wash said many years later, "We never knew why he left Princeton."

Grandpapa put him on the strictest of written-out home schedules, every hour accounted for, and pondered what to do with him. Dr. Douglas Southall Freeman wrote, "He [Washington] must have concluded that for him the management of boys was indeed more of a challenge than the management of men."

Enforced order and regularity, however, had no effect on the teen-ager. Belief in his system shaken, Washington appealed to the boy's stepfather, Dr. Stuart. "He will forget what he does know, so inert is his mind," he wrote.

St. John's College in Annapolis had an excellent reputation and so in February Grandpapa packed the lad off there with a note outlining his shortcomings and saying, "His friends (and none more than myself) are extremely desirous that his education should be liberal and polished."

Almost seventeen, handsome, wealthy and likable, Little Wash received a warm welcome from the townspeople but his family was shocked to hear before long rumors of his engagement. This time Mrs. Stuart, his mother, was sent to talk sense to her son, who claimed he only had told the girl he would like to marry her if he were old enough.

Coldness fell between Grandpapa and his namesake and letters from Annapolis went unanswered despite pleas from the culprit, who finally provoked an answer by asking whether he was expected to return to the school next autumn. Washington wrote, "The question, 'I would thank you to inform me whether I leave it entirely, or not, so that I may pack accordingly,' really astonishes me! For it would seem as if *nothing* I could say to you made more than a momentary impression."

That summer, however, Little Wash cajoled Grandpapa into permitting him to shoot deer in the Mount Vernon deer park, and crawled back into Grandpapa's good graces. He took a great interest in Washington's desire to develop a good domestic breed of sheep, and he began to look at the lands he himself would inherit. Grandpapa never mentioned returning to school to him, telling Dr. Stuart he considered it utterly useless to pursue a course to which the boy was totally indifferent.

Nelly did not marry Charles Carroll despite nationwide rumors and her brother's wishes, but on February 22, 1799—the general's last birthday—was married to Lawrence Lewis, Grandpapa's favorite nephew, with all her sisters and family in attendance.

Delighted with the wedding Grandpapa gave the couple 2,000 of his nearby acres for a handsome still-standing home to be called Woodlawn. William Thornton, architect of the Capitol, made the plans. Nelly's first child, named Martha Elizabeth, was born at Mount Vernon that November.

The following month Little Wash and his brother-in-law were in lower Virginia inspecting Custis farms when Grandpapa died unexpectedly from a serious cold which turned into pneumonia. The Lewises continued to live at Mount Vernon until Grandmama's death in 1802 and, of course, so did Little Wash.

In his will Washington left Mount Vernon (at the death of his wife) to Bushrod Washington, a nephew, and made bequests to his other nephews.

"Next [came] his children—his and Martha's—for her grandchildren had been in every sense like their very own, 'more especially . . . the two whom we have reared from their earliest infancy.' "

To Nelly and husband the 2,000 acres, together with the mill, distillery, and other houses and improvements on the premises. To Little Wash 1,200 acres on Four Mile Run, adjoining an acreage the lad would inherit from his mother, and Square 21 in the new Federal City.

Executors, including Little Wash (when he reached twenty-one) were instructed to sell the remaining part of the estate and divide the money into 23 equal parts. Full parts went to Eliza Law, Martha Peter and Nelly Lewis. Little Wash shared a part with two nephews.

When Mrs. Washington died she left her grandson a large portion of her furniture, silver, china, and family portraits, her famous iron money chest, the general's desk, and a fourth of her bottled wine. He tried unsuccessfully to buy Mount Vernon, but bought much from remaining furnishings and livestock auctioned at two sales. He bid recklessly for relics closely associated with Washington—such as his coach, war tents of the Revolution, flags of battles. He owed $4,545 when the sales ended, but never regretted the debt it took him years to pay off.

Little Wash crammed his possessions into a small 4-room

brick cottage on 1,000 acres he owned immediately across the Potomac from the Federal City. There he built on the highest bluff an imposingly pillared yellow mansion called Arlington, and there it still stands, surrounded today by Arlington National Cemetery.

Remarkably enough, each of the four Custis grandchildren still has a home standing in Washington or nearby: *Arlington,* where Little Wash lived until his death, is now the Custis-Lee Mansion and belongs to the National Park Service. *Woodlawn,* sold for $25,000 in Nelly's lifetime, is administered by the National Historic Trust and Council; *Tudor Place,* the gorgeous yellow mansion which Martha and Thomas Peter built in Georgetown in 1805, still is occupied by their descendants. The lovely but more modest Federal home in which Eliza and Thomas Law first lived is the community center of an extensive new urban redevelopment project in southwest Washington. The much finer home they built on Capitol Hill later was razed to make room for the second office building needed by the House of Representatives.

Little Wash perhaps never became the man the general wished him to be, but Grandpapa surely would have approved of the Arlington sheep he developed and his lifetime of work in behalf of American agriculture. Some call him the one-man forerunner of the Agricultural Extension Service. He held famous sheep shearings at his Arlington Spring, breaking out the war tents to cover long tables piled with food for contestants and onlookers.

He wrote some of the very first plays with an American background and they delighted audiences in several cities. One of them was *Pocahontas.* Another, *The Indian Prophecy,* started a continuing vogue for Indian plays. Joseph Jefferson had the lead in *The Rail Road,* one of his operettas. Another operetta was *The 8th of January, or Hurrah for the Boys of the West*. It extolled Andrew Jackson, the first President he really admired after Grandpapa.

An ardent Federalist, like all his family except Eliza, he deplored Jefferson and all his followers. He became a Fourth of July institution whose orations were widely attended. He devoted his life to pushing agriculture, keeping the memory of Washington fresh, and supporting controversial causes such as the Irish Revolution for Independence and freedom of the press.

He married Mary Lee Fitzhugh and their only child, Mary Anne Randolph Custis, married young Lieutenant Robert E. Lee. Arlington became Lee's home when stationed in Washington and always at Christmastime. All his children were born there. When Little Wash died he left the home to his oldest grandson, Custis Lee—and it was at Arlington that General Lee made his fateful decision to cast his lot with the Confederacy. Arlington was seized as a military installation during the Civil War and its grounds became a Federal graveyard.

Beautiful Eliza's later years were highly dramatic. At nineteen she had married Thomas Law, an eccentric Englishman twice her age and by him had a daughter also named Eliza. Then when he was on a trip to England she left him and took her daughter with her. He obtained custody of the daughter, however, in the ensuing divorce.

Almost all that is known for sure of Eliza's divorced years is in letters written over a period of 20 years to David Bailie Warden, who was attached to the U. S. Embassy in Paris.

Eliza admitted to a desperate love for a Frenchman named De Greff, a refugee from the French Revolution, and hoped to marry him—perhaps in the White House, an idea with which she said President and Mrs. Madison were in full accord. De Greff went to France to recover some of his property and never returned. After that, Eliza never again wrote Warden about being willing to follow the man she loved to the ends of the world, but she did reveal the wish that she had gone to France (a country she loved), made contact with the Lafayette family and remained there.

Her life was a lonely one indeed. The daughter was not permitted to live with her, but she followed her to Philadelphia when she went to school there, lived near her, dressed her for parties and wrote how wonderful she was—but refused all invitations for herself. The daughter married Lloyd Rogers of Baltimore and again Eliza went to live near her. She wrote heartbrokenly of young Eliza's death at age twenty-six and of her joy in being permitted to keep her three grandchildren with her in Georgetown, where she rented a home. Lafayette visited her there and she reported he thought the children as adorable as she did.

Her happiness was short-lived, however, because Rogers remarried and took the children away. (His second wife was President Monroe's granddaughter.)

Nelly, after a lapse marked by illness and the deaths of her first two children, resumed her correspondence with her school friend Elizabeth Bordley. At the time she was the mother of two small daughters named Parke and Agnes Friere and a six-month-old son Lorenzo—and changing her mind about country living. "Oh, for a house on Chestnut Street," she wrote, thinking of schooling for her children. When she later sent Parke and Friere to school in Philadelphia her friend kept an eye on them.

Nelly kept up her music and played for the wedding when Little Wash's daughter married Robert E. Lee. She shunned White House events, because she did not like the politics of its inmates, and was resilient when misfortune struck her family, as it did with regularity.

Friere died in her early teens and Parke married George W. Butler, a military man of whom Nelly disapproved. A third daughter, Angela, married a New Orleans lawyer, Charles Magill, whom she adored. When Angela died very young he sent his two sons to school in Georgetown so they could be near their grandmother. Lorenzo, the only son, went to school at Yale and Princeton, took a New England wife and more than fulfilled his mother's hopes for him.

After her husband's death, Nelly went to live with Lorenzo at Audley in western Virginia and died there in 1852. Lorenzo sold beautiful Woodlawn for $25,000 "as best for his children."

The namesake granddaughter Martha had perhaps the happiest life of all: a successful marriage, no money worries, and a family which still flourishes. Her husband was the son of Georgetown's first mayor, who was also a rich merchant. Her sizable inheritance from Washington she put into expansions for Tudor Place, where her descendants still live, and she gave her three daughters the remarkable names of Columbia Washington, America Pinckney, and Britannia Wellington. Her three sons, all older, were named John Parke Custis, George Washington, and Daniel Parke Custis.

The children and grandchildren of Martha, Little Wash, and Nelly were good friends and constant visitors, but there is no record that they visited with Eliza's daughter.

John Adams's Flock of Four

ONE A FUTURE PRESIDENT

EVERY time John Adams, a chunky but nonetheless handsome member of the Continental Congress sitting in Philadelphia, heard from his letter-writing wife in faraway Massachusetts a pleasant family picture formed in his mind. Or so he wrote her.

He saw himself and her, two children on either side, walking the fields of their farm at Braintree—"Charles in one hand, Tommy in the other, Nabby on your right and John upon my left." This vision sustained him during spells of homesickness and was sharply before him as he posted a canister of scarce tea to help them through the risky medical venture of "taking the smallpox."

His wife, the incomparable Abigail, had not intended him to know about this bit of daring but such important news seeped through to him via couriers who kept the road hot between Boston and the City of Brotherly Love. Along with the tea came a note from John Hancock, president of the Congress, suggesting that she use his fine Boston house during the quarantine period. (Hancock was rich enough to have his wife in Philadelphia with him.)

Naturally Abigail wrote her husband all about the great experience. The inoculation took on her and Johnny at once, his case being a mild one, hers making her dreadfully sick. When Nabby, the only daughter and oldest child, broke out she "displayed 1,000 pussels as large as a green pea," but at the end of a week neither Charles nor Tommy had a single eruption.

Charles, not erupting until the third week, almost died. Tommy's case was a light one. The family slept on straw mats which could be easily burned, ate only fruits and unsalted vegetables, slept with windows open and tried to walk daily in the Hancock yard. At the end of their five weeks of confinement they had only a few pits to vouch for the ordeal they had endured.

Ages of the children in that year, 1774, were: Abigail Amelia (Nabby), nine, John Quincy, seven, Charles, four, and Thomas Boylston, two.

Nabby, a feminine version of her father in looks, was gentle and placid. She and Johnny were exceedingly good friends. When he was a baby she had sung him lullabies of her own composition, one of them having the refrain, "Come—Papa, come home to Johnny."

Johnny, contrary to what he became later, among other things the only son of a President to become President himself, was sunny and lighthearted, very talkative and always laughing. He was so gay that his mother once cautioned him that famous men never laughed much.

Charles was the most handsome member of the good-looking family. He had a bright quick mind and an ingratiating manner which made him easily the pet of his relatives. Tommy was the baby and had the attention of all, never needed any personality of his own.

When Papa wrote home he enclosed notes for the children, adding one for Tommy after he cried when being told he was not old enough to read. Even a baby knew that in the John Adams family not being able to read was something rather awful!

Johnny, to whom a legible handwriting did not come easily, struggled and struggled to improve his penmanship for letters to Papa. In one he wrote:

> Mama says you will accept my endeavors and that my duty to you may be expressed in poor writing as well as good. I hope I grow a better boy and that you will have no occasion to be ashamed of me when you return. Mr. Thaxter says I learn my books very well. He is a good master. I read my books to Mama and we all long to see you. I am, sir, your dutiful son.

He learned to be the family postrider so he could ride the sorrel mare into Boston and hasten back with Papa's letters. He knew how much they meant to Mama. Once he gave her one, watched her face glow and then, with a low bow, produced two more while they both went into gales of laughter.

Thus began the famous Adams letters which would turn into the most voluminous family record in American history, now requiring more than 608 reels of microfilm to hold them.

The tragedy of the family—if such it can be called, since it resulted in so many delightful letters—was that after 1774 its members rarely ever were all together again: not during the growing up of the children, not during John Adams's Vice-Presidency, and not once while he was President.

When she was First Lady, Abigail wrote her sister, "We are a scattered family. I long to have all my children with me, but fear that may never be." John Quincy was a diplomat in Europe during all but the last few months of his father's terms in the two highest offices, and Tommy was with him as secretary for some of the time. Charles, who married against his father's wishes, and developed a drinking habit, paid only rare visits during the Presidency. Nabby, clinging to an unfortunate marriage, spent only one Presidential winter with her parents: too proud, despite parental urgings, to partake of the honors without her land-speculator husband. John Quincy married in London while his father was President, with Tommy the only family member present.

Separations among the children began in 1778 when Congress sent John Adams to Europe to help bolster the French alliance and seek economic aid elsewhere on the Continent for the struggling colonies. He took John Quincy, then eleven, with him. Mama acquiesced as an aid to her son's education, stripped Boston and Braintree to supply the bedding and foods needed for the six-week crossing.

Sea passengers in those days had to supply their own wherewithal for survival. Abigail supplied six chickens (to lay fresh eggs), two sheep, five bushels of corn, a barrel of apples, fourteen dozen eggs, thirty weight of brown sugar, a ten-gallon keg of rum, two bottles of mustard, two weight of tea and chocolate, a box of wafers, and sundry other goodies to ward off hunger and scurvy for however long the voyage took.

For writing purposes she supplied three reams (1,500 sheets) of paper, a stout bottle of homemade ink, twenty-five quills, and two books for Johnny—one for a record of his expenses, the other to be his diary. It would have been unthinkable for an Adams to run out of paper and ink.

Johnny was put in school at Passy, went sightseeing with Papa in Paris on weekends and learned to fend for himself when Papa traveled elsewhere. The venture worked so well that when the two came home briefly, almost two years later, Charles was permitted to return with them. Both went to school in Passy, where Charles made a great hit with the other students.

When Papa was reassigned to the Netherlands he put the boys in a school to prepare them for Leyden University, one of the great learning centers of the world. At examination time both were prepared scholastically, but Charles was not yet twelve, the minimum age for acceptance. Without his brother, he was miserably homesick and Papa sent him home in care of a friend by way of Portugal. Looking back later, his mother regretted having permitted Charles to accompany the more self-sufficient two to Europe, wondered whether the turndown at the university and his inability to conquer homesickness haunted Charles in later years.

Then, in 1784, she left Charles and Thomas in care of her sister to continue in school while she and Nabby set off to join Papa and John Quincy in England, where John Adams was to be the first U. S. Minister to Great Britain. At the time, she had not seen her husband and oldest son for five years. Nabby, a grown-up young lady, was in the midst of a romance and Papa, who still thought of her as a mere child, was furious when he heard that "my other self . . . my princess" was thinking of marrying a man he had never seen. He grudgingly consented to a tentative engagement and ordered his women-folk to cross the ocean.

John Quincy, who meantime had been all the way to Russia as secretary to Charles Dana, was seventeen and a handsome young man of the world when they were reunited. He and Nabby had a few wonderful months in London and Paris before he hastened back to America to attend Harvard—the school to which all Adams sons went automatically.

It happened that the secretary at the U. S. Legation in London was a dashing Col. William Stephens Smith, who was a member of a prominent Long Island family and had been an aide to George Washington. He was ten years Nabby's senior and most attentive. Nabby's fiancé did not possess the Adams facility for communication. He failed to write, although Nabby at first put a letter for him on every departing boat.

The colonel and Nabby were married by the Bishop of St. Asaph, no less, which was the best the Puritan Adamses could manage in a land ruled by the Church of England. But he had sided with the colonies during the Revolution, and that made him forgivable. The happy couple went to live on Wimpole Street and took their meals with the Adamses, who lived on fashionable Grosvernor Square. Their first child, William Steuben Smith, was born in London—and the five came back to America together so that John Adams could become our first Vice-President.

Mama Abigail established herself on Richmond Hill in New York City and hastened out to Long Island, where Nabby lived with her numerous in-laws, for the birth of the second Smith baby, promptly named John Adams.

It was Johnny Smith, this grandson, who most often is thought of in connection with President John Adams and children. It was he who had Grandpapa playing horsey and piggyback during the Vice-Presidency. He and his brother William were at Richmond Hill almost every day.

Meantime, John Quincy graduated from Harvard and was struggling along as a lawyer in Boston when President Washington named him Minister to the Netherlands and started him on his long diplomatic career. When Adams became President he, on written advice from Washington, reappointed his son to Portugal and then Berlin—and Tommy went to join him.

Charles, at times called the best dancer and most handsome young man in Boston, graduated high in his Harvard class. His parents deplored some of his fast company and escapades but loved it when he came to New York and established himself as a promising young lawyer.

But Charles was unable to maintain his parents' high standards. He fell in love with Sally Smith, a sister of his brother-in-law, and the Vice-President absolutely forbade the marriage —seeing it as beyond belief that a son of his would marry before he could support a wife adequately. Charles waited a while and married Sally without his father's consent. He was twenty-five, but that was younger than his father had married or than his brothers would. It was not in the Adams pattern. John Quincy relinquished a romance rather than face his father's displeasure. He and Thomas were both over thirty and had parental consent to wed.

After the capital was moved to Philadelphia, Charles paid his parents very few visits. His mother stopped to see him on her trips to and from Braintree and in 1797, the first year she was First Lady, wrote her sister:

"Charles lives prettily but frugally. He has a lovely Babe and a discreet woman, I think, for his wife, quite different from many of the family." This last was in reference to her son-in-law, who had a fondness for get-rich-quick schemes and at times disappeared—from his creditors and family—for months at a time. At times he lived like a lord, but at this writing Nabby and the children—who by now included a lovely daughter named Caroline—were living at East Chester on Long Island, or as Abigail called it, "20 miles from anybody."

Nabby refused to discuss her husband with her mother and declined to go live with her in the President's House. Abigail wrote her sister:

> My reflections upon prospects there took from me all appetite to food, and depressed my spirits—before too low. The Col. had gone on a journey, I know not where. I could not converse with her. The boys are fine lads. I wish they were under your care.

Thus is was with this First Lady as she journeyed to Philadelphia to move into the President's House vacated by the Washingtons: two children in Europe, the other two uneasily in her mind. She and the President lived family-less during their first Presidential years, except for twelve-year-old Louisa Smith, daughter of the First Lady's dead brother. Louisa would spend the remainder of her life in the Adams household and be a godsend to all its members.

Next summer on her way to Braintree the First Lady stopped again at East Chester and although unable to take Nabby home with her, did persuade her daughter to part with William and John, who that autumn were left in school in Massachusetts.

Not until October, 1799, did she persuade Nabby and Caroline to spend a winter in the President's House. Threat of war with France had enabled Colonel Smith to receive a military assignment. His regiment would be stationed at Scotch Plains, New York, and until the encampment was ready Nabby and daughter lived most happily with her parents. She and "other young ladies" of Philadelphia went to hear the President deliver a message to Congress and Mama sent home to Braintree for trunks filled with finery from other days. Some of the accessories were right in style and Nabby found ways to salvage silks and satin dresses worn during her London years.

To brighten the President's House even more there was news of John Quincy's wedding in London to Louisa Catherine Johnson—AND the return of Thomas, who brought great reports of his brother's career and glowing words about his new sister-in-law. This was the only winter, the third of four, in John Adams's Presidency that the Presidential mansion contained some of the family happiness and closeness for which Abigail and her husband, too, longed.

Thomas, although not so brilliant as his brothers, was a joy to them always and under his spell the First Lady, always most formally correct and Puritan in her entertaining, softened enough to permit a dance right under the Presidential roof! She was somewhat apologetic, but proud of it, too, when she wrote her sister that she did not mind at all "because it was unplanned and completely spontaneous." It was after a gala dinner for 28 young people that Tommy whispered in her ear to ask permission.

This son settled down happily to practice law in a Philadelphia office and the winter's only family gloom was worry about Charles—and the prospect of having to move the Presidential household to Washington next winter. Abigail never approved of moving the capital to a new Federal City located so far South and she dreaded it—but it was her son Charles who worried her most.

She had stopped to see him the autumn before and written Mrs. Peabody her delight with Charles' children, Susanna, three, and Abigail, one:

> They are sprightly and lively children. Susan is very forward and intelligent for three years, and would stand all day to hear you read stories, which she will catch at a few times repeating, and has all Goody Goose stories by heart as her uncle J. Q. Adams did Giles Ginger Bread. She tells me her letters and would read in a month if she had a good school.
>
> Abby went alone [walked alone] at nine months, and is very pretty. More so than Susan, having the advantage of sprightly eyes. Both have fine complexions. But I cannot look upon them, my dear sister, with the joy you do upon yours. . . . When I behold misery and distress, disgrace and poverty brought upon a family by intemperance my heart bleeds at every pore.

Nabby and daughter Caroline left the President's House in March of 1800 to join the colonel at his encampment, but his regiment was disbanded shortly thereafter and he was out of work again. His father-in-law, who had no support from his Vice-President, Thomas Jefferson, and was not popular with his Cabinet, was unable to manage a permanent military commission for him. So once again that summer Nabby's mother went home to Massachusetts worried about Nabby and Charles.

In New York that autumn she found Charles near death and his family destitute. She took his daughter Susan, "a four-year-old mite in a black dress," on to Washington with her and Susan would be the first young child to live in the new White House.

In Philadelphia she and her party spent a night in the inn into which the old President's House had already been converted. By then it was November 10 and she already knew within reason that John Adams had been defeated for reelection. Sitting there with Thomas, who was to complete the journey with her, she could "scarcely persuade myself that tomorrow I must quit here for an unknown and unseen abode." She wrote a sorrow-filled letter to her sister:

> At N. York I found my poor unhappy son, for so I must call him, laid upon a bed of sickness, destitute of a home. . . . A distressing cough, an affliction of the liver and dropsy will soon terminate a life which might have been valuable to himself and others. . . . His physician says he is past recovery. I shall carry a melancholy report to the President, who, passing through New York without stopping, knew not his situation.

Charles died on November 30. His father heard the tragic news almost at the same time that final returns from the Southern states convinced him beyond doubt that he had lost the election.

He gave much time to prayer and reflected to Thomas on the inscrutable ways of God and men. "That I might have died for him if that would have relieved him from his faults as well as his disease," he cried to his youngest son.

Why this talented second son of the Adamses fell in with "bad company" and took to drink is not really known. Had they not been in the Presidency, however, they might have had more time for forgiveness and aid. The Presidency is a harrowing post at best and for those with family problems which cannot wait it can be devastating indeed.

Granddaughter Susan had some mishaps in the White House. Her grandmother described a night when the First Family lost sleep due to one of her illnesses:

> Last night Susan was threatened with the quincy, which alarmed me very much as she went well to bed. I was waked in the night by a strange noise. She sleeps in a little chamber next to mine. I went in, and found her laboring with a dreadful hoarse cough, a sound which indicated medical aid.
>
> We sent for the physician nearest us, who gave her calomil, put her feet in warm water, and steamed her with vinegar. She puked, and that seemed to relieve her. She has coughed all day, but not with so much hoarseness. I think she has worms. . . .

Grandmother also reported, three months later, that Susan had "hooping cough."

Of her days in the White House Susan herself recalled that Uncle Thomas gave her a doll of which she was exceedingly proud and a fine toy tea set which she prized highly. A little friend named Ann Black came to have "tea" with her and the doll and, in envy—Susan thought—smashed some of the pretty dishes. Susan, whose temper would make her an unruly teenager, returned the visit and, without saying a word, smashed the head of Ann's doll.

Susan returned to Massachusetts with the Adamses the next spring and lived with them until her marriage.

Abigail did not let her husband's defeat nor the unfinished condition of the White House conquer her spirit. She said to Thomas regarding the election, "Well, my dear son, South Carolina has behaved just as your father always said she would. . . . We retire from public life. If I did not rise with dignity I can at least fall with ease, which is much more difficult."

She moved mountains to get fuel enough for White House fireplaces and to lessen aches from her rheumatism, which worsened in the damp and newly plastered structure. She moved through workmen to determine that the unfinished East Parlor would be an adequate place to hang the laundry. She put the Presidential furniture into place, bemoaning the smallness of mirrors when placed in rooms with tall ceilings. Some of the furniture, bought for Washington, was damaged and lost in transit from Philadelphia—and much of her own good china was smashed. She considered the little port of Georgetown, where White House grocery shopping had to be done, "quite the dirtiest place of business" she had ever seen.

But she wrote Nabby, after unburdening herself about how awful the whole house was—still without adequate inside and outside steps and with only a few rooms completed—to say that she liked it fine and that the view down the Potomac was excellent. She returned all the calls ladies made on her. She gave the expected official dinners and on New Year's Day, 1801, she inaugurated a custom which was to linger until well after World I: a public reception with a vast assortment of refreshments, including syllabub and mulled cider.

Anyone climbing the steps to the upstairs Oval Room that day would not soon forget the Adamses, he in his velvet knee pants and powdered wig, with silver buckles at his knees and on his slippers; she in stylish brocade. A large fire roared up the chimney and the view down the Potomac was enhanced by crimson curtains at the windows. Nor would history forget the words with which he ushered in his few months in the White House:

> "I pray heaven to bestow the best of blessings on this house, and all that shall hereafter inhabit it. May none but honest and wise men ever rule under this roof."

Abigail received the President-elect, Thomas Jefferson, whom she once had termed one of the earth's most gorgeous people, with all the correct formality—and coldness—which she had seen Queen Charlotte display at the Court of James's so many years ago. She did not tarry for his inauguration but set out for Quincy in late February to dry out her rheumatism and forget about public life. Her husband was not far behind her.

But during his last days in office Adams struck a great blow for the happiness of his daughter. He named Colonel Smith surveyor of the Port of New York, term limited only by bad behavior, so that Nabby could enjoy some peace of mind. Also, he ordered John Quincy home from Europe, not wanting to leave Jefferson the satisfaction of doing it.

Living again as private citizens after 35 years in public office had its compensations, the Adamses learned. They at last met John Quincy's wife and baby son, the latter named George Washington. Adams liked his refined daughter-in-law, Louisa, who was London born and bred—although of Maryland ancestry—but Abigail had some doubts at first. As for Louisa, it took her quite a while to grow accustomed to the Adamses.

Fresh from the gaiety of the Prussian court, she found the life of her in-laws rather primitive. "Country dress and country manners, the nasal twangs, the Indian puddings and boiled potatoes," all made her feel as though she had fallen in with a strange tribe. She admitted ruefully years later, "I was literally and without knowing it a *fine* lady."

John Quincy picked up his law practice in Boston, but soon was appointed to the U. S. Senate and went to live in Washington. His second son was named John Adams and his third Charles Francis. In 1809 President Madison named him Minister to Russia. George, eight, and John, six, were left with their grandparents to attend school in Massachusetts, but Charles Francis, less than a year old, went to old St. Petersburg with his parents.

In 1815 John Quincy became Minister to Great Britain and

his sons went to join their parents in London. The Adamses were delighted with this appointment because it showed that their favorite son was following in his father's footsteps.

Thomas Boylston moved his law practice from Philadelphia to Boston, married Ann Harod and became the father of seven children. He never caused his parents a sleepless night.

But the fate of their only daughter continued to haunt them. The colonel returned to his land speculations and took his family to live "on the frontier of new lands" in western New York. After an absence of three years, beloved Nabby returned home, the victim of cancer. Her distraught father wrote his old friend, Dr. Benjamin Rush, who advised an operation, and the Adams home became so much of a hospital that George and John, John Quincy's sons, were sent to live with Grandmama's sister for a while.

Remarkably, Nabby recovered—temporarily—and returned to the frontier. About a year after the operation, however, she came home to die and at her death Caroline continued to live with her grandparents, with whom her Cousin Susan also was living.

Grandmama Abigail found Susan an impetuous handful—but Caroline was sheer delight. Susan, a self-willed but most engaging girl, married at sixteen, against her grandparents' wishes, and when soon widowed returned with her daughter to live again at the home until her remarriage.

Abigail loved to remark that a feather would control Caroline but a cable would not hold Susan! Caroline, as beautiful as she was good, made a very happy marriage to Peter De Windt of New York and frequently brought her large family to summer at the Adams home.

John Quincy Adams was Secretary of State when his mother died at age seventy-four. His lament for her filled several diary pages, and she would never see him President. His father would, however.

John Adams lived to be almost ninety-one, surrounded by grandchildren who helped him carry on a voluminous correspondence with his old friends, including Thomas Jefferson, erstwhile friend and political enemy and then friend again. Two of Jefferson's grandchildren came by to see him, Thomas Jefferson Randolph and his sister Ellen, who had married a Bostonian.

On July 4, 1826, when John Quincy Adams had been President more than a year and was busy with a Fourth of July celebration in Washington, his father died at his old home —and Jefferson died on the same day at his beloved Monticello. President Adams hastened to his father's funeral while all over the country the populace read that the second and third Presidents were dead. These two Founding Fathers were wholly unlike each other politically and as parents, but grew more alike when they both became fond grandfathers.

Jefferson's Two Daughters

AND A BEVY OF GRANDCHILDREN

ALTHOUGH public offices kept Thomas Jefferson so much separated from his family during the earlier part of his career that he once—most unhappily—described himself as a "vagrant father," it would be difficult to imagine a more constantly devoted parent or grandparent than our third President.

When duties of the Presidency became tedious, he once wrote his younger daughter Maria, only two things made his existence endurable: thoughts of his family and thoughts of his farm at Monticello. Of these, he assured her, the "ineffable pleasure of family society" invariably came first.

He resigned the governorship of Virginia to devote more time to his young family, promising his fragile wife never again to leave her for a public assignment. Twice during her final illness, Congress importuned him to accept the title of Minister Plenipotentiary and go to Europe to work with Benjamin Franklin and John Adams to win favor and economic aid for the struggling colonies. Each time he refused.

After her death at age thirty-three, in 1782, he accepted. She left him three daughters: Martha (named for Martha Washington and usually called Patsy), aged ten, Maria (Polly or Mary), a mere four, and Lucy Elizabeth, not yet a year old.

He took Maria and the baby to his wife's sister, Mrs. Francis Eppes, to be kept in custody for him; but he was determined that come what might he would take Martha, his oldest, to Europe with him. Until the red tape connected with his assignment could be cleared he put her in school in Philadelphia and to her, there, he began the correspondence which well could be headed "Education of a Daughter."

In his first letter he wrote:

> MY DEAR PATSY—
> With respect to the distribution of your time, the following is what I should approve:
> From 8 to 10, practice music.
> From 10 to 1, dance one day and draw another.
> From 1 to 3, draw on the day you dance, and write a letter next day.
> From 3 to 4, read French.
> From 4 to 5, exercise yourself in music.
> From 5 till bed-time, read English, write, etc. . . .
> Take care you never spell a word wrong. . . . It produces great praise in a lady to spell well. . . . I have placed my happiness on seeing you good and accomplished. . . . Keep my letters and read them at times, that you may always have present in your mind those things which will endear you to me.

He expected a letter from her each week for sure, and by each post if possible. That way he could watch her progress.

The wife of a friend suggested that the school's head mistress was not careful enough about the dress of her charges, so he wrote his daughter:

> Be you, from the moment you rise till you go to bed, as cleanly and properly dressed as at the hours of dinner or tea. A lady who has been seen as a sloven in the morning will

never efface the impression she has made. . . . Nothing is
more disgusting to our sex as a want of cleanliness and delicacy
in yours. . . .

Patsy was a tall and sympathetic girl, had red hair like her
father and was an excellent student. When she and Jefferson
reached Paris he placed her in school at the Abbaye de Panthe-
mont just outside the city, had her home for weekends and
continued to write her, especially when he was elsewhere on
the Continent. The stay in Europe stretched longer and
longer, and he often wished for his other daughters.

When Lucy Elizabeth died of whooping cough before she
was four years old, he became determined that Maria should
join him and Martha in Europe. Persuading Polly and her
aunt that she should cross the ocean required great diplo-
macy. Jefferson wrote that he had a fine doll for her. Polly
asked him to send it to her, but said she wanted to remain with
her Aunt and Uncle Eppes.

"I know, my dear Polly," her father replied, "how sorry you
will be, and ought to be, to leave them and your cousins; but
your sister and myself cannot live without you, and after a
while we will carry you back again to see your friends in Virginia."

"Dear Papa," Polly wrote him more than a year later, "I
should be very happy to see you, but I cannot go to France.
. . . I want to see you and sister Patsy, but you must come to
Uncle Eppes. . . ."

"Although I am distressed when I think of the voyage,"
Jefferson wrote Mr. Eppes, "yet I know it is necessary for my
happiness. . . . It would be most unfortunate through life,
both to her and to us, were those affections loosened which
ought to bind us together."

Eight-year-old Polly, still unreconciled to the trip, was escorted to Baltimore by several of her cousins who stayed with

her while she became accustomed to life aboard the ship. They left her asleep one afternoon and, in the company of a young Negro girl, she sailed for London to stay with Abigail Adams, wife of the U. S. Minister to England, until Papa could send for her. A most affectionate child, she became so attached to Mrs. Adams that she did not want to leave her.

"A finer child I never saw," Mrs. Adams wrote. "I grew so fond of her. . . . She would sit sometimes and describe to me the parting with her aunt till the tears would flow down her cheeks. . . . Papa would break her heart, she said, by making her go again. . . . She clung to me and I could not help shedding a tear at parting with her. . . . She is a very beautiful girl, too. . . ."

Polly arrived in Paris on the eve of her ninth birthday. "She neither knew us, nor should we have known her had we met with her unexpectedly," Jefferson wrote Mrs. Eppes.

"Her sister came and staid a week with her, leading her from time to time to the convent, until she became familiarized with it. . . . She retains all her anxiety to get back to her country and her friends."

Slight and lovely, like her mother, Polly became a convent pet. She busied herself with her classes and making new friends, but rarely finished a letter to Aunt Eppes. "She starts them over and over," her father wrote. "Her face kindles with love when she hears your name. She and Patsy will be with me tomorrow and if she has a scrap of her pencil with her I shall inclose it. . . ."

Polly never became the student her sister was. Perhaps to prevent Patsy's becoming too bookish, Papa began to remind her of the customs she would find back home.

"Do not neglect your needlework," he begged her. "In the country life of America there will be many moments when a woman can have recourse to nothing but her needle for employment. In dull company and in dull weather, it is ill manners to read; it is ill manners to leave them; no card-playing there among genteel people."

Patsy grew up quickly, loved the school and its religious atmosphere. At fifteen she wrote asking Papa's permission to become a nun. Papa did not write a reply but came in person, had a talk with the Abbess and took his daughters back to Paris with him. Neither then nor later, Martha told her own children many years after, did he discuss her request, believing it only a fancy attached to growing up. "He knew me so well," she said.

So Patsy, looking more than her years, was presented to the brilliant French court of pre-French Revolution days and became a part-time hostess for Papa. A miniature of her done about this time—and now in the U. S. Embassy in Paris—reflects her bright coloring and her joy of life.

Among visitors received at the Jefferson home in Paris was a handsome young cousin, Thomas Mann Randolph, who had just graduated from the University of Edinburgh and was traveling on the Continent. He and Patsy fell in love and in the February after the Jeffersons returned home, when Patsy was seventeen, they were married in a gay ceremony at Monticello.

Polly, enchanted to be home, spent much time with Aunt Eppes—but when Jefferson became Secretary of State and then Vice-President he kept her part of the time with him at Philadelphia in school. His letters to her are filled with "How does your Don Quixote go?" "I did not write you last week because you owe me four letters already." "Where are you, Maria? With your aunt or your sister?" Polly cared little for letter writing, however, and most of his questions went unanswered.

At age eighteen Polly married Aunt Eppes' son, John Wayles Eppes, whom she had loved all her life.

By the time Jefferson became President, in 1801, Martha

was a mother six times over and Maria was expecting her first baby. Both his sons-in-law were in Congress and stayed with him in the White House—but his daughters did not visit him until his second winter there. Then the presence of his seven grandchildren created a stir among the Washington elite.

The two oldest, Anne Cary aand Thomas Jefferson Randolph, twelve and ten, attended parties for the younger set, but not even the babies lacked for attention.

Margaret Bayard Smith, chief social chronicler of the time, told what a pretty picture Mrs. Randolph made "sitting on a sopha with the President surrounded by her lovely family," of how the children piled all over Grandpapa, who permitted them to play with his watch, told them stories and read them poems—and sent Mrs. Madison on shopping expeditions for the latest toys and clothing. Mrs. Smith's favorite was a golden-haired six-year-old named Ellen, who loved poetry.

The other Randolph grandchildren at the time were: Cornelia, four, Virginia, three, and Mary, an infant. Maria's son, Francis Eppes, was almost two. Rarely has the White House harbored such an abundance of children at one time.

Mrs. Smith also described the Jefferson daughters: "Mrs. Eppes is beautiful. Simplicity and timidity personified when in company, but when alone with you of communicative and winning manners. Mrs. Randolph is rather homely, a delicate likeness of her father, but still more interesting than Mrs. E."

Maria had not wanted to make the trip to Washington. Not only timid, she thought the trip would cost her father too much—since he always insisted on paying all costs when his children and grandchildren were involved. Also, she grew vexed when always complimented about her beauty. To her it indicated that beauty was her only accomplishment.

Ill almost from the time of her marriage, Maria's innate fears and tendency to worry increased as her health declined. Jefferson went to great lengths to soothe and assure her, and especially he sought to erase her often-expressed belief that surely he must love Martha better.

"No, never imagine," he wrote her from the White House, "that there could possibly be a difference to me between yourself and sister. You have both such dispositions as to engross my whole love and each so entirely that there can be no greater degree of it that each possess."

He made two trips to Monticello each year during his Presidency, one in the early spring and one in midsummer—and he wanted all his family there.

His namesake grandson wrote how he would come to Edgehill, the Randolph home, for breakfast the morning after arrival and refuse to leave until the whole family went home with him.

The trips to Monticello were hard on Maria, who lived farther away. She died there in the spring of 1804, when she was only twenty-five. Her son was five years old by then and she also left a tiny daughter, Maria, who died shortly thereafter. After her death the President insisted that Martha and her children return to Washington with him.

Martha's second son, her eighth child (counting a daughter who died in infancy), was the first child born in the White House. She promptly named him James Madison in keeping with her avowal to name all her sons for famous Americans. (This son lived to be twenty-eight and died unmarried.) After him, Martha gave birth—but not in the White House—to children named Benjamin Franklin, Meriwether Lewis, Septimia (her seventh daughter), and George Wythe. Twelve of her thirteen children lived to adulthood and most of them married.

Thanks to her, Jefferson is the President with the most descendants living today.

Jefferson always treated his grandchildren as his very own, became upset when his Eppes son-in-law kept Francis too long away from him. When Thomas Jefferson (first called Tom, and later Jefferson) Randolph was fifteen he came to the White House with Grandpapa on his way to school in Philadelphia. "He examined my wardrobe as my mother would have done and sent me to his tailor with a list of articles that he thought I required," Tom said.

In Philadelphia the grandson stayed with Jefferson's old friend, Charles Willson Peale, who did a charming portrait of him and sent it as a gift to the President.

This grandson, the solace of Jefferson's old age, was considered a bit heavy and humorless as a child. Grandpapa insisted he learn French so they could talk it together and he often lugged a French grammar around with him. Anything he lacked in gaiety of spirit, however, he more than made up for in devotion.

He came to Washington to be with Grandpapa during the festivities of Madison's inaugural and to accompany him home. The Randolph family, at the President's insistence, had moved to Monticello. Young Tom lived there for two years after his marriage and then "colonized" four miles away. This distance was too great to satisfy Grandpapa, so Tom moved two miles nearer and Jefferson graded a smooth road between their farms.

Nothing affecting the children was too small for Grandpapa to notice. Cornelia and Francis learned to write at about the same time, and the President sent them both congratulations. When Anne married he wrote, "Who is going to help me with the gardening or let me know when the first bulbs come up?"

"He could see into our hearts," Ellen wrote. "He gave me my first silk dress, my first good writing desk, my first leghorn hat. From him seemed to flow all the small blessings and joyful surprises of my childish and girlish years." He gave Ellen a new Lady's saddle and bridle just as she was becoming ashamed of her childish one. She wanted a watch more than almost anything. He sensed this and sent her one.

(The Monticello museum today holds many watches and pieces of jewelry he gave his granddaughters.) "My Bible came from him," Ellen said, "My Shakespeare . . . What, in short, of all my small treasures did not come from him?"

Virginia, too young to learn to write while Grandpapa was away from home as President, worried always that she had no letter from him to cherish. Cornelia, when about ten years old, said she'd never had a silk dress in her life—and Grandpapa, overhearing, got her one next day and included pretty frocks for Mary and Virginia, too.

Virginia longed for a guitar. She bartered with a neighbor moving West to purchase hers secondhand, but the price was more than she could afford. Grandpapa said that if she would promise to learn to play it she could have it. "I shall never forget my ecstasies. I was but fourteen, and the first wish of my heart was unexpectedly gratified," she wrote.

Jefferson knew before his death that Monticello and its furnishings would have to be auctioned to pay his debts. His acres had lacked good management for too long and an agricultural depression left him stripped of hopes that he could leave Martha an inheritance.

His oldest grandson, in a devotion far beyond the call of duty, intervened to make Grandpapa's last years easier. He took over management of the farm and pledged to make good all his grandfather's drafts. The ex-President parted with his library, one of the best in the country, but the $23,950 which Congress paid him for it was quickly devoured in debt payments.

A few weeks before his death an accounting showed that his grandson had "interposed himself between him and creditors to the amount of $58,536." When the estate was auctioned, it was found that his debts still exceeded the value of the property by $40,000. Tom pledged himself to pay them—which he did over a period of several years, while rearing his own large family and helping his brothers and sisters.

It distressed the country that the writer of the Declaration of Independence, who in his old age was even then engaged in launching the University of Virginia, should be dying penniless. The Mayor of New York raised $8,500 to send him on behalf of New York citizens. From Baltimore came $3,000, from Philadelphia $5,000.

He died at eighty-three, having said good-bye to his grandchildren individually and leaving a letter filled with love and gratitude for Martha to open later.

Tom took his younger brothers "to my house to be maintained and educated and restrained until they could get on their feet, which they all did with energy and capacity and blessed me by their confidence and affections. I served my Grandfather, Mother, and her children with as much fidelity as I could have served my God. . . ."

Martha educated all her daughters, with only an occasional tutor. After her father's death she considered opening a school for girls so that her unmarried daughters could teach in it. She dropped the idea when the legislatures of Louisiana and South Carolina voted her $10,000 each as a token of their esteem for Jefferson.

Her husband obtained a job running the boundary between Georgia and Florida and she decided to take her two youngest sons to board in Boston near her daughter Ellen, who was married to Joseph Coolidge, so they could go to school there. She did this for two winters, until her husband's death.

Her daughter Virginia meantime married Nicholas P. Trist, and Henry Clay gave young Trist a job in the State Department at $1,400 a year with the understanding that Martha would live with the Trists in Washington. This she did, in an adjoining small house, until Trist—who became a valued and successful diplomat—was able to secure a structure large enough for all of them. Each year, however, she spent time with Ellen in Boston and with her oldest son at Edgehill.

Her return to Washington occasioned much rejoicing. Few women ever were more admired and respected than Martha. She was invited everywhere and entertained a great many callers. President Jackson called on her at least once a year and gave her son, Meriwether Lewis Randolph, a handsome young lawyer, a good appointment in the Territory of Arkansas.

This son married Elizabeth Martin, the niece of Emily Donelson who was President Jackson's White House hostess. His career was cut short by death and his widow, by one of those odd interminglings of White House families during the years, later married Emily's widower husband, Andrew Jackson Donelson.

Martha died at the home of her oldest son in 1836 at the age of sixty-seven.

Youngest of the Randolph children, George, whom his mother reluctantly permitted to join the Navy, became Secretary of War in the Confederacy Cabinet of Jefferson Davis. During the Civil War almost every shred of finery in the way of attire or curtains which the family still possessed was used for bandages or reworked into clothing. Martha is represented in the Smithsonian's Hall of First Ladies, which includes hostesses, too, by only a fine cashmere shawl.

Madison's Stepson

PAYNE TODD WAS A HEARTACHE

WHEN James Madison became the fourth President in 1809 his stepson, Payne Todd, was a handsome, precocious and polished lad just turned eighteen, a student at St. Mary's College in Baltimore.

His polish began at age three, when his mother married "the great little Madison" and shed her Quaker grays for the glitter which surrounded the levees given by President and Mrs. Washington in Philadelphia. Almost one could say that it began at birth, for no less a man of the world than Aaron Burr was his godfather.

That he was the apple of Dolley Madison's eye everybody who knew her knew. They also knew that her heart was set on his becoming a dazzling social success who would travel in Europe, meet crowned heads and dance with princesses.

Payne lived up to her expectations on the social front, at least for a while, but also he became such a wastrel that the wealth of czarist Russia—the first country he visited—might never have satisfied his mania for extravagance.

He succeeded in making Madison's last years painful indeed and caused his aged mother to live in such penury that Daniel Webster often brought her baskets of fruits and vegetables when he came to call.

He was the son of Dolley's first husband, John Todd, a Philadelphia lawyer who died in the yellow fever epidemic which swept the second capital city in 1793, sending President Washington, his Cabinet and the Congress scurrying to Germantown and other nearby areas. John Todd left his worldly goods to his beautiful wife, knowing she would be "an affectionate mother to my little Payne and the sweet babe with which she is now enciente." The baby died soon after birth and Dolley returned home with Payne to live with her mother.

Mrs. Payne ran a boardinghouse frequented mostly by Members of Congress. Her husband, John Payne, a devout Quaker, had freed his slaves and moved his family from Virginia to the City of Brotherly Love so that his children could be reared in the Society of Friends. When his business failed, Mrs. Payne took in lodgers.

It was Burr who brought James Madison, a taciturn bachelor of forty-three, to call on Dolley. She accepted his quickly given proposal of marriage, although she worried about the difference in their ages. She was only twenty-five.

The legend is that Martha Washington helped her decide by declaring, "We both (the President and I) approve, think he will make you all the better a husband by being so much older."

Dolley put the Todd inheritance in trust for her son. It was not a large fortune, but a comfortable patrimony with which to launch Payne in a professional career. In the same settlement, she promised to rear her son in the Quaker faith.

On her wedding day she wrote her best friend to say, "My little Payne will have a generous and tender protector." And Madison, the record shows, always was a generous stepfather to the lad, who called him Papa. Just how tender and affectionate he was is another matter. Those are not adjectives usually attributed to Madison, but any lack of them on his part was more than made up for by Dolley. Love and tenderness were her specialties. Payne was never neglected.

Once when he was ill his mother wrote her sister, ". . . Payne continues weak and sick. My prospects rise and fall to sadness as this precious child recovers or declines."

Dolley had to be in Philadelphia for an operation and wrote her husband, then Secretary of State: "To find you love me, have my child safe and my mother well seems to comprise all my happiness. . . . Kiss my child for me." In the same letter she asked, "Did you see the Bishop, or engage a place at school for Payne?"

By the time Dolley returned, Madison had seen Bishop Carroll of Maryland and entered Payne in St. Mary's College, a new school for boys run by the Sulpician Order, but open also to non-Catholics.

The school stressed foreign languages, particularly French, and of this Madison approved because he always regretted his own lack of languages. Also, Madison thought that Payne needed stricter discipline than he received at home, where he already was evidencing his wayward tendencies.

It pleased Dolley that Mrs. Jerome Bonaparte, American wife of Napoleon's brother (and said to be the most beautiful woman in America at the time) promised to keep an eye on the lad in Baltimore and see that he met only the best people.

In 1812, when Dolley was First Lady, she wrote her sister, "Payne is in Baltimore yet and as much admired and respected as you could wish. He writes me that Mrs. Patterson and Mrs. Bonaparte are very kind to him and he is invited out all the time. We intend to send him a few months to Princeton. . . ."

The Princeton plan never materialized, however. The President's secretary became ill and Payne came home to fill in for him at the White House for six months. Evidently he turned in a satisfactory performance.

In 1813 he was permitted to go on a Presidential mission which hastened his undoing. Czar Alexander of Russia offered to mediate a settlement in the War of 1812 and a peace conference was scheduled in St. Petersburg, where John Quincy Adams was the American Minister. Payne, now twenty-one, went as secretary to Albert Gallatin, one of the negotiators.

He was the nearest thing to an American czarevitch ever seen in Russia and, Adams wrote in his diary, his importance was exaggerated out of all proportion. He was given a near-royal status and attended court balls from which other members of the delegation were rigidly excluded.

Madison had sent with him a package of documents for Gallatin. In it was a letter in which he enclosed "a draft for $800—to be a fund in your hands for J. P. Todd. He has his own $200 more, which is the estimate called for. Should this be too little you may draw a draft to my account."

The peace mission was a premature failure, the British by no means willing to negotiate. The delegates disbanded to meet again next year in Holland and trust for better luck. Gallatin decided to send young Todd home, but Payne chose to leave St. Petersburg by the Swedish route, was snowbound in Scandinavia—and missed the boat.

Dolley, hearing that her son was separated from Gallatin somewhere in Europe, wrote Mrs. Gallatin, "I am distressed at Payne's leaving Mr. Gallatin. What could have led him to do so? Nothing but anxiety to get home, I hope. . . ."

Payne was out of funds when he reached Gallatin, and the older man established credit for him with Baring Brothers of London. Gallatin still was eager for Payne to go home and not await the reconvening of the peace mission—but Payne wanted to see Paris. This pleased his mother. She wrote, "My precious Payne is going to France, and I hope to see him highly benefitted."

His intended three weeks in Paris stretched into ten and, to Gallatin's chagrin, the young man missed another boat and also wanted to remain with the negotiators.

During the long peace conference Payne evidently intended, at least once, to go home. His luggage arrived in Philadelphia without him. This was the time he missed the same boat twice, once at Le Havre and then again—after a mad dash to England—at Plymouth, too. His mother wrote Mrs. Gallatin please to have the captain of the boat send on to Washington Payne's clothing and "the several items he has bought for us in France."

When the British burned Washington in the autumn of 1814 Payne wrote his stepfather: "Dear Papa—I wish I could have been in Washington to help the family during the fire. I am enclosing a newspaper article, the author of which [apparently Madame de Staël] requests me to make known to you her high regard."

He wrote Madison later that the peace mission was working also on a trade treaty with Great Britain, giving the President the first details he had of this accomplishment. His time was not wholly wasted, it seems, and if he had been too much out of line at any time it is unlikely that Adams would have failed to note it in his diary.

The treaty finally was signed on Christmas Eve of 1814, in time to be a Christmas gift by today's standards—although the fighting continued into January.

Payne lingered in Europe and the President received a statement of $6,500 owed to Baring Brothers. He wrote Gallatin, "I was not prepared for the heavy expenses of J. P. Todd. I thank you for lending your responsibility; but being unable in my present situation to do better for repaying the Barings I enclose my check for $6,500 with the request that you will turn it into means of an adequate remittance." Later he paid the accrued interest and cost of exchange.

In June of 1815 Payne wrote his uncle, Richard Cutts, from London: "I have again found it necessary to make use of your name in preference to the President's or my mother's in drawing a bill at 30 days sight . . . amount of $320. You will please accept and receive the amount from my mother." He thanked Cutts for the similar assistance he had given during his student days in Baltimore, indicating that Madison never had known how much it cost to keep his stepson in school.

In the autumn of 1815 Payne was back in Washington and expected to meet some school friends at the Georgetown races. One of them wrote, "Our friend Payne is semper Payne. He arrived at the race after the races were over."

When the Madison terms ended, Payne refused to go with his parents to Montpelier, their country home in Virginia. A cosmopolite now, he "had blossomed into the full maturity of his extraordinary power to distress his family." He haunted the larger cities, relying on Madison fame to clear his way. Rarely alone, he and his changing groups of buddies, made the rounds—not so much to be in the social whirl, it seems, as to visit the races and gaming tables.

One Christmas Eve, Dolley wrote Payne that she was ashamed to tell visitors "how long my only child has been absent from the home of his mother. . . . Your papa thinks as I do that you should have the appearance of consulting your parents on subjects of deepest account to you." Payne had asked her for money and she sent him more than he asked, reporting that she also had paid $400 on his local debts.

When next she heard from him, he was in Philadelphia and asking for stage fare home. She forwarded it, but he neither came nor wrote.

Meantime his stepfather paid his $500 debt to a Washington lottery house and wrote the friend who had made the loan so as to keep Payne out of debtor's prison that there might have been more friendship in refusing to make the loan. "But," he added, "would it serve any purpose to send him to prison?"

He wrote his stepson that he could not begin to describe his mother's distress should he go to prison. "It would inflict new and untold tortures on her. Come then, I intreat and conjure you, to the bosom of your parents who are anxious to save you from tendencies and past errors and provide for your comfort and happiness."

Payne escaped prison this time by taking $300 which the postmaster of Philadelphia loaned him, out of loyalty to Madison, and going to New York. By now he had added liquor to his expenses.

Madison took mortgages on his farms to raise $5,600 to pay Payne's notes. Every mortgage was a drain. Crop failures and a depression made money exceedingly scarce.

Shortly came the chilling news that Payne again owed more than $3,000. By selling his tobacco crop, taking another mortgage and obtaining a loan, Madison was able to hold off the inevitable a little longer. But in June of 1829 Payne went to prison in Philadelphia, and finally wrote his mother.

"My dear child," she wrote in reply, "boarding within prison bounds! . . . Every feeling of my soul is wounded." She pointed to the poor state of her husband's health but said his anxiety and hope to aid were as great as any father's. This time Madison borrowed $400 from John C. Payne, Dolley's brother. But next year he heard from his old friend, Anthony Morris, that Payne was again in prison, his creditors wanting $600 in cash and notes to let him go. The funds were furnished and Payne did come home, seemingly chastened and eager to use his time in the country to improve his knowledge of geology!

Madison, in agony from arthritis which crippled his hands, nonetheless worked long hours on his books and papers. Payne did some of the copying. Shortly before his death Madison showed Dolley's brother a package to examine and to show to his wife when he was gone. It revealed that he had paid about $20,000 on Payne's debts without her knowledge.

After Madison's death Dolley returned to Washington to live, leaving Payne in management of the farm, which—naturally—he could not handle. In a few years it had to be sold. Congress bought Madison's papers from her for $30,000 which disappeared quickly. She pawned her silver to help Payne.

Dolley ranked as a Dowager Queen in Washington, remained tireless in her friendships and kind deeds. Almost as many flocked to see her on New Year's Day as called at the White House. Her nieces surrounded her with love and attention, and her servants remained devoted.

During Jackson's administration Congress bought the remainder of Madison's unpublished papers and letters from her for $25,000, but did not pay it as a sum. It was put in trust to be received in installments, to prevent Payne from spending it all in one weekend.

"My poor son," Dolley often said. "Forgive him his eccentricities. His heart is good and he means no harm." Payne never saw that he did any harm, either. "I have been my own worst enemy," he said on his deathbed, "have harmed only myself."

Dolley died at age eighty-one and left her home, near the White House, plus her other shrunken possessions, jointly to Payne and to Anna Payne, the niece who lived with her. Payne did not like the idea of sharing with Anna, and unavailably contested the will. He succeeded in getting one of his creditors, a professional collector, named one of the estate's administrators, however. Several Madison papers and letters disappeared by that route and showed up in private collections years later, the Library of Congress repurchasing many of them.

Payne died of typhoid at sixty-one, nursed by his mother's devoted servants. Her niece, Lucia B. Cutts, who edited her *Memoirs and Letters,* failed to record for him a redeeming feature—in fact, seemed to regret having to mention him at all.

Monroe's Two Daughters

THEY DID NOT REMAIN FRIENDS

➤➤➤-➤➤➤❮❮❮-❮❮❮

WHEN popular James Monroe returned to America in 1808 after a lengthy diplomatic sojourn in France, Spain and England, many old friends rushed to see him. They almost forgot to discuss politics with him, though, so intrigued were they with his liveliest French import: a four-and-a-half-year-old daughter born in Paris and named Maria, pronounced with a long "i" in early American style. She was an enchanting surprise for them.

Maria was blondish and frisky and had brought a French puppy home with her. Also, she was wearing a fashion not before seen in America: pantalettes for little girls.

No less a statesman that Judge St. George Tucker quickly posted a letter urging that small females of his Virginia family be put into them immediately. His description of the youngest Monroe and her attire was:

> She was dressed in a short frock that reached half-way between her knees and ankles, under which she displayed a pair of loose pantalettes, wide enough for the foot to pass through with ease, frilled around with the same stuff as her frock and pantaloons. . . . The little monkey did not fail to know the advantage of the dress. She had a small spaniel dog, and the general opinion seemed to be that she turned and twisted more than the spaniel.

In contrast, the other Monroe daughter, Eliza, was a tall and aloof young lady of twenty-one with "large soft black eyes and glossy black hair." A graduate of Madame Campan's famous school for girls on the outskirts of Paris, she additionally had enjoyed a social season in London while her father was U. S. Minister to the Court of St. James's. Her luggage included an Irish harp on which she played stylish Continental airs.

Eliza had spent much of her life in France, having entered the Campan school at the age of seven when her father was Minister to that country on an earlier assignment. There she became the lifelong friend of Hortense de Beauharnais, the stepdaughter of Napoleon who later became Queen of Holland. Although Hortense was four years older they worked happily together on the chores and "good works" with which Madame Campan interspersed book lessons and worldly knowledge.

Three times a week, for instance, the girls cooked and carried food to the poor. They learned to cut out and sew clothing, clean and mend lace, make out and check laundry lists, etc. Madame Campan, once the teacher of royalty, founded her school with lessons of the French Revolution in mind and thought to make her charges self-sufficient. "If a girl loses her money and has only a humble pallet it should be decent," she said, "and the girl remains every inch the lady."

Eliza loved the school and the first time remained almost three years, her father visiting her frequently. Once he was extolling American democracy to Madame Campan when his daughter broke in with, "Yes, Papa, but there are no fine streets like these in America." "Very true, my dear," he replied. "We are in want of many things but we possess the finest of all—Liberty."

Recalled, he became Governor of Virginia. "Papa is teaching me geography, history and other subjects," Eliza wrote the headmistress. "I would appreciate it beyond expression if you can send me a doll fashionably dressed, as Papa intends to let me go to some balls and other public places." She was happy indeed when President Jefferson returned Papa to France and she could reenter the school.

Monroe and Eliza were very good friends. Eliza's mother left everything, including letter writing, up to him and he supervised his daughter's upbringing.

Born so many years apart, Eliza and Maria never spent much time together until their father became President in 1817— after which they had eight years together, but not always happily, under the White House roof. By then Maria, still petite and frolicsome, was fourteen and Eliza was the sedate mother of a seven-year-old daughter named, naturally, Hortensia.

Eliza's husband, George Hay, an attorney noted for his prosecution of Aaron Burr in the latter's trial for treason, became a White House secretary and Eliza was stand-in hostess for her mother. The friend of royalty, she was inclined to be domineering and her lofty decrees about protocol made enemies. She and Hortense, now married to Napoleon's brother, corresponded regularly. Hortense sent her namesake godchild portraits of herself and brother and a gold chain "which I pray she will wear as a souvenir of me."

Maria's education and friends were much less romantic. While her father was Secretary of State under Madison she attended the local schools of Washington, lived quietly with her family at 2017 I Street, Northwest, in the still-standing home the Monroes continued to live in for almost a year after the election. The White House, burned by the British in 1814, was not completely rebuilt and needed a full set of furnishings.

Monroe placed orders for French furniture, using $50,000

appropriated for the purpose, and set out on the first of his trips around the country to bind sectional wounds and usher in his Era of Good Feeling.

The ladies of Washington, accustomed to the social fanfare of Dolley Madison's eight years, were aghast at Mrs. Monroe's failure to make calls and stage parties—but thought all would change once the White House was habitable.

The old (rebuilt) mansion was reopened with a large public reception on New Year's Day, 1818. The furnishings were beautiful. When the $50,000 had not been enough the President, in a gesture he was to regret, sold the government his own collection of priceless French antiques, porcelain and silver for about $9,000 to fill the gaps.

The ladies were happy, but not for long. Mrs. Monroe intended neither to make nor return calls and Eliza, as her stand-in, to make none, and to be very selective about the ones she returned. But there would be a weekly "at home" at the White House plus all the "required" official parties, of course. To the ladies, including the wives of Congressmen, this was heresy.

They boycotted the Monroe at-homes and extended their stay-away decrees to parties given by wives of Monroe's Cabinet members. Mrs. William Seaton, wife of the town's leading editor, wrote, "The drawing room of the President was opened last night to a row of beggarly chairs," and another time—"Mrs. Adams [wife of the Secretary of State] invited a large party which we attended at which there were not more than three ladies."

Today it sounds like a small tempest in a smaller teapot, but from Martha Washington's day on, calling and returning calls had been a definite part of the White House picture. And every time Eliza tried to explain the rules now being followed she seemed to make it worse.

The President, who would have liked to live above such trivia, began to receive letters from Senators—no doubt influenced by their wives—asking wнo was supposed to call on them. He referred them to John Quincy Adams, his Secretary of State, who in his diary blamed Eliza for having raised "this senseless war of protocol."

Had he searched the globe, Monroe probably could not have found two people with fewer hospitable impulses than Adams and his older daughter. With friendliness and tact she could have soothed the women and he could have made the diplomatic corps feel less embattled.

James Fenimore Cooper, who attended a White House dinner, called the atmosphere "cold and unimaginative rather than formal." "A great gravity of mien marked most of the company," he said, "and there was neither any marked exhibition of spirit nor any words of grace."

Eventually the atmosphere changed under Monroe's record as a good President and with the return visit to America of Lafayette which sent the country into a long period of jubilation. But it did not change quickly enough to prevent Maria's wedding from being mismanaged by her sister and the resulting estrangement between the sisters.

Maria's parents thought of her as a child although she considered herself to be grown up. Her mother's nephew, Samuel Lawrence Gouverneur, came from New York to be junior secretary to the President, and Maria at once set her cap for him. They courted in the sparkling new White House and wished to get married when he was twenty-one and she sixteen. Reluctantly, the Monroes consented and Eliza took charge of the plans.

As a result, Maria, the first daughter of a President to marry in the White House, had the quietest nuptials imaginable. News of her engagement leaked to the diplomats and, scenting a thaw in their White House relations, they sent a representative to ask Mrs. Monroe whether their wives might entertain Maria or call on her.

Mrs. Monroe referred the problem to Eliza, who ruled that since she herself had not called on diplomatic families her sister "could not receive and return their visits." She stressed that the wedding would be "New York style" with only relatives and a few close friends of the family present, and suggested that the diplomats "take no notice of the marriage." This meant that Maria received no gifts from any foreign countries, something her descendants still regret.

Maria and her cousin were married in the oval parlor known as the Blue Room on March 9, 1820, her tiny feet on the center spread eagle of the new rug. Her dress was white and trimmed in silver lace. She wore it a week later in the receiving line when the Monroes gave a reception for the couple.

Local newspapers a few days later ran a front-page notice:

> MARRIED on Tuesday evening last in this city by the Rev. Mr. (William) Hawley, Samuel Lawrence Gouverneur, Esq., of New York to Maria Hester Monroe, youngest daughter of James Monroe, President of the United States.

There were no society reporters in those days and even if there had been Eliza would not have furnished them with fuller information.

Several parties outside the White House were scheduled for the couple, but only one was given. It was a dance and supper party by Commodore and Mrs. Stephen Decatur, who lived on neighboring Lafayette Square in a handsome home built with bounties won by the dashing Commodore in his battles against the Barbary Pirates.

The Commodore that same week fought his fatal duel and all other festivities planned for Maria and Samuel were canceled as the city went into mourning.

Maria's first child, named James Monroe Gouverneur, was born in the White House and the same Reverend Hawley, rector of St. John's Episcopal Church, did the christening. The Gouverneur marriage was happy but the young husband never forgave Eliza's "meddling" and saw to it that her rules no longer applied to Maria.

"The Gouverneurs can be quite highhanded themselves. He rebelled against Mrs. Hay's domination and it infuriated her," is the way Laurence Gouverneur Hoes, Maria's great-great-grandson, director of the James Monroe Memorial Library, puts it.

Family life at the White House did not always move smoothly after that and the saddest thing about it was that eventually the break between the sisters became complete. Two sets of Monroe descendants lived as strangers to each other. Family papers, letters and records were scattered and lost, many of them forever.

During his two terms in office Monroe was building Oak Hill, a lovely Virginia home for which his idol and mentor, Thomas Jefferson, had drawn the rough plans. Eliza and her family moved there with the Monroes when his Presidency ended. Maria and family moved to New York to live.

The new President, John Quincy Adams, repaid some of his debts to Monroe by making Eliza's husband judge for Virginia's eastern district and appointing young Gouverneur Postmaster of New York City. Everybody was happy about the moves which separated the sisters.

Hortensia, an unusually beautiful but strong-willed child, married at Oak Hill but much against her mother's wishes. She was but sixteen or seventeen (few Monroe dates are certain) and her husband was a widower with three young children. (He was Lloyd Rogers of Druid Hill near Baltimore, the same wealthy Marylander who had married Eliza Custis Law's daughter.)

Judge Hay died at Oak Hill shortly thereafter and in the same year Mrs. Monroe died after a brief illness. The former

President, shocked and bereft, went to live with Maria and her family.

He died at her home in New York on July 4, 1831, and was buried there. In his will he left Oak Hill not to Eliza but to Maria and—ironically, although evidently without malice— he commended Eliza "to the fraternal care and protection of my son-in-law, Samuel L. Gouverneur." This was a legacy sure to cut Eliza to the quick.

The will explained that he already had given Eliza an estate and wished to give Maria a like amount and then divide his remaining property between them. His papers he left to Gouverneur, who supposedly would edit and publish them, Eliza to get a third of any profit from them. (Gouverneur, sportsman and man-about-town, neglected the editing assignment.)

No doubt feeling unloved and an alien in her own country, Eliza returned to France to visit her friend Hortense and while there became a Roman Catholic, Pope Gregory XVI himself converting her while she and Hortense were in Rome.

She may have returned to this country briefly, but she died in Paris and is buried at Père Lachaise, the resting place of many another exile. It is believed that she took the vows of a religious order in Paris and spent her last days in a convent.

Maria and family returned to live in Washington and at Oak Hill. One family legend is that Maria kept the best silver hidden to prevent her husband from selling it for gambling debts. Once he said to a son, "For God's sake, have your mother get the silver out. We're going to have guests."

The Gouverneur son born in the White House died before he was a teen-ager. The second son, Samuel L. Jr., served in the Mexican War and was a comfort to his mother. The only daughter, Elizabeth, married Dr. Henry L. Heiskell in a large Washington ceremony attended by President Tyler and John Quincy Adams.

Maria in her will left Oak Hill and its contents to her husband, who then remarried and, at his death, left everything to his second wife. His son had to sue in the Orphans Court for his mother's personal effects. Not all were recovered, but gradually through purchases and gifts Mr. Hoes has collected and assembled a large showing for the memorial museum and library in Virginia. Oak Hill, still beautiful, is today in private hands and not open to the public.

John Quincy Adams's Sons

A VERSATILE, NOT ALWAYS
HARMONIOUS TRIO

>>>->>>)(((-(((<

IMMEDIATELY after breakfast on Christmas Day, 1820, Secretary of State John Quincy Adams made a captive audience of his three sons—George, John and Charles Francis, all home for the holidays—and read them Pope's "Messiah," a poem he not only felt suited to the day but one he had loved since childhood.

In his diary he wrote that he did it as an experiment to test the literary tastes of the younger generation, and sadly he reported its failure:

"Not one of them, excepting George, appeared to take the slightest interest in it, nor is there one of them who has any relish for literature. Charles has a great fondness for books and a meditative mind, but neither disposition nor aptitude for public speaking or correct reading. Charles must teach himself all he learns. He will learn nothing from others." He failed to mention his middle son but John's grandmother, Abigail Adams, already was on the record that John was "inclined to a quickness of passion and a stiffness which needs subduing."

The father could not resist comparing his sons' indifference to poetry to his own youthful eagerness to master all the books

his parents loved. But he probably forgave the boys as he recalled the tears he had shed trying to understand Milton's
"Paradise Lost," a parental favorite. He had struggled with
their copy of it in a shed at Braintree, Massachusetts, and
learned to smoke during his long period of frustration. He was
thirty years of age, he recorded, before Milton said a thing
to him.

Ages of his sons at the above Christmastime were: George,
nineteen, John, seventeen, and Charles Francis, thirteen. All
were alert and attractive. George, born in Berlin while his
father was U. S. Minister there, was a senior at Harvard, and
the other two lived mostly with their grandfather, the ex-President, so as to attend better schools than were generally avail-
able in Washington at the time. The Secretary of State in
actuality did not know his sons nearly so well during this
period as his father did. (He had spent more time with Charles
than the other two.)

The older boys stayed behind with their Adams grandparents when John Quincy Adams became U. S. Minister to
Russia, but Charles, only two, went along on the 6-year assignment to old St. Petersburg. When his father went to Holland
on the peace mission which ended the War of 1812, Charles
and his mother remained in Russia until sent for and then
made a fabulous 40-day trip by carriage in the dead of winter
to join the father in Paris in 1815. Napoleon had made his
spectacular escape from Elba at the time and Charles never
forgot seeing him in his uniformed splendor addressing a
frenziedly happy mob from a balcony. Then John Quincy
Adams was made U. S. Minister to Great Britain and sent
for his other sons. In London Charles became reacquainted
with his brothers.

When George and John, ages fourteen and twelve, sailed off
to join their parents and brother in England in 1815,
the grandparents loaded them with pencils and diaries, cau-

tioning them to record every detail of the journey and stay. A trip not written down, Grandfather said, leaves no memories.

Grandfather apparently had outlived the grumpiness which marked his Presidential days. He delighted in his grandchildren, all of whom seemed to adore him. As for Grandmother Abigail, she was venerated. Charles Francis could not believe his eyes when he finally made it home to Massachusetts and saw how his older brothers got tears in their eyes when they even thought they had displeased Grandmother.

The three brothers had two happy years together in England. George and John went to school in Ealing, and Charles went to a school nearer home.

Their father was proud of them and noted in his diary that they persuaded him to go to the theater and take them on excursions to historic sites. "George is studying Greek to your heart's content," he wrote his father. When he was called home to become Secretary of State to President Monroe the lads again lived happily with their grandparents to be near Harvard.

George graduated and began his struggle as a lawyer in Boston. John, along with the whole senior class, was expelled for "rioting and insubordination." Charles Francis entered the school at fifteen and graduated on schedule.

The boys did not miss all social events in Washington, however. They decorated many of their mother's parties and looked forward to their winter holidays with the family. Also, the summers were spent together at the family home at Quincy and all three sons adored their fragile English-born mother, who could express her affection for them more readily than their father was able to do.

Living in the John Quincy Adams home during this period were two young and pretty nieces: Mary Catherine Hellen, orphaned daughter of Mrs. Adams's sister, and Abigail Adams, daughter of the Secretary of State's brother, Thomas Boylston. All three sons were at one time or another in love with Mary Hellen, who either unwittingly or by flirtatious design caused the family many hours of unhappiness.

George, the oldest son, and Mary Hellen were engaged by January 8, 1824, the ninth anniversary of the Battle of New Orleans, and the date on which the Adamses gave their most impressively successful party. It was in honor of Gen. Andrew Jackson. The sons and nieces helped decorate the Adams home on F Street. The floors had chalk drawings of eagles and the Stars and Stripes, plus a decorative bit of lettering reading WELCOME TO THE HERO OF THE BATTLE OF NEW ORLEANS. Tissue paper festoons and evergreens took more than a week to put up. Niece Abigail considered that the effect was very beautiful and also wrote that an 8-piece orchestra furnished delightful music.

An almost unheard of 1,000 persons came to this party, partook of a lavish supper and danced until 1 A.M. Their carriages made so much noise dashing over the cobblestones that people not invited complained of inability to sleep.

The ball was a prelude to that year's elections in which John Quincy Adams won the Presidency, although Andrew Jackson received more popular votes and the close decision had to be made in the House of Representatives.

Son John, dismissed from Harvard, was free to become his father's White House secretary and to read law under his father's tutelage. He was a loyal companion who accompanied the President on daily horseback rides—usually before breakfast and at times eighteen miles long—and often went swimming in the Potomac with him.

Son George, busy getting his law practice started in Boston, was not around to keep up his courtship of Mary Hellen. Charles Francis came to the White House after his graduation,

which was shortly after his father's inauguration, and duti-
fully warned George that his romance seemed to be in serious
trouble.

Neither the President nor Mrs. Adams was too eager for
George and Mary Hellen to marry but they worried when it
became evident that the flirtatious niece now had set her cap
for John. The romantic situation in the White House was definitely sticky, but not known to the public.

Charles Francis had a gay time in the White House and
treated his stay of almost two years in Washington as a postgraduate course in men and politics. Then he returned to Boston to clerk in the law office of Daniel Webster and to pursue
his courtship of Abigail Brown Brooks, daughter of Boston's
leading merchant.

The First Lady wrote him that John and Mary Hellen
planned to marry and that she was having nothing to do with
the wedding. When George heard the news, he refused to
write John his congratulations. Charles Francis wrote in his
diary that, in his opinion, George's reaction "betrays more
littleness of spirit than I had wished to suspect in him.

Meantime, the plans were canceled and reset several times.
Finally John wrote inviting his brothers to attend his marriage on February 25, 1828. Neither accepted and Charles
Francis wrote in his diary that he feared his refusal to attend
would be "misconstrued and productive of future coldness."

So the only wedding of a President's son in the White House
was not attended by his brothers, and the First Lady was less
than enthusiastic. Nonetheless, it seems to have been a brilliant affair. Young Abigail and three other girls were bridesmaids. Abigail wrote that "the bride looked very handsome
in white satin, orange blossoms and pearls." The wedding
was in the Blue Parlor, which was "arranged with flowers and
ribbons," and the day following there was a White House
reception for the newlyweds.

Two days after the event *The National Intelligencer* listed in its "Marriages" column: *On the 25th inst., by the Rev. Mr. Hawley, Mr. John Adams to Miss Mary Catherine Hellen, daughter of the late Walter Hellen, Esq.*

One of the groomsmen recorded that the President, "usually so grave and unsocial, unbent for the nonce, and danced at the wedding ball in a Virginia reel with great spirit." Another called the wedding "a high-spirited affair with many guests and much laughter."

The President, concerned about the coolness among his sons, sent Charles Francis a piece of the wedding cake and asked him to wish for the happiness of the marriage and wrote that his prayers were for its success just as they would be "equally fervent for the prosperity of your own, in prospect."

Both family matters and politics were painful to the Adams family that year. The father found the Presidency tedious beyond belief, knew that his popularity was low and suspected that he, like his father before him, would have only one term in office.

On December 2, of 1825, President and Mrs. Adams's first grandchild was born in the White House. She was named Mary Louisa for her mother and grandmother, and her grandfather called her "Looly" right away. He must have loved her dearly, because in his diary forever afterward are scattered references to this Louisa. He taught her to read and write and when she was eight years of age he gave her a Bible in which he later pasted one of his poems. The poem is titled "The Casket"—which in those days meant a box for precious things.

Like his father before him, this Adams President did not attend the inauguration of his successor but on the day before it, moved to a home he owned on Meridian Hill, putting an announcement in the papers to say that since his residence was so far from downtown he expected nobody at all to call on him on inaugural day.

As soon as the accumulations of his dozen years in the capital could be packed he expected to move home to Quincy. He wrote his son George to come down and help him with the move. John and Mary were to continue living in Washington, where John would manage a gristmill which his father had purchased on what is now Adams Mill Road.

George did not relish the assignment his father gave him and delayed as long as he could, but on April 27 he told Charles Francis that he had received another letter and must make the trip. "He seemed very much disarranged. As usual, delay has done him no service," the youngest brother noted in his diary. Poor Charles Francis and all his family, however, were totally unprepared for the next news about George.

It is explained in the following report which appeared in the New York *American* of April 30, 1829:

A very melancholy occurrence took place last night on board the steamboat Franklin, on her passage from Providence to this city. George Washington Adams, eldest son of the late President of the United States, was on board on his way to Washington. During the day and evening he evinced no symptoms of indisposition till near bedtime, when he complained of a violent pain in his head, and said he would be bled as soon as he got to New York.

He, however, retired with the other passengers but rose about 2 o'clock, dressed himself in a hurried manner and awoke one of the passengers complaining they were plotting against him, and particularly asked one of them what it was he had said about his (Mr. Adams') jumping overboard. Nothing of the sort had been said, and the thing passed off, Mr. Adams going upon deck and the passengers resuming their slumbers.

The only subsequent trace of the unfortunate young man was the finding some hours afterward of his hat upon the deck

forward of the wheelguard whence he is supposed in a high
state of fever to have jumped overboard. Mr. Adams was a
lawyer of promise, a young man of considerable acquirements,
and has been several times one of the representatives of the
Massachusetts legislature of the city of Boston. He was unmarried.

Charles wrote in his diary: "My father almost lived in him
[George] and the loss indeed to him will be dreadful. . . ."
His father wrote him a week later that the first shock of "this
heavy dispensation of Providence is past" and that he and his
wife were relying on "Him who chasteneth in mercy" and
"still look for consolation in the affectionate kindness of our
remaining sons."

In going through George's effects, his brother learned that
his father's financial affairs were in great disorder (George
was his father's business manager) and, even more shocking
to him, that George was heavily involved in an affair with a
chambermaid by whom he had fathered a child. In retrospect
Charles could understand why his brother could see no way
out of his problems.

He wrote: "I have been forced to the unpleasant conclusion
that it [the death] was not untimely. He would have lived
probably to give much misery to his friends and more to himself . . . now his memory will be cherished by his friends
and his end lamented."

George was twenty-eight when he died.

Charles was deeply worried about his father's future. "A
more pitiable situation I do not think I know than that of my
father and mother," he wrote. He went out to Quincy to get
the Old House ready for them and found it in a most rundown
condition. He knew his father was no good at managing finances, and wondered how he ever could make a living again.

Charles, with a good law practice and about to marry into
a rich family, was the only member of his family who

was doing well at the time. When he learned that his father wanted to run for Congress he strongly opposed the whole idea. Charles thought that the ex-President, at sixty-three, was too old to attempt it, and also, Congressmen at the time made only $1,500 a year.

This Presidential son, however, swallowed his doubts, made himself his father's financial guardian, and never again doubted his father's greatness. The father threw himself into his race with great enjoyment and youthful energy. He served in the House of Representatives with notable distinction until his death at age eighty.

Charles married his Abigail and they had seven children. When his father-in-law died he left each of his sons-in-law $75,000 and divided his huge fortune among his daughters. Charles stopped his law practice and carved an illustrious career for himself editing his grandmother's letters and his grandfather's papers, editing a newspaper, serving in the state legislature, going to Congress and during the Civil War becoming—like his father and grandfather before him—U. S. Minister to Great Britain.

His brother John died at the early age of thirty-two years, leaving his wife and two charming little daughters, Louisa and Georgiana Frances.

The Old House at Quincy, today a national historic site run by the National Park Service, descended to Charles Francis and there every summer the descendants of the second and sixth Presidents were expected, and came—for many years.

Andrew Jackson's
"Chosen" Children

The children of President Jackson's family request you to join them on Christmas Day at 4 o'clock, P.M., for a frolic in the East Room.

Almost every child in the official social swim of the capital city on December 19, 1835, received this missive and was on hand when the appointed hour came—and went home the ecstatic pal of Andrew Jackson.

For a man with no children of his own, nor any blood kin which he knew about, the seventh President did more baby-sitting, monitored more weddings, followed more school grades, and had more youngsters of all ages swirling about him than any of the other Presidents would have cared to manage.

Six children below the age of ten were with him in the White House when the above invitation was hand delivered to more than 100 households. What is more, three of the six had been born there—where he could oversee their arrivals and sponsor their christenings. Their names and ages were: Mary Rachel, six, John Samuel, three, and Rachel, eighteen months. (Mary Rachel, in self-defense, later changed her name to Mary Emily to lessen the confusion.) They had an older brother, Andrew Jackson, nine, who was born before "Uncle Jackson" became President.

All of these were the children of Andrew J. Donelson, his secretary and a nephew of his dead wife Rachel, and of Emily Donelson, his White House hostess and also Rachel's niece. The President had supervised A. J. Donelson's upbringing, abetted his marriage to a first cousin—the more of Rachel's relatives around the better—and paid for their wedding trip.

The other two children belonged to Andrew Jackson Jr., Rachel's nephew who was adopted at birth, and Sarah Yorke Jackson, a demure and talented Quakeress from Philadelphia whom the President was happy to call daughter. These two were: Rachel, three, and Andrew Jackson, III, aged eighteen months. The young Jacksons were spending the holidays in Washington but regularly lived at the Hermitage, the President's acred home in Tennessee.

For these six the President did all but change the diapers. He walked the floor with them when they had colic, let them chew on his Rachel's miniature when they were teething—a deed for which he would have shot anybody else—and loved it when their parents went on visits leaving them in his total care. When manly little Jackson Donelson was sent to school in Langley, Virginia, the President wrote him much more frequently than his parents did, loaded him with enough good advice to sink a battleship and let him know he was loved. He had held this one, then two and a half years old, on his knees almost the whole way to Washington when he had come to "clean out the city" and be inaugurated. ׀

Games played by the happy young elite at the Christmas frolic included Blind Man's Buff, Hide and Go Seek, Puss in the Corner, and forfeit games like Spin the Plate. Vice-President Martin Van Buren, one of the adults on hand to keep the fun in high gear, failed at plate spinning and incurred the penalty. Others long remembered the sight of him standing on one leg to chant:

> "Here I stand all ragged and dirty.
> If you don't come kiss me,
> I'll run like a turkey."

No child "redeemed" him, so he strutted across the floor like a game gobbler and amid peals of laughter, most of it from the grown-ups.

The Marine Band played when the youngsters tramped into the State Dining Room for refreshments. The tables were heaped high with an edible array of "confections of every conceivable design." Towering pyramids of snowballs and icicles were topped by a large gilt cock to form the centerpiece and, wonder of wonders, the snowballs were to throw.

Each snowball contained a French kiss and was made to explode in a flurry of artificial snow when thrown at a frolicmate. Mary Emily years later wrote about the party in a little book called *Christmas Under Three Flags*.

She wrote also of the afternoon before when the President took the four older children with him to distribute gifts at the orphan asylum.

In the carriage they talked of Santa Claus. Johnny asked Uncle Jackson whether he would come that night and what he would bring. "We can only wait and see," said the President. Then he told them, obviously referring to his own desolate childhood, "I once knew a little boy who not only never had a toy in his life but after the death of his mother, a pure and saintly woman, had neither home nor friends."

Then at 8 A.M. there was a family breakfast, for which a large Yule log was burning. Under standing orders from the President children always were served first at his table. "They have better appetites and less patience," he explained, "and should not be required to wait until their elders are served."

In all, it has been estimated, Jackson and his beloved Rachel "raised" eleven children at the Hermitage. Their love of children was legendary in several states. Old friends on their deathbeds would arrange to have their sons sent to Jackson so that he could oversee their upbringing. He took them in, cared for their inheritances, sent them off to school and prodded them to keep up their studies.

Always, though, Rachel yearned for a child of her very, very own. This was not to be, but Providence smiled her way on December 22, 1809—when she was forty-two.

The fragile wife of her brother gave birth to twin boys. Please, begged Rachel, give me one. Her brother and wife agreed and on January 10, 1810, after Jackson had rushed through adoption papers, she stepped from her carriage at the Hermitage with Andrew Jackson, Jr. She and the general felt like real parents at long last.

Andrew J. Donelson, almost ten at the time and growing up as a son of the family, recalled how the general would sit before the open fire on a wintry night with a baby lamb and his toddler son between his knees. Andrew Jr. was a most satisfactory child, and pleasing to the general always. "Kiss our dear Andrew for me and tell him I am coming home" became a constant refrain in his letters. When Congress voted him a medal for services in the War of 1812, he sent it to Rachel with the instructions:

> Tell my son how anxious I am that he may become the worthy possessor of the things that a grateful country has bestowed on his papa.
> Tell him to read and learn his book. . . . His happiness through life depends on his procuring an education now; and on all occasions to adhere to the truth. . . . Having experienced so much inconvenience from the want of a perfect education myself makes me so solicitous.

Jackson was careful when visiting boys came with their parents, as they did in great numbers, to keep the games manly but not permit rowdiness. He did not want his son to have the angry battles he himself had had and, perhaps most of all, he did not want him to kill anybody in a fight, as he once had done in a duel.

He need not have worried on that score. Young Andy was completely unwarlike and always would be.

He was sent early to old Cumberland College in Nashville to become a polished gentleman. If he had swaggered a bit it would have been understandable, since the students and faculty often turned out en masse to welcome Jackson home from battles—but Andy Jr. was never one to swagger.

The son's nineteenth birthday, which fell between Jackson's election and inauguration, was a day of deepest mourning at the Hermitage because Rachel Jackson, First Lady-elect and his devoted mother, was dying. She collapsed while buying clothing to take to Washington and was buried on Christmas Eve, her husband never doubting that scandals loosed against her during his second bid for the Presidency had killed her.

It was a sad little group which boarded the steamboat *Pennsylvania* at a wharf near the Hermitage and set out for the capital city on a bleak and drizzly January 18, 1829.

Accompanying Jackson, his son, and the three Donelsons—A. J., Emily, and their baby son—were Mary Eastin, a beautiful sixteen-year-old great-niece of Rachel's who would have a White House wedding and Maj. William B. Lewis, a military aide whose brother-in-law, John Eaton, recently had jolted Washington society by marrying Peggy O'Neal Timberlake, the innkeeper's daughter whose social status became the *cause célèbre* of the Jackson administration.

Andy Jr. was to remain in Washington only a few weeks before returning home to prove that he could manage the Hermitage acres. He enjoyed the inaugural festivities and evidently made a good impression. Anne Royal, the hard-bitten female reporter who rarely complimented anyone, wrote, "His countenance is sweetness itself, his eyes as soft as dewdrops." She asked him how he would like to be President. He replied, "Not at all, ma'am, not at all."

He had something ever so much more important than politics on his mind. He was discovering girls, a subject in which he lacked education and which he tackled, the new President was to learn, in sledgehammer fashion. During the inauguration he met the pretty daughter of Major Francis Smith, who lived in Virginia, and decided immediately to stop and woo her on his way back to Tennessee.

So eager was he to begin the courtship that he tarried only two or three nights at the White House. Miss Smith was outraged by his unscheduled advances and wounded his pride so severely that he returned to Washington and his father. Surely one of the most tender stories about Andrew Jackson is that his son came to him for solace, and the way he handled the debacle. He never had coached his son in girl culture, but he began now by writing a letter for Andy Jr. to take to Colonel Smith. In it the President said:

> I fear he has committed an error. If he has I trust you will ascribe it to his youth, diffidence and inexperience, and allow him to make atonement for it, for which purpose I send him to you. . . .
> He has erred in attempting to address your daughter without first making known to you and your lady his honorable intentions and obtaining your approbation, but he has been admonished of this impropriety and now awaits upon you to confess it.

Then, not wishing to hurt his son's chances, if any, he added:

He has been reared in the paths of virtue and morality by his pious and amiable mother, and I believe has walked steadily in them. He is the only hope by which I look to the continuation of my name, and has a fortune ample enough. . . .

Miss Smith never thawed, however, and young Andy went on to the Hermitage to court a girl named Flora, who obviously enjoyed a spirited flirtation now and then. The concerned President was happy when this romance ended. He wrote his son:

> I expected the result you name with Flora. She is a fine little girl . . . but as I told you she has given herself up to coquettry. . . . Treat her with kindness, but I assure you I am happy at the result, as I seldom ever saw a coquett make a good wife. . . . All I have to request is that you will engage in no other affair of heart without first obtaining my advice.

Andy Jr. met and fell instantly in love with his future wife while visiting his twin brother in Philadelphia. She was a tiny black-eyed orphan named Sarah Yorke, a demure and educated Quakeress.

The President was delighted and wrote:

> MY SON . . .
> I have pursued with interest the letter of Sarah's which you have submitted to me. . . . Your happiness will insure mine for the few years I expect to live. The amiability of her temper and her other good qualities which you represent is a sure pledge to me that she will unite with you in adding comfort to my life.
> You will please communicate to her that you have my full and free consent that you be united in the holy bonds of matrimony; that I shall receive her as a daughter and cherish her as my child. I find that you are engaged to each other; the sooner this engagement is consummated the better.

Unable to attend the wedding, the President sent Ralph E. W. Earl, the artist who had married one of Rachel's nieces, with the ring of pearls which had a lock of his hair entwined —and many affectionate messages.

The newlyweds came immediately to Washington. As their carriage turned into White House grounds on November 24, 1831, Andrew said, "Look, Sarah, to see if you can distinguish father." She replied, "Oh, there he is—like Saul among his brethren, head and shoulders above them all."

No one ever cherished a daughter-in-law more than Jackson did Sarah. He proudly presented her at a large reception, at which she wore her silk and lace wedding gown, and gave several large dinners for her. In the spring the young couple journeyed on to Tennessee. "You, my dear," the President told Sarah, "are mistress of the Hermitage." Emily Donelson remained mistress of the White House, which the couple visited often, and after Emily's untimely death Sarah was hostess there for part of a year.

Titian-haired Emily was only twenty-one when she became White House hostess. She and Uncle Jackson got along beautifully on all subjects, except that she would not accept Peggy Eaton socially. She sided with the Washington women who considered Peggy unworthy of notice. That Emily was among his enemies on this ticklish and continuing problem the President could not understand.

This was not permitted to spoil the fine East Parlor christening for Mary Rachel, Emily's new baby, however. "Spare no expense nor pains," the President said. "Let us make it an event to be remembered; we will do honor to the baby."

He gave this baby a personal maid and companion, drawing up this unique document to do so:

Be it remembered that I, Andrew Jackson, have this day given to Mary Rachel, daughter of Andrew J. Donelson and

Emily Donelson, a mulatto girl slave, about eight years old called Emeline, which I give to her and her keeps forever.

The President, frustrated at Emily's refusal to agree with him about Peggy Eaton, decided to banish her back to Tennessee, muttering that he could get along without his family as well as they could get along without him.

At the last minute he piled into the carriage with Emily and the children, and went along, too.

Emily's husband returned with Uncle Jackson that autumn but Emily remained with her mother. Uncle Jackson missed her and made some overtures to her, but they always were accompanied by "if you will do your duty by Mrs. Eaton." Finally he sent the Eatons off to the governorship of Florida and then on to Spain. Then the prodigal could return and the President have "his children" again.

Two Donelson nieces came back to the White House with Emily: Mary Eastin again and Mary McLemore. Mary Coffee, a third one, came later. Then the President invited Mary Ann Lewis, daughter of Major William Lewis, to come to the White House, too—and was in his element with all the pretty young marriageable beauties around him.

He gave Mary Eastin and Mary Ann Lewis weddings in the White House, took happy credit for bringing Mary Coffee and his ward A. J. Hutchings together. Also, he promoted and was proud of the romance between Elizabeth Martin, who was visiting him, and Jefferson's grandson, Meriwether Lewis Randolph. He backed his interest in this latter wedding by giving young Randolph a fine job in the Territory of Arkansas.

The nuptials of Mary Ann Lewis to Alphonse Joseph Yver Pageot, Secretary of the French Legation, on November 29, 1832, were in every way unusual. Miss Lewis not only was marrying a foreigner, but a Catholic. Father William Matthews performed the ceremony and was present a year later to christen Andrew Jackson Pageot in the Red Parlor. Then the Pageots went off to France, from whence they returned later when he became French Minister to the United States. All the marriages Uncle Jackson monitored seemed to work well.

For Emily and A. J. Donelson, who had meant so much to him, he bought acres adjacent to the Hermitage and had built for them a beautiful home called Tulip Grove.

Emily went home to furnish it in the spring of 1836 and never returned. A victim of rapid tuberculosis, she died there in December with Elizabeth Martin Randolph at her side and her husband rushing homeward.

Andrew Jr., unhappily, was no farm manager and had a way of losing on land deals from which he expected fortunes. His father advised him, exhorted with him and refused to blame him—although he cost the President a pretty penny.

It was sad for Jackson to leave the Presidency in debt because of young Andrew. Francis Blair, his Postmaster General, tried to give him $100,000 outright but the old warrior—ever a good businessman except when his emotions were overly involved—refused the great kindness.

He threw himself into the Hermitage operation, pulled its fertile acres out of the red, paid his son's debts. After his death, however, the son reverted to debts, endangering the livelihood of Sarah and their children. Out of love for Jackson, the State of Tennessee bought the Hermitage so that the family could live there free and the home be saved.

The Civil War made inroads into the lives of Jackson's White House family. John Samuel Donelson, born in the White House, died at Chickamauga fighting for the Confederacy. Mary Emily, a lock of whose hair went into the cornerstone of the Treasury Building when Uncle Jackson smacked it right in the path of Pennsylvania Avenue—where it remains today—returned to Washington as Mary Emily Wilcox, the widow of a Confederate Congressman.

President and Mrs. Grant invited her to sleep in the White House in the room in which she was born. She accepted a clerkship at the Treasury Department with no embarrassment at all and was much respected as one of the city's first "working women."

Today the Hermitage (and adjacent Tulip Grove) is a beautifully kept public heritage supervised by the Ladies Hermitage Association. Uncle Jackson's racehorses have gone and the suburbs have come, but the fields and buildings remain a delightful oasis.

Van Buren & Sons

ALL OF THEM LADIES' MEN

THE ladies who admired an elegant young widower named
Martin Van Buren during his first winter in Washington
(1821-22) would have been upset to know how much thought
he gave each day to the proper rearing of his four handsome
sons: Abraham, fourteen, John, eleven, Martin (Mat), nine
and Smith, four.

They lived with relatives in Kinderhook, New York, the
little Dutch village in which Van Buren was born and in which
English still was the second language. He, the new Senator
from New York, lived in the capital city as a carefree bachelor.

He was thirty-seven years of age and, although below medium
height, had a fine head of burnished curling locks which gave
him a pleasing appearance, and an urbane gloss which made
his charming manners most acceptable at social gatherings.

He played whist at family parties, called on matrons to
bring them choice news from Capitol Hill, and could be relied
upon to be at that most respectable gathering of the elite, the
bedside of sick children of the prominent—where "sitting up
at night" was a high civic virtue. Also, he was much in evidence
at the little city's gala balls.

He had married his pretty Dutch cousin, Hannah Hoes,
and at her death took their children to live with their aunts

and uncles, but he continued to supervise their upbringing. He was devoted to their welfare and they remained devoted to him, putting his career ahead of their own always.

Abraham, who went to West Point, might have had a brighter army career had he not taken military leave whenever his father needed him to be his secretary, confidant and general factotum. John, who became an attorney, might have held higher offices had he not spent so much time promoting his father's ambitions.

Van Buren needed Abraham when he became Secretary of State for Andrew Jackson and began his climb to the Presidency. They moved into Decatur House on Lafayette Square and lived intimately near the White House family, with John a frequent visitor. The Van Buren boys were attentive escorts for visiting relatives in the Presidential household.

Jackson knew Van Buren not only as an able politician but also he valued his status as a father. Smith Van Buren, who was thirteen at the time and in a New England school, wrote that he had been disciplined for a misdemeanor which he said that he had not committed. His father showed the President his letter. All sentiment when young people were concerned, Jackson said of the letter:

"What a gem! Cherish it. . . . I would not take a *million* for such a son and I protest against his sense of propriety being subdued by despotism. . . . Never let him change his position unless the superintendent atones for the punishment of innocence. . . ."

At the beginning of the Jackson administration Van Buren felt sure that he soon would solve the Peggy Eaton problem which had Washingtonians divided into two warring social camps. As a widower, he could afford to take the President's side and be charming to Peggy, wife of the Secretary of War. But try as he would, he could not influence the *good* women of the city to accept her.

Finally he evolved a plan so daring that he almost was afraid to tell the President, with whom he went horseback riding most mornings. Abraham, who agreed with his father about the plan, sympathized when he returned from three rides without mentioning it. On the fourth ride, however, Van Buren came home elated. Jackson had seen the logic in having *all* his Cabinet resign so as to get his Secretary of War and wife out of town.

Peggy did not appreciate it when her husband became Governor of Florida and so he soon was made U. S. Minister to Spain, a country in which she was supremely happy—and very popular. That was Van Buren's message: a President has many jobs at his command, can move his appointees around until both parties are reasonably satisfied with the results.

In the "fruit basket turnover" Van Buren himself was named U. S. Minister to Great Britain. "The Fox of Kinderhook has done it again," it was said on Capitol Hill. Abraham went back into the army and Van Buren, accompanied by John, set out for London—although the Senate had not yet ratified his appointment. Washington Irving, a longtime Van Buren friend, settled into the London residence as visitor and John continued to the Continent on a sightseeing tour.

The Senate, when it got around to voting on the Van Buren assignment, was evenly split and the Vice-President, John C. Calhoun, untied it by voting against confirmation—thus widening the gap between himself and the President, and insuring that Van Buren would become Vice-President during Jackson's second term.

Abraham wrote his father, gleefully, that the lack of confirmation was a boon, not a disaster. Van Buren wrote John to end his travels in Rome and join him for the voyage home—and he did become Vice-President that same year.

This time Abraham, now a major, and Martin Jr. lived with their father in Washington. Smith was studying to be a lawyer, and John established himself in New York City as an immediately successful attorney with a lucrative practice. Witty and self-confident, John was an eloquent speaker who matched wits with lawyers twice his age. Rumors that he was drinking heavily reached his alarmed father, however, and remembering the difficulties he had experienced with John when he was an undergraduate and a somewhat wayward student at Yale, he wrote him:

> What you may regard as an innocent and harmless indulgence will take you years to overcome in public estimation. . . . The light and vain feeling of desiring to be regarded as a dashing fellow is surely gratified at too great an expense in this way. Washington is full of reports at your expense. It was no longer than last evening that I was informed by a friend—well-meaning but fond of gossip—that Major Fane said you had been twice carried drunk from the race course. I knew of course that this was untrue. . . .

Martin Jr. was quiet and self-effacing, had a sense of history and was interested in keeping his father's papers in order, but he was in ill health much of the time. Smith, the youngest, was developing a nice literary style and becoming a pleasing conversationalist. He sought his father's advice about the study of law; in fact, asked him to outline a complete study course.

The Vice-President set down some general observations as perhaps more beneficial and serviceable than the outline of particulars which Smith requested. He wrote:

> I am convinced that I lost much valuable time in deliberation upon and in discussion of the superior advantages of one course over another. . . . Rather than cogitating so much on this I should have taken up the first of the usual books: Blackstone.
>
> The only way to acquire fondness for law is to read constantly. A month's study is made completely unprofitable by

a moment's abstinence. Read Blackstone's commentaries and then the revised laws and opinions, how modified and dropped by the courts. Write up a summary of this. To resolve yourself to it you must keep at it. Keeping at it, you will grow half fond of it.

All four sons lived with Van Buren when he became President in 1837. They ran a womanless and, for them, a happy White House.

Van Buren did the mansion over most elegantly and began to live in an exclusive manner. White House doors no longer were open to the masses. The gold spoons and emerald finger bowls were put into everyday use, and small dinners replaced the great public affairs sponsored by Jackson. The widower and the bachelors screened their guests most carefully.

John, whose first trip to Europe was cut short, set out for a longer stay in 1838. The President, knowing the Jackson name carried more prestige than his in England, asked the former President for an introduction for his son to the Duke of Wellington.

"My son John is called to England on professional business," he wrote. "He proposes to sail the middle of May and I should be proud to have him bear a letter of introduction from you to the Duke of Wellington."

Jackson replied immediately and sent the letter.

With the duke as sponsor, the President's son was received by the royalty and nobility of Great Britain. Shortly after his arrival Queen Victoria gave a state ball and John was among the guests. British newspapers detailed the magnificence of the entertainment, the splendor of costumes and jewels, the rich foods and costly wines—all widely reported in America.

Henceforth the second Van Buren son was known as "Prince John" in papers throughout America. Congressmen devoted speeches to the un-Americanism of hobnobbing with royalty.

Abraham joined John in England in the spring of 1839—

on a somewhat belated honeymoon. The previous autumn he had married Angelica Singleton, a twenty-one-year-old beauty from South Carolina. Angelica, a member of a wealthy and prominent family, had come to Washington to visit her relatives, Senator and Mrs. William C. Preston—and Dolley Madison. It was Dolley, her cousin, who eyed the womanless White House with misgiving and promoted the romance.

The President proudly presented his daughter-in-law at a large New Year's Day reception of 1839, where she won praise for four hours of standing to help receive guests and for her charm.

Angelica's uncle, Andrew Stevenson, was the American Minister at the Court of St. James's and his wife planned a lavish entertainment schedule for the honeymooners in London. Mrs. Stevenson was no admirer of the Van Buren family but wrote a relative that she liked Abraham very much.

"He is very different from Prince John, who resembles his father in using his fellow men as a ladder upon which to mount and when he is up he kicks it down and without scruples of conscience denies he has had any aid."

She obtained for Angelica an invitation to the Duchess of Northumberland's grand ball "but John Van Buren persuaded her that he had procured it for her," she continued.

Queen Victoria received Angelica graciously and the young beauty was "perfectly enchanted" at the Queen's ball, or so her aunt reported, describing in detail the dresses her niece wore and what the royal family served at meals. The aunt also wrote that Angelica had come to England with extravagant expectations and that she pitied the "unfortunate being whose duty or necessity it may be to give the rousing shake . . . to awaken one from such a dream as hers. . . ."

The major and Angelica went on to the Hague and then to France, where King Louis Philippe entertained them at dinner.

Angelica loved the dresses she wore at European courts and often received in them at the White House, seated on a raised platform and greeting her guests with a formal bow.

The President should have known better than this, even if his daughter-in-law did not. It added to her aunt's opinion that she was living in a royal dream world—when in reality, as later years showed, she was a modest and sweet person afflicted only by youth and inexperience.

After his father's defeat for reelection, Abraham returned to military service as a colonel and served during the Mexican War. He and Angelica became the parents of three sons, none of whom lived to reach manhood. In their later years they lived in New York and were acclaimed for their generous hospitality.

"Prince John" became a famous defense lawyer in the same city. He was noted for winning his cases and for being a gay blade about town.

One of his most sensational cases was in defense of Edwin Forrest, the noted tragedian, whose wife sued him for alimony. Each charged the other with adultery. Newspapers gave much more space to "Prince John's" handling of the case than to the other side. He lost the case but the loss did not lessen the demand for his legal services.

John served in the national House of Representatives, where he devoted much time to defending his father's record as President, and he worked tirelessly for his father when he was the unsuccessful candidate for reelection twice on the Democratic ticket and once on the Free Soil slate. He married Elizabeth Van der Pool, daughter of a prominent Dutch family, and fathered three daughters.

Martin Jr., lacking the robustness of the other sons, served his father as secretary during the Presidency, but liked research more than political sparring and began collecting data about his father's early life and arranging it so that his father could write his autobiography. Had he been in better health the book would have been written much sooner.

After the Presidency, Van Buren persuaded Martin to seek medical aid in Europe. It was a long and losing battle. Martin, a bachelor, died in Paris at age forty-two.

In his old age Van Buren leaned heavily on Smith for advice about property sales and to get his memoirs finished. He himself worked on his papers from time to time but made slow progress. He wrote Smith that if he worked three hours every day, including Sunday, it would take him more than two years to finish—and that at age seventy-six he considered his chances rather risky. He wanted Smith to complete the job for him. He wrote Smith that in his will he was leaving the papers and the writing he had done to him and did hope he soon would finish the project.

Smith married Henrietta Eckford Irving, a niece of Washington Irving, and began to edit his father's papers. "To the last he, like all the Van Buren sons, labored to defend his father's career and to exalt his fame. . . ."

Tippecanoe and Ten Children

NONE WAS IN THE WHITE HOUSE, THOUGH

"I FIND that my nursery fills much faster than my strong-box," young Captain William Henry Harrison wrote to President Thomas Jefferson in 1806. "If our future progress in this way is as great as it has been and our government should accept the Roman policy of bestowing rewards on those who contribute most to the population of the country I do not despair of the highest award."

The thirty-three-year-old captain, already the father of six, was writing from old Vincennes, formerly a French trading post and now capital of the new Territory of Indiana—of which he was Governor and Superintendent of Indians, although he had wished for a post nearer civilization. By then, it seemed to him, he had been on the frontier a lifetime.

He had gone West from Virginia when he was eighteen after the death of his father, Benjamin Harrison, a Signer of the Declaration of Independence. For financial reasons and because the lure of the West was so strong he had relinquished his desire to become a doctor and joined General "Mad" Anthony Wayne as his aide on the Western frontier.

He might have returned home long before 1806 except that into the old Northwest Territory shortly after his arrival rode a dimpled brunette named Anna Symmes, the finished product of Isabella Graham's School for Young Ladies in New York City. Anna's father, John Cleves Symmes, held title claims to more than a million acres in Ohio and vicinity. Anna accompanied him and his third wife when he was taking another caravan of colonists to settle on some of his acreage, and the lieutenant spied her right away.

A lieutenant's salary did not strike Mr. Symmes as adequate for Anna and he looked askance at the lad's courtship of her, but one day when he was gone from home Anna and the handsome lieutenant marched out and married. "I hear you have married Anna," the irate father-in-law exclaimed. "Now how do you expect to support her?" "By my sword and my good right arm, sir," declared the brash lieutenant.

Harrison and Anna would have ten children and they would be born in four different places. This would make him the President who had fathered the most children at the time he took office. But his Vice-President, John Tyler, had seven children when he succeeded him. Then after Tyler's Presidential term ended, he had a second family of seven more. Thus Tyler wrested from Harrison the Presidential fatherhood prize. But William Henry Harrison remains the President who had the most grandchildren and great-grandchildren to date, and the only one to be grandfather to a President.

The first Harrison child, Elizabeth, was born at Fort Washington in a 4-room log cabin the lieutenant built for Anna on the banks of the Ohio River. The second, John Cleves Symmes, was born at Vincennes and the third, Lucy Singleton, was born in Virginia during a visit of her parents to the Harrison home. Then five in a row—William Henry Jr., John Scott, Benjamin, Mary Symmes, and Carter Bassett—were born at Vincennes. The ninth, Ann Tuthill, was born in Cincinnati because the family had to evacuate Vincennes during the War of 1812, and the tenth, James Findlay, was born at North Bend, Ohio, after his father had become a general but had resigned from the army and, he thought, left government services forever.

At Vincennes the Harrisons lived in the first brick house in the whole area, one Harrison built on a grand scale with his ancestral home, Berkeley, in mind. It was two and a half stories, had lookout stations on top, and its living room was really the council room in which the Governor met to trade and treat with the Indians. From this fortress mansion he and his troops marched off frequently to fight the Indians when the treaties which he made with them were broken. Four-fifths of the population over which he ruled were Red Men.

Living at Vincennes became decidedly unsafe for women and children during the War of 1812, when the British spurred the Indians to ever greater activity and furnished then an abundance of ammunition. Families of the troops were evacuated to Ohio and Kentucky, and many white settlers fled the territory.

It was in this war that Harrison won his lasting nickname of Old Tippecanoe. In a spectacular battle at Tippecanoe, an Indian settlement on the Wabash River in Indiana, he defeated The Prophet, brother of the great chief Tecumseh. The Prophet considered that it was he who was destined to turn back the tide of encroaching white men and free his people forever.

President Madison sent his compliments and Harrison was given the rank of major general. Later that year he defeated the combined forced of British and Indians at the Battle of the Thames, in which Tecumseh himself was killed and the war in that part of the country brought under control.

Next year, when he was forty-one, he resigned his commission and decided to be a farmer. Anna's father had given her 3,000 rich acres in the North Bend of the Ohio. They moved their original 4-room cabin 16 miles up the river to this spot and continued adding to it until it had 22 rooms, all of them needed by the large family and their stream of Sunday visitors. There the final child was born and died when he was three years of age. All the other Harrison children lived to adulthood and marriage.

Life on the farm was pleasant enough, but cash became scarce and educations for the children occasioned mortgage after mortgage. Harrison was not the farmer he envisioned and began to seek public office to augment his income. He served a term in Congress, was three years a U. S. Senator, and John Quincy Adams appointed him Minister to Columbia.

His third son, John Scott, relinquished the study of medicine to move onto the farm—in a brick house his father built for him—to be the real farmer in the family. He was the steadying influence around whom the family rallied in time of trouble—and he was the father of Benjamin Harrison, who became our twenty-third President.

Nobody visiting the farm in early 1840, the year the Whigs nominated General Harrison for the highest office, would have dreamed there was one future President there, let alone two. Only two of the Harrison sons were still living: John Scott and Benjamin, and the latter—a doctor who had served with distinction in the Mexican War—was seriously ill.

The oldest son, Symmes, who married Clarissa Pike, daughter of the man who explored Pike's Peak, died at thirty-two. He had become Secretary of the Territory of Indiana and was removed from office for cashing worthless checks. His father assumed responsibility for his debts of $12,000. Meantime the second son, William Henry Jr., became a talented and popular lawyer who ruined his life by excessive drinking and died when he was only thirty-eight. Carter, the youngest son, also became a lawyer and died after a brief illness when he was only twenty-five.

Benjamin, the doctor son, did not live through the noisy campaign in which his father was elected President. Visitors poured into North Bend in such numbers that editorial writers said they perhaps prevented recovery. Mrs. Harrison, having suffered the loss of four sons and two daughters within a comparatively short span of years, became desperately ill for the first time in her life—and at one time it seemed that no member of his family would accompany Old Tippecanoe on his victorious trip to Washington.

Only a widowed daughter-in-law, Mrs. William Henry Harrison, Jr., and her sons, James, aged sixteen, and William Henry III, fourteen, from the immediate family—were able to make the journey. Mrs. Harrison's seventy-three-year-old aunt, Mrs. James Findlay, of Cincinnati, accompanied them and doctors said that the First Lady-elect could join the group by early summer when roads over the mountains were easier to travel.

The inaugural was as spectacular as the campaign had been: a great festival attended by jubilant masses and highlighted by two gala balls. The Whigs were beside themselves with zip and joy—and the new President-elect celebrated with them every step of the way. He arrived in town several days early and stayed in the home of W. W. Seaton, Washington's mayor.

March 4 was bitterly cold and he rode "a mean white charger" to the Capitol without a topcoat and stood bareheaded on the Capitol portico to read the longest inaugural address on record. It ran almost two hours, although Daniel Webster had shortened the original manuscript and brightened its language. The parade was long and loud: log cabins, cider barrels, and canoes rolling along on wheels and everywhere old soldiers and new troops marching by with slogans and songs.

The President received the procession in sections at the White House. The *Intelligencer* wrote:

> The crowd at the President's house was immense, and the marvel is that serious accidents did not occur.
>
> In the procession was one huge car, drawing a log cabin filled with people, and bearing upon the logs outside the names of Whig states and the majorities cast by each. There was another car of great size, containing a cotton-mill and a loom in actual operation. As fast as the cloth was woven slips were cut off and thrown to the people.

Rockets were blazing throughout the evening and fire-balloons were sent aloft. Witnesses at the two balls spoke of the President's excellent health and of his strong and popular Cabinet. Young James and William doubtlessly had the time of their lives. However, there is no actual record of how they spent their month in the White House.

A friend wrote of those days:

> General Harrison at first did his own marketing, but only for a few days, for the worry of office and the importunities of office-seekers interfered with his domestic activities, and drove him to depend solely on his steward.
>
> The lady of the White House was the President's daughter-in-law, an attractive young widow.

It was said that Mrs. Findlay, the aunt, in deference to her age, was seated at the head of the table and always served first. It is known that a Virginia niece of the President was in the house too, and possibly other relatives, but the President evidently treated them all as guests and ran his own establishment.

A letter to the defeated Martin Van Buren described a Harrison White House dinner:

> The dinner on Saturday was such an affair as I never expected to witness—and such a one as I am quite sure was never before seen in that house. . . . There were about 40 people—3 more than the table would hold, and they were put at a side table. Before dinner the poor old man was bustling and fidgeting about—running out 3 or 4 times into the dining room. The ladies did not appear. . . . The dinner was scarcely over before he began giving toasts. You were the subject of a toast . . . certainly well meant. . . .

President Harrison, although sixty-eight, was not the "poor old man" which this letter indicated until he caught a miserable cold during his inaugural festivities and was unable to cure it. It developed into pneumonia and he died on April 4, after exactly a month in office.

His death was a shock and his funeral a most elaborate one. The White House exterior was draped in black. The pallbearers, wearing white scarves and with bands of black crepe on their sleeves, numbered twenty-six: one for each state in the Union. Ten thousand persons marched or rode in his funeral parade, which extended for two miles. The family members who were in the White House, including the grandsons, rode in carriages behind the funeral caisson, which was draped in black velvet.

The body was placed in the public vault at old Congressional Cemetery to be sent home when the roads were better, and the family scattered back to Ohio and Virginia.

The Whigs had lost after all because Vice-President John Tyler, who succeeded to office, was not a Whig either in his heart or behavior.

Mrs. Harrison, nearing recovery in North Bend, moved into the home of John Scott and lived to see numerous grandsons, including Benjamin, march off to war on the Union side before she died in 1864 at age eighty-nine. Of her ten children, only John Scott survived her. Congress voted her the remainder of her husband's $25,000 salary for the year, and followed that custom for widows of Presidents who died in office until a regular pension for First Ladies was established many years later.

The youngest of the two grandsons who lived in the White House for the month, William Henry, III, died single in 1849. James married and increased the number of Harrison great-grandchildren.

And Tyler, Too . . .

HE FATHERED FOURTEEN!

◀︎≫≫-≫≫-≪≪-≪≪▶︎

SOON after he so unexpectedly became President, suave
John Tyler gathered his seven children about him in the
White House and delivered a code of ethics to guide them
during his days as Chief Executive.

"Now, my children," he supposedly said, "during the next
few years we are to live in the home of the President of the
United States. I hope that you will conduct yourselves with
more than usual propriety and decorum. . . . You are to
know no favorites. . . . You are to accept no gifts whatsoever. . . . You are to allow no one to approach you on the
subject of office and favors."

This happened more than a month after he took the oath
of office at noon on April 6, 1841, which was two days after
Harrison's death. As Vice-President, Tyler attended the inaugural festivities in Washington, turned his duties as presiding officer of the Senate over to a president pro tem and returned to his home in old Williamsburg, Virginia, where he
hoped to continue living for most of his time in office.

News of Harrison's death reached him at 5 A.M. on April 5.
He and his two oldest sons, Robert, twenty-four, and John Jr.,
twenty-two—both married and preparing to practice law—left
with the messengers immediately.

Other family members came on more leisurely, after purchasing additional wardrobes and packing belongings which they wanted around them in the White House. The move was complicated by the fact that Mrs. Tyler was a victim of paralysis and lived mostly in a wheel chair. The others were:

Mary, twenty-six, the oldest child and perhaps the President's favorite, although he called them all "my treasures." She had been married for five years to Henry Lightfoot Jones and was the mother of a young son named Henry Jr.

Letitia was twenty and named for her mother. She was beautiful and high spirited, and newly wed to James A. Semple, nephew and heir of a prominent Williamsburg judge. Letitia would visit the White House frequently and after her husband went to sea as a purser in the U. S. Navy would be hostess there for a few months.

Elizabeth was seventeen and lovely. She was engaged to William Nevison Waller and would marry him in the White House. Until that gala event, the only social affair at which Mrs. Tyler appeared, she spent most of her time in attendance on her mother.

Alice, fourteen, a strong-willed girl with dark shoulder-length curls, was the self-avowed protector of the youngest child, Tazewell, a sensitive little lad of ten who often felt lost amid the swelter of adults and infants who peopled the Tyler administration. At times he went to school in Georgetown but always Alice took him to old St. John's Episcopal Church, just across Lafayette Square, on Sundays.

One Sunday they were late and found two ministerial students in the Presidential pew. The students jumped into the aisle to hold the pew gate open. Alice, fearing they intended to sit beside her, shoved Tazewell ahead and slammed the gate behind her. The congregation smiled behind prayer books as the blushing young men found seats elsewhere. One of them, Henry Mandeville Denison, decided then that he would even the score some day by marrying Alice. He did, but it took him almost a decade.

Robert's wife was Priscilla Cooper Tyler, the daughter of Thomas Abthorpe Cooper, a distinguished tragedian of his day, and Mary Fairlie Cooper, a New York belle whose regal mother much opposed her daughter's marriage to an actor, however handsome. When the family fortunes waned, Priscilla toured with her father. She was playing Desdemona to his Othello in Richmond when young Robert Tyler first saw her. The audience gave her a standing ovation, but Robert stood the longest of all. He went backstage later and never let Priscilla go. His father was his son's best man when they married at Priscilla's home in Bristol, Pennsylvania.

It was logical that charming Priscilla should become her father-in-law's hostess at the White House—and a more delightful one the old mansion never had. She kept a diary in which she wrote the vivid truth, and letters to her sisters about her experiences there were frequently hilarious.

Robert and Priscilla had a two-year-old daughter named Mary Fairlie for her grandmother, who was the Sophy Sparkle of Washington Irving's *Sketch Book*.

During the first Cabinet dinner at which Priscilla was hostess, the only woman present, Mary Fairlie was ill. She had expected to be overwhelmingly happy but she was miserable, imagining her child at death's door. Daniel Webster, the Secretary of State, sat on her right and consoled her. Known as "a cathedral in britches," he was so learned and unapproachable, Webster and Priscilla became great friends. She consulted him frequently on matters of protocol.

Another dinner at which Priscilla sat beside Webster was almost as much of a catastrophe. Things were "going merry as a wedding bell," she reported, "when for the first time in my life I fainted dead away." Webster picked her up and "Mr.

Tyler [Robert] with his usual impetuosity threw ice water on us, ruining my new dress and causing, I fear, a decided coolness between him and the Secretary of State."

Reason for the fainting was not hard to find. Priscilla's second daughter was born in the White House a few months later and named Letitia for the invalided First Lady.

Robert, as an oldest son and usually a superb example of rectitude, was "idolized by his parents, profoundly loved and respected by his brothers and sisters," his wife said. Priscilla appreciated this but profoundly wished his own career could be forwarded. Robert never had a paying job before his father became President. He and Priscilla had lived with his family all their married life.

Priscilla's thrifty soul was shocked by extravagances in the Tyler family's way of life. Tyler would have liked nothing better than to have all his children living with him all the time. He opened charge accounts for his "beloved new daughter," Priscilla, but she tried not to use them. If she needed a new paper of pins, she tested herself on how long she could do without them, and she made her old wardrobe do. She wrote her sisters that her dresses "are very French, either Toulouse or Toolong, I hope you get the meaning."

When it developed that Robert was to have a job in the Land Office and make $1,500 a year in Washington, she splurged on new attire including a silk dress with rosebuds in the sleeves "that would set you crazy," and a clip straw bonnet in which to call on the ladies of the capital city.

John Jr., who had married Martha Rochelle when he was only nineteen—almost a year before Robert married Priscilla —continued to live at home while he finished his education and studied law at William and Mary College. His wife remained much of the time with her own parents. Perhaps John Jr. married too young or his father took too much of a hand in salvaging his education—looking toward the fulfillment of a dream that one day he and his two oldest sons would practice law together.

At any rate, young John's marriage was a failure and in later years he liked the bottle too well. He became "major domo" of the White House and was his father's secretary until near the close of the term, when the President fired him. Martha, his wife, must have been in the mansion off and on. At one time the President asked the Rochelles to go in with him and buy the couple a home near Washington, but nothing came of the suggestion. Some years later the couple separated and John advised Martha to take back her own name.

Elizabeth celebrated her eighteenth birthday in the White House and announced her wedding date for January 31, 1842. There was a great family gathering for this gala event in the large East Parlor. Some of her bridesmaids expressed surprise that she would give up life in the White House to live in a country town—but in reply to this Secretary of State Webster quoted:

> "Love rules the court, the camp, the grove,
> And love is heaven; and heaven is love."

Priscilla wrote her sisters:

> Lizzie has had quite a grand wedding, although the intention was that it should be quiet and private. This, under the circumstances, though, was found impossible. The guests consisted of Mrs. Madison, members of the Cabinet with their wives and daughters, the diplomatic corps, a few personal friends, and relatives.
>
> Lizzie looked surpassingly lovely in her wedding dress and long blonde lace veil; her face literally covered with blushes and dimples. She behaved remarkable well, too, and any quantity of compliments were paid to her. . . .

Priscilla thought her mother-in-law the loveliest person at the wedding, however. "She gained by comparison with all the fine ladies about her," she wrote. Her health was growing worse, though, and the President wrote his daughter Mary that her mother needed her. So Mary came with her child and husband to stay until her mother's death in September. Her second son, Robert, was born in the White House during this period.

Tyler's first wife died in the White House and, while still President, he married a sensational belle named Julia Gardiner from Gardiner's Island, New York, who was thirty years his junior—six years younger than his daughter Mary. Julia, after his term ended, would mother seven more children for him, all as completely devoted and loyal to him as the first seven.

Thus, Tyler became the greatest father among the Presidents. When he died at seventy-one his youngest daughter was not two years of age. As late as 1885, after he had been dead more than twenty years, one of his second group of sons, Lyon Gardiner Tyler—who headed William and Mary—published *Letters and Times of the Tylers,* a labor of love and the sort of vindication for actions in office which not all our early Presdents enjoyed.

Historically, Tyler may not rank as a great President but he was an interesting one, and not the least of his charms was the attention he lavished on two sets of his children.

After her mother-in-law's death Priscilla wrote, "Nothing can exceed the loneliness of this large and gloomy mansion— hung with black—its walls echoing our sighs. . . ."

She decided to usher in the 1843 social season with a gay costume party to celebrate Mary Fairlie's third birthday. The honoree was dressed as a fairy, her wand, wings and crown all aglitter. Baby Letitia was a little Dutch girl. The small guests came as pirates, sultans, Turkish ladies with veils, dancing girls, and whatever. Grown-ups were invited to watch them at games.

With Letitia's husband at sea this daughter was free to become her father's hostess, and Priscilla was more than eager for Robert to establish himself as a lawyer in Philadelphia. They moved to that city in March, 1844, among their goodbye presents being two dozen champagne glasses from Daniel Webster.

Julia was only twenty-four, about the age of her stepdaughter Letitia, when she and the fifty-four-year-old President married in New York City on June 26. John Jr. was his father's best man—but to the Tyler daughters the wedding was a bombshell surprise. The father had not even confided in Mary, let alone young Alice who was now almost seventeen and looking forward to a belleship of her own.

Mary adjusted to the unwelcome situation, and young Elizabeth made a token surrender, but Letitia carried on a vendetta with her stepmother for several years. Alice was extremely difficult until Julia made her a member of the White House "Court" of girls who served as an honor guard at Julia's receptions. Tazewell was no problem, and both John and Robert greatly admired Julia.

Julia's advent ushered in eight of the gayest social months the White House had ever known. Her wardrobe was as sensational as her marriage. She usually received her guests while seated on a raised platform before south windows of the Blue Parlor, bowing most regally. She was such a friendly extrovert that everybody admired her, nonetheless.

Julia became as interested in the annexation of Texas as the President was and gave a great party to celebrate the final victory. It was the one at which the President quipped, "They call me a President without a party, but look at this!" The marriage was an unusually successful one. Julia's delight in "the President," as she always called him, never diminished.

After the election in which James K. Polk became President the ex-President took Julia to Sherwood Forest, a many-acred place he had bought for her on the James River—and which still remains in the Tyler family. Mary and her husband had supervised the needed repairs and additions.

Far from being a displaced Northerner who was lonely in the South, Julia became politically and emotionally an ardent Southerner.

In rather quick succession she became the mother at Sherwood Forest of: David Gardiner, John Alexander, Julia, Lachlan, Lyon Gardiner, Robert Fitzwalter, and Pearlie, who was born in 1860.

Popular Alice became a confirmed flirt, probably because her stepmother was forever lining up eligible men for her to inspect. She visited her relatives, flitted in and out of Sherwood Forest as the mood struck her, resisted all Julia's efforts to marry her off. She finally married the Rev. Mandeville Denison, by then a distinguished clergyman. Alice, sadly, died when only twenty-seven and her husband died in a typhus epidemic not long afterward. Her sister Letitia took their infant daughter, Elizabeth, to rear.

Meantime Mary had died at age thirty-three and beautiful Elizabeth had lived only 8 years after her White House wedding.

Ex-President Tyler was a leader in the ill-fated Peace Convention held in Washington in February, 1861, as the Civil War neared. The number of Tylers in the Civil War was almost countless. No other Presidential family lost and suffered so much in the holocaust.

The ex-President himself led the way by running for the Confederate Congress. He was in Richmond for a session when he died in January of 1862. Julia and Pearlie, then one and a half, were with him only because Julia, who believed she had second sight, foresaw his death in a dream and rushed from

Sherwood Forest. He seemed in perfect health as he greeted them, delighted that Pearlie recognized him with cooing and outstretched arms—but he died that night.

Robert was forced to leave Pennsylvania, barely escaping a Philadelphia mob which cried, "He ought to be lynched."

Priscilla and their five children—Robbie, a baby in arms, and four daughters—left their home with a pass through the lines about a month later. It was their daughter, Letitia, born in the White House, who raised the Confederate flag over the capitol at Montgomery later.

Robert became Register of the Confederate Treasury. John Jr. became assistant Secretary of War, and gave up drinking. Tazewell was a Confederate surgeon. Their sister Letitia's husband resigned from the U. S. Navy to join the Confederacy. William Waller, son of the White House bride, resigned from West Point to be a Confederate soldier and during the war married the youngest sister of Mrs. Jefferson Davis. His brother Henry died "defending his mother's grave," as he saw it. Mary's son Robert, born in the White House, was promoted for gallantry at Gettysburg.

Among the second family, Gardie and Alex tried their best to become Confederate heroes. Gardie, only fifteen when war came, refused to be evacuated North when his mother took her other children to her mother's home on Staten Island.

Tyler papers were stored in a Richmond warehouse—later burned—and the Tyler silver in a bank, which also burned although the silver was salvaged with scars. Sherwood Forest, which Julia was unable to sell either during the war or afterward, was ransacked and pillaged. Alex, unhappy in New York, nagged so much to go South that his mother finally permitted it. He tried unsuccessfully to join the Confederate Navy, by then almost nonexistent.

At war's end, thanks to an inheritance from her mother, Julia was able to send Gardie and Alex to complete their education in Germany. Gardie did not care for the sojourn, came home to study under General Lee and bring Sherwood Forest back into productivity. Alex became an engineer and remained in Germany long enough to try his hand at fighting: with the Germans briefly during the Franco-Prussian War. He married a Gardiner cousin and his mother badgered the government to give him a job.

Robert and Priscilla were left penniless in Montgomery. He became the respected editor of the Montgomery *Advertiser* and eventually headed the Democratic party in Alabama. Priscilla, despite all hardships, remained witty and charming. Robert's sister Letitia divorced her husband and ran a school for girls in Baltimore before coming to live in Washington. She lived until 1907.

Tazewell never forgave his stepmother for leaving Sherwood Forest during the war, claimed that his father had told her not to—although Julia maintained he had urged her to "take the children North." Tazewell went to California to practice medicine and died there.

All Julia's children received good educations. She moved to Washington to put her two youngest in school, Fitz in Georgetown University and Pearlie in the Visitation Convent school.

Pearlie married Major William M. Ellis and had eight children. Julia visited them often at their home near Roanoke, loved it when her son Lyon Gardiner—whom she called Lonie —produced the volumes on his father's life and times. She lived 27 years after her husband's death and Pearlie lived until 1947. From the first Tyler child's birth to Pearlie's death was a stretch of 132 years!

Zachary Taylor's Family

HE WAS A ROUGH BUT READY FATHER

"IT is perhaps as well if not better not to make too favorable calculations in favor of our children in early life for should they fail to meet or come up to them the disappointment will be felt with double the effect it would under different circumstances. . . ."

This was General Zachary Taylor writing to his son-in-law, Dr. Robert C. Wood, from the Mexican War in September, 1846. Dr. Wood, an army surgeon, was stationed at Fort Polk, Texas, but the general was down in Mexico near Monterey. The subject for discussion was Ann Mackall Wood, Taylor's oldest child, and her children. Ann had been left in Detroit, a place she did not like, and with four children who were a handful.

The doctor, as he often did, turned to his father-in-law and in writing pondered what he should do about the children, who should be in better schools, and wondered whether it was time for the oldest one—John Taylor, sixteen, who wanted a Navy career—to be sent to Annapolis.

Never too busy to take a hand in family decisions, the general cautioned the doctor to go slowly in deciding on the Navy for John and advised that Ann and the children spend the war in Baton Rouge, Louisiana, with her mother and sister Betty.

There was a "tolerable" school for boys there, he wrote, and he felt sure that a teacher could be located for the girls.

Ann was thirty-five at the time and, in addition to John, her children were Robert Cooke Jr. (Bob), fourteen, Blandina (Puss or Nina), twelve, and Sarah Knox (Dumple), nine. Birthplaces of the four reflected their frontier life. John was the first white child born in what is now Minnesota. Bob was born at another army post in the same state, Puss at Prairie du Chien in Wisconsin, and Dumple at Tampa Bay, Florida.

There were two other Taylor children: Mary Elizabeth (Betty), who was twenty-one and recently home from school when Ann and the children came to Baton Rouge, and Richard, nineteen, the youngest child and only son.

Richard, never robust, was never educated to be a soldier. As a lad he was sent to New England schools to become a scholar. As soon as he graduated from Yale University, however, he rushed to join his father in Mexico. The general sent the tall and thin young man home again. He did not want a son on his staff and, also, he did not believe that Richard—who looked tubercular to him—could withstand the rigors of battle. He urged him to spend a year or so building up his health and suggested that he try the hot springs of Arkansas and Virginia.

The son decided against visiting the health resorts, but the general took the news calmly, merely writing the doctor:

> All hopes of his benefitting from that quarter or I greatly fear from any other is at an end, if he is not returned to health by the operation of nature. . . . If gentle advice will not have the proper effect, nothing else ought to be thought of in regard to controlling him. . . .

There had been a third Taylor daughter, beautiful Sarah Knox, who died under tragic but romantic circumstances which caused her father to soften his ideas about parental discipline.

General Taylor, frontier fighter, had lived at so many rugged army posts and moved so often that his children one by one had been sent East to relatives and schools. He felt that the life was too harsh on his wife and the separations too painful.

He was sad when Ann married an army man, but consented —thinking conditions were changing rapidly and she would have an easier time, perhaps. It soon became evident, however, that Ann's lot was to be a duplicate of her mother's, and so he took an oath that no other daughter of his could marry an army man.

He took the vow at an unfortunate time, as it turned out, because Knox shortly came home from schools in Maryland and Kentucky and immediately fell in love with a young lieutenant named Jefferson Davis. Adamantly, the general forbade the lieutenant to enter his house. For two years Knox and Davis courted secretly and then, without parental blessing, were married at the home of an aunt in Kentucky.

Less than three months later Knox was dead from malaria, and still unforgiven. It was the family's greatest sorrow and two letters from her were Mrs. Taylor's most worn keepsakes.

On her wedding day, June 17, 1835, Knox wrote from Louisville:

> You will be surprised, no doubt, my dear mother, to hear of my being married so soon. When I wrote you last I had no intention of leaving here before fall; but hearing that the part of the country to which I am going is quite healthy I concluded to go down this summer and will leave here this afternoon at 4 o'clock.
>
> I will be married as you advised, in my bonnet and travelling dress. I am very much gratified that sister Ann is here.

At this time having one member of the family present I shall not feel so entirely destitute of friends. . . .

But you, my dearest mother, I know will still retain some feelings of affection for a child who has been so unfortunate as to form a connection without the sanction of her parents, but who will always feel the deepest affection for them whatever may be their feelings toward her.

Say to my dear father I have received his kind and affectionate letter, and thank him for the liberal supply of money sent me. Sister will tell you all that you wish to know about me. I will write as soon as I get down and as often as my mother may wish to hear from me, and do, my kind Ma, write. I shall feel so much mortified and disappointed if you do not.

I send a bonnet to sister [Betty], the best I could get. I tried to get you some cherries to preserve, but could not. Sally has kindly offered to make your preserves this summer. Farewell, my dear mother. Give my best to Pa and Dick.

Believe me always your affectionate daughter,

KNOX

Knox and her dashing husband went to his plantation home in Mississippi, which might have been safe enough in midsummer perhaps, if one were acclimated, but Knox was not. On August 11, she wrote her mother:

MY DEAREST MOTHER,

I have just received your affectionate letter forwarded to me from Louisville; you may readily imagine the pleasure it afforded me to hear from you. . . . Have you been much annoyed with visitors this year? Do tell me who you have been obliged to entertain.

How often, my dear mother, I wish I could look in upon you. I imagine so often I can see you moving about attending to your domestic concerns—down in the cellar skimming milk or going to feed the chickens. . . . Tell Dick I have a beautiful colt, prettier than his I expect. When did you hear from dear little Betty? Give my love to Dr. Mr. Davis sends his best respects to you. Did you receive the letter he wrote from St. Louis?

My love to Pa and Dick. . . . Remember me most affectionally to sister and the Doc. Kiss the children. . . . Do not make yourself uneasy about me; the country is quite healthy.

Davis became a six-year recluse after his bride's death, spending most of the time in his library. Then he married a striking and unusual girl named Varina Howell and came to Congress. Varina could not understand it when Davis resigned his Congressional seat and went to the aid of his beleagured ex-father-in-law in Mexico. He and his regiment served gallantly, especially at Buena Vista, and he and the general became friends again.

Less than two years after the Mexican War Zachary Taylor, who never had voted nor been interested in politics and was not sure whether he was a Whig or Democrat, was elected President. He was swept into office on a great wave of popular acclaim for his military feats, and on a wave of sympathy, too.

President Polk, irritated by Taylor's unorthodox strategy, had sent Gen. Winfield Scott to supercede him in Mexico and ordered many of his best troops to join General Scott at Vera Cruz. This left Taylor's troops desperately exposed during the great battle of Buena Vista—but they won it, nonetheless.

On the battlefields Taylor became a folk hero and a legend. He rode about camp in a non-issue uniform on Old Whitey— a horse which became so well known that by the time he grazed on the White House lawn his tail was "sparse from loss of hairs to souvenir hunters." He talked to his men as a father or uncle might and led a charmed life as the shots whizzed by.

The difference between him and the always correct Scott was evident in their nicknames. Taylor was "Old Rough and Ready"; Scott was "Old Fuss and Feathers." Even today it is

obvious which of the two would win votes in an election. All
the Whigs had to do was get up a few campaign songs like the
one which began:

> Come fall in boys, eyes right and steady,
> And raise a shout for Rough and Ready. . . .

To move into the White House so recently vacated by the
scholarly Polk was a plum not many generals could have refused and Taylor did not fight the honor.

(The Polks had no children and ran the first childless White
House. Young nieces visited from Tennessee and Andrew
Johnson's daughter, at school in Washington, spent at least
one vacation with them but no children actually lived with
them.)

Taylor wrote his doctor son-in-law, who had been transferred to Baltimore:

> My election has no doubt astonished those in power, who
> resorted to every measure to break me down as far as they
> could do so, when in a foreign country in front of the enemy,
> and to destroy me with vilest slanders. . . .
>
> I expect to leave for Washington about Feb. 1 [1849] but
> on account of feeble health Mrs. T. will not accompany me.
> She will remain with Dick, who will accompany her to Balti-
> more or Cumberland in May or June, where I will join her
> and he will return South.
>
> I do not want him to locate at or near Washington, or to
> fill any office. . . .

These plans for entering the capital city changed somewhat,
but Taylor's son never lived in the White House. He super-
intended his father's Louisiana lands and came up for
occasional visits. His health was much improved and, "like all
the Taylors," he could be fascinating in conversation. He had
a cynical outlook on life and was very much the gentleman,

not at all the rough and ready type. In later years, to his surprise, he found himself much interested in politics.

Mrs. Taylor, the new First Lady, had been looking forward to the general's retirement and not to the White House. She thought her husband, at sixty-four, was mistaken to consider the Presidency and stated firmly that she would take no part in official entertaining. The general loved to tell White House guests how she had prayed fervently that he would lose the election.

Betty was her father's ally and hostess. In preparation for her White House social duties, she decided to get married before coming to Washington. Her choice was Col. William S. Bliss, her father's adjutant. Bliss had entered West Point at age thirteen and graduated high in his class. He was fluent in foreign languages as well as in English, and gave the general's reports a gloss they otherwise would have lacked. In all respects he was so admirable that his nickname was "Perfect Bliss." He was his father-in-law's confidential secretary in the White House.

Also, the general was lucky in that Ann and his four grandchildren were stationed in nearby Baltimore and could come over frequently. Puss and Dumple adored their White House visits. John did go to Annapolis and Grandfather got Bob into West Point. A niece, Rebecca Taylor, was at school in Washington and used the White House parlors as places to entertain her beaux.

The old mansion was not lonely during Taylor's little over a year there, and the inaugural festivities were enough to gladden any President's heart. Three balls were going at once. Betty and her resplendently uniformed new husband attended all of them. She wore a simple white dress and had a single white flower in her hair. She won instant acclaim. Her fresh charms were contrasted glowingly to the charms of ladies in more colorful satins and jewels.

Betty had soft black hair parted in the middle, a superb complexion, lovely large eyes and a laughing mouth. Her charms also included a natural poise and tact, and a disarming friendliness. One contemporary, Jessie Benton Frémont, whose father had been a noted Missouri Senator and whose husband, the Western explorer, was then in the Senate, ranked Betty with Dolley Madison as having "the same charming nature."

"With the directness and singleness of her soldier-father, she blended a sweet, gentle gayety," she wrote. Mrs. Frémont, as one who needed to take the wives of her husband's constituents to the White House, may have been prejudiced—but Betty did receive an unusually good press.

She was hostess at dinners twice a week and receptions thrice a week, and every Saturday put in an appearance at a band concert on the south lawn.

The President, not particularly supported by the Whigs who elected him and having no program of his own, at times grew so tired of office seekers that he plunked on his tall hat and went for walks about the little city in his black broadcloth suit—made on purpose—two sizes too large for him.

He had only one Christmas in the White House and all four grandchildren were his honored guests. The program, such as it was, was built around them. The Christmas party was purely family but on New Year's Day, following the public reception, he and his grandchildren were "at home" to officials who wished to bring their families by.

Next Fourth of July was abominably hot. For days ahead the newspapers ran tips on how to beat the heat and cautioned everybody against "flooding the stomach with ice water." President and Mrs. Taylor received a Sunday school group of children that morning and then he set off without her for a Washington Monument celebration.

There were two *very* long speeches, including one, sad to

relate, by G. W. P. (Little Wash) Custis, who could talk longer than anybody still living. The President comforted himself as best he could on ice water and went back to the White House to drink chilled milk and eat ripe cherries before his dinner.

The doctors were called that night and diagnosed his ailment as cholera morbus, one symptom of which was painfully acute indigestion. He lived until July 9, having served a term of one year and 127 days.

Mrs. Taylor, who returned to Louisiana with the Blisses, never wanted the White House mentioned in her presence again and died two years later. Colonel Bliss died shortly thereafter. Betty married Philip P. Dandridge and moved to Winchester, Virginia, where her home became the gathering place and the solace station for the Taylors during the Civil War and afterward.

Richard became a prosperous sugar planter, known in all the best clubs and banks of New Orleans. He served in the state legislature and was opposed to secession. When war came, however, he joined the Confederacy as the only course he saw open to him. He became a general and wrote a book of his Civil War experiences.

At the end of the war his wife and two of his children were dead. He sent his remaining two daughters to live in the care of his sister Betty in Winchester and died in New York while his book was being published.

Ann, one must assume, suffered the greatest Taylor heartbreak during the Civil War, however. Her sons, John and Bob, served with the Confederacy, John resigning from the U. S. Navy to be on the staff of Jefferson Davis and Bob having gone south before the war to become a sugar planter. But her husband, the doctor, remained loyal to the U. S. Army and served the Federals with distinction.

At the end of the war John went to live in Nova Scotia rather than remain in "the land of his fathers" and his mother, Ann —the doctor dead—went to live in Germany. Blandina (Puss) had married Baron Guido von Grabow of the German Embassy staff in Washington, and took her mother and sister to live with her in Europe. Ann died there and Dumple, who never married, returned to live with her Aunt Betty.

Fillmore's Son and Daughter

HE DESTROYED THE FAMILY PAPERS

WHEN Vice-President Millard Fillmore ascended to the Presidency at the death of Zachary Taylor, his wife and nineteen-year-old daughter, both named Abigail, were in Buffalo, New York, not only to escape Washington's midsummer heat but to be with their son and brother, twenty-four-year-old Powers Fillmore, a practicing attorney.

Powers, a Harvard graduate and a bachelor, had entered his father's law office as a clerk when he was only fourteen and was exceptionally well trained for his profession. He, however, lacked the drive which had brought his father from sheerest poverty, put him in Congress and caused him to be thought of for Vice-President.

Fillmore, the thirteenth President, had been apprenticed to a clothmaker and never went to school until he was nineteen. His first teacher was Abigail Powers, a twenty-year-old student who never stopped learning. She became his friend and mentor and, eight years later, his wife.

Also, almost unheard of in her day, she continued to teach after their marriage so that he could study law. After her husband came to Congress she taught herself to play the piano, never missed a Washington lecture and began to teach herself French.

The daughter Abbie had a much more vivid personality than her brother and, although not so pretty as Powers was handsome, she was an extrovert who made friends more easily. Gay, radiant and charming, she became very popular in the capital city. She had graduated from the Sedgewick School in Massachusetts and then attended the State Normal School in Albany, determined to become a teacher.

One rule of the school was that each graduate must teach at least three months and although Abbie's father became Vice-President before her apprenticeship ended she completed her contract before joining her parents in Washington.

Powers returned to the capital city with his mother and sister after his father became President and was a loyal White House secretary during his father's less than three years as President.

Mrs. Fillmore, the eternal student, was shocked that the White House possessed no books, not even a dictionary or a Bible. Congress was shocked, too, once its members thought about it, and gave her $5,000 to remedy the situation. She made the second floor Oval Room into a library, put her piano and Abbie's harp in it and used it as the family sitting room. There she and Abbie played duets for visitors and the family had evening songfests, Powers and the President often joining in the singing of such melodies as "Sweet Vale of Avoca," "The Desert a Fountain Is Springing," and a brand-new tune called "Old Folks at Home."

After Taylor's death the newspapers had staged a campaign to make the White House more modern and livable and among the modern conveniences added was a new cooking stove. The chef, well able to cook a dinner for thirty-six on an open fire, could not master the range—so the new President went to the Patent Office to study the drawings and taught him how to manage the drafts and regulate the heat.

For their first Christmas in the White House, the President

invited his former law partner, Solomon G. Haven, and Mrs. Haven to be their guests. He wrote:

> The busy week is nearly ended, the last letter read—but not answered—and the last office-seeker bowed out of the room.
> I seize this precious moment simply to say that I am anxious that you and Mrs. Haven should come to visit us this winter. We have one spare bedroom in this temple of inconvenience, neatly fitted up—and just the thing for you and Mrs. H. . . .

The Havens came and had a good time, as did nearly all guests of the Fillmores, who not only gave a large dinner each Thursday but often a small one on Saturday, held a public levee each Friday evening when Congress was in session, and received guests together each Tuesday morning.

Mrs. Fillmore was not in the best of health. She had an injured knee which made standing in receiving lines painful for her and at times she called on Abbie to take her place. Abbie also managed some of the housekeeping details and sought other ways to make her mother's life easier.

For the family's second Christmas in the White House the visitor was one of Abbie's close childhood friends, Julia Miller. Julia always thought that Abbie's handsome father would be President some day because he was such a pleasant father and eager for Abbie's friends to have a good time.

As children they had argued because Abbie insisted she would be a teacher while Julia said, "No, you will be living in the White House." They settled the argument by agreeing that Julia would visit her both places. She had attended Abbie's class one day and thought her a good teacher, and now she was fulfilling the second half of the bargain.

Julia arrived with two trunks filled with pretty dresses on the Saturday before the first Monday in December—which was the day Congress opened in those days—and her escort was Mr. Haven, the law partner who was a new member of

Congress. She kept a journal of the visit and in it gave a vivid description of the New Year's Day reception of 1851.

She stood with the Cabinet wives in a second receiving line "a little behind and to the side" of that formed by the First Family. Mrs. Fillmore looked regal in a wine-colored velvet dress trimmed in Honiton lace and a diamond brooch. "Abbie wore a silk of changeable green and red, a patterned brocade with three flounces and with fine muslin embroideries at the waist and on the sleeves. . . . I wore a Napoleon blue silk with black velvet trimmings and embroidered muslin sleeves."

The diplomatic corps came through the line first and she especially noted Count Bodisco, the Russian ambassador who was "past seventy and she [his wife] just twenty-eight." The countess was dressed in heavy white silk with three richly embroidered flounces, wore a white velvet bonnet with plumes on it.

"It was a beautiful sight," Julia wrote. After the diplomats came the Cabinet members, then Judges of the Supreme Court and their wives. Some of the ladies remained during the whole reception. "Those who remained did so by invitation and were unbonneted. Everybody else came in handsome street costume. Then anybody and *everybody* came, and were without exception sober, decent and well-behaved. . . . By three o'clock the reception (which began at 11 A.M.) was over, and we were glad enough to get upstairs."

Julia and Abbie attended parties in the city together and made many calls. One afternoon they spent several hours with Mrs. Alexander Hamilton, who was ninety-two years of age and very entertaining. Julia decided that Washington "is a museum filled with people."

Fillmore did not expect to win a term on his own and when his partial term ended he and his wife planned to make a long-wished-for trip to Europe, so that the First Lady could try her foreign languages. Powers would return to his law practice in

Buffalo. Abbie would keep house for him and establish herself as a teacher. Also, she would study sculpture. One of her schoolmates, Harriet Hosmer, had become a well-known sculptress and Abbie was eager to try it.

The family packed in February and moved to the Willard Hotel so that the Franklin Pierces could move into the White House before the inauguration should they so desire. Everything was planned and the tickets purchased. Mrs. Fillmore, fatigued and partially ill, hoped to avoid most of the inaugural festivities.

Her dream was not to come true, however. The Pierces' only child, eleven-year-old Benjamin (Bennie), was killed in a train accident and Mrs. Pierce too stricken to come to Washington with her husband. The President-elect arrived in the capital city unaccompanied by any woman member of his family and Mrs. Fillmore rallied to do what she could to help him through the inaugural.

It happened that both William Makepeace Thackeray and Washington Irving were in town. She entertained them and went with "both Presidents" to hear Thackeray's lecture. Then on the cold inaugural day she sat with them on the windswept Capitol platform while Pierce took the oath of office and made his address.

That afternoon she went to bed with a cold, which turned to pneumonia. She died at the Willard amid her packed trunks. Her death shocked the nation, which was already in mourning for Bennie.

Nor were the Fillmores' sorrows ended. Slightly more than a year later Abbie died of cholera while visiting her aged grandparents at East Aurora, New York. She was twenty-two at the time.

Her death shocked Buffalo even more than her mother's had. The Buffalo *Commercial Advertiser* for July 24, 1854, apologized for what was considered at the time to be an intrusion of family privacy but "wished to soothe or express the feelings of that intimate circle of friends which her many attractions had drawn about her," ran a lengthy comment. In part it read:

> Miss Fillmore's character was written on her face. It was not beautiful, yet so full of vivacity and intellect, of cordiality and of goodness, that it attracted more than any beauty and as it arises before us now its expression only suggests the simple thought,
>
> How good, how kind. And she is gone!
>
> In that character were mingled, in just proportion, almost masculine judgement and the most feminine tenderness. Its leading feature was excellent common sense, united with great vivacity of temperament, genuine sensibility, and real intellectual force. With a keen sense of the ridiculous, overflowing with wit and humor, all her views of life were nevertheless grave and serious.
>
> . . . fidelity to her own sense of duty had led her to cultivate all of her talents; and it is no exaggeration to say that she was among the most accomplished young women we have ever seen among us. . . .
>
> In Washington, the etiquette of the place and her mother's feeble health combined to devolve upon her, almost unaided, the entire performance of social duties incident to her father's station. . . . She was but a young girl fresh from school. . . .
>
> She was eminently social and latterly her conversational powers were of the first order. . . . She clung to her old friends . . . was constantly thinking of some little surprise, some gift, some journey, some pleasure, by which she could contribute to the happiness of others. . . .

Four years later her father married Mrs. Caroline C. McIntosh, a comely widow with a comfortable fortune. They bought a turreted Gothic home in a fashionable part of town and entertained all the celebrities who came to Buffalo.

Powers at first practiced law, then obtained a position in the

Federal Court as a clerk, rising to higher posts through the years until he became United States Commissioner. There is nothing to indicate that he participated in politics more than the average citizen did, nor that he attended the political convention at which Fillmore was nominated for President on the Know-Nothing ticket in 1856. He continued to live with his father and stepmother.

The ex-President in his will wrote that if his wife and his son "shall survive me, I hope and trust that they may love each other as I have loved them; and, as both will be orphans indeed, I hope also that they will naturally render to each other every assistance due from a most affectionate parent to a beloved child and from a most affectionate and dutiful child to a beloved parent. . . ."

Outwardly the two observed the injunction but after a while Powers moved to the third floor of a downtown business building in which, it so happened, Grover Cleveland also had bachelor quarters. The two became warm friends.

The second Mrs. Fillmore, in her will, wished to leave to her relatives the Fillmore library, a costly silver service set and other valuables, including a huge cask of Madeira wine which Commodore Perry had brought to President Fillmore on the same warships with which he had opened the Japanese islands to American trade. Powers did not want to drink the wine, which later was auctioned along with the family silver, but he contested the will—and won.

Then into his will Powers, who never married, wrote a most unusual provision which read:

"I, Millard Powers Fillmore, particularly request and direct my executors at the earliest practicable moment to burn or otherwise effectively destroy all correspondence or letters to or from my mother, sister or me. . . . I hope to be able to do that before my death. . . ."

The last of his family alive, he destroyed his father's letters, scrapbooks and journals—leaving an irremediable blank in Fillmore family history.

His reasons were his own and he never explained them. He lived to be sixty-one and died at the Taft Hotel, where he had lived in his later years, spending his evenings in the lobby talking or playing a game of cards with friends. Newspapers reported, "He had no living relatives."

Pierce and Buchanan

BEREAVED FATHER AND A BACHELOR

DURING the administrations of Franklin Pierce and James Buchanan, or for the eight years prior to the Civil War, no children lived in the White House.

A main reason that Pierce, the dark horse candidate who served during a dark period of growing sectional differences, wished to be President was to advance the future career of his beloved eleven-year-old-son Benjamin (Bennie or Benjie), an only child.

But Bennie, who was looking forward to celebrating his twelfth birthday in the White House in early April, was killed in a tragic train accident on January 6, 1853, two months before his father's inauguration.

The President-elect, accompanied by his wife and Bennie, boarded the train in Boston that morning for their home in Concord, New Hampshire, to finish preparations for their move to the capital city.

Bennie was chatting merrily as the train left the station, his parents giving him their usual close attention. Less than a mile out "there was a sudden snap and jar, then a violent shock as the car in which they were seated toppled off an embankment and rolled into a field."

The parents escaped with minor injuries. Bennie, caught

in the wreckage, was crushed to death before their eyes. It was a shattering experience from which neither parent ever fully recovered, and it cast a pall over Pierce's four years in office. For reasons to do with Mrs. Pierce's semi-invalidism and her morbidly fearful attitude toward politics, the parents had built their life around Bennie. Without him, their main interest in life was gone.

Two other sons were born to them earlier: Franklin, Jr., who died as an infant, and Frank Robert, who lived to be four. Mrs. Pierce associated the latter's death with what to her was the miserable life she lived in Washington as the wife of a Congressman.

After Bennie was born, to appease his wife and establish a family environment more to her taste, Pierce resigned from the U. S. Senate and practiced law at Concord. He wrote President Polk, who wanted him to be Attorney General, that his wife's illness was such that he would never accept public office "except in defense of my country."

Bennie was a beautiful child, popular with his classmates and devoted to his parents. He was sensitive and delicately built, as was his mother, but in excellent health and spirits.

Mrs. Pierce was in Boston visiting relatives during the deadlocked National Democratic Convention of 1852 and as the days wore on her husband realized that he probably would become the nominee. Fearing its effect on his unsuspecting wife, he rushed from Concord to be with her when she heard the unwelcome news. As he expected, she fainted when the message arrived.

As she grew accustomed to the idea, however, she adjusted to the new situation and became proud of her popular husband. Bennie was much impressed by the things he could learn and the fun it might be to live in the White House. The little family was a happy and harmonious one indeed as it boarded the train in Boston.

The loss of an only child under such circumstances would have been a shattering experience for any parent, and for Mrs. Pierce it was devastating. Her collapse was complete and, in her nervous state, she again associated the death of a child with her husband's interest in politics.

Roy F. Nichols, Pierce's biographer, said that in the wreck the new President lost not only his child but his rapport with his wife and his will to succeed. "He could not undertake his duties with that buoyant and confident assurance which so often in itself invites success."

Mrs. Pierce, accompanied by her aunt, Mrs. Abby Means, who would remain as her companion, came to the White House in late March but did not appear publicly until the next New Year's Day, when she helped her husband receive. She was a pretty woman of forty-seven and created a good impression in her dress of black velvet, worn with diamonds. Although large groups made her nervous, she was a charming hostess at small dinner parties and made several warm friends in Washington.

Pierce sought renomination in 1856, but lost to James Buchanan, a sixty-five-year-old bachelor who had wanted to be President for a long time. After this election the Pierces traveled extensively in Europe, visiting many health resorts. In Rome the ex-President renewed his old and happy friendship with Nathaniel Hawthorne, who was shocked at the change in him. "Something seemed to have passed away out of him," Hawthorne wrote, "without leaving any trace." He came to Concord to be with Pierce in December, 1863, when Mrs. Pierce died.

Buchanan had no children, but he did have a lovely twenty-seven-year-old niece named Harriet Lane, who became one of the most popular hostesses the White House has had. She had selected Uncle James to be her guardian when she was orphaned at the age of nine.

This was a bit awkward for the bachelor, as he never had cared much for children and was away from home most of the time, serving in the U. S. Senate and other government posts.

He supervised her upbringing and kept her in good schools, and when he became Ambassador to England he permitted Harriet, then twenty-three and a beautiful blonde, to join him as his hostess. She was a success in London and then for four years she ran the White House with graciousness and efficiency.

"After the sadness of the Pierce administration," wrote Margaret B. Klapthor of the Smithsonian Institution, "the city was delighted with the new First Lady, who filled the White House with flowers and who enlivened social gatherings with a mixture of spontaneous gaiety and charm.

During the troubled administration of James Buchanan, she guided the White House social life successfully by the force of her youthful personality."

"Harriet" became a favorite name for babies all over the country. Ships and perfumes were named for her, too, and a new song, "Listen to the Mocking Bird," was dedicated to her—its doleful words not reflecting her verve and energy, but the melancholy mood which then was so popular in verse and song.

Rumors of her engagement kept tongues wagging, but she did not marry until she was thirty-six years of age. Her wedding to Henry Elliott Johnston of Baltimore was held at her Uncle James's home in 1866. She gave birth to two sons, but both died as young boys and at her death in 1903 she left the bulk of her fortune to a children's wing for Johns Hopkins University to be dedicated to their memory—stating that sick children of all races and creeds should be treated there regardless of financial ability. She left her art collection to the Smithsonian to form a nucleus for today's National Collection of Fine Arts.

The Lincoln Sons

"FREE, HAPPY AND UNRESTRAINED"

>>>-->>><<<-<<<

ON a bright day in early November of 1847 a proud Congressman-elect named Abraham Lincoln from Springfield, Illinois, alighted from the train in Lexington, Kentucky. He was accompanied by his beaming twenty-eight-year-old wife, Mary, and their two children: Robert, four, and Edward, a mere one and a half. They were on their way to Washington and had detoured a bit so that Mr. Lincoln could make a first visit to his in-laws.

The family carriage met them and they rode the short distance to the charming and comfortable home of Robert S. Todd, Mary's father.

A fellow passenger, Joseph Humphreys, unknown to them but who happened to be the nephew of Mary's stepmother, arrived before the Lincolns did, however. He had more or less run the distance.

"Aunt Betsy," he exclaimed fervently, "I never was so glad to get off a train in my life. There were two youngsters aboard who kept the train in a turmoil. Their long-legged father, instead of spanking the brats, looked pleased as Punch, aided and abetted the older one in his mischief.

"Good Lord," he gasped, glancing out the window. "There they come now." Whereupon young Humphreys found an exit and was seen no more during the memorable visit.

Radiant Mrs. Lincoln, five years wed and with, in her opinion, a fine husband and two of the sweetest cherubs in the world to show for it, entered her old home carrying little Eddie. Behind her came Lincoln with Bobby in his arms. (This mode of travel for the children was completely in character, incidentally. A Lincoln boy, and there would be four of them, never needed to walk—except on escapades or by desire—until well beyond the age of four. Once a sister-in-law scolded Lincoln for carrying a seven-year-old offspring down a Springfield street. "Oh!" he said in surprise. "Don't you think his little feet get tired?")

Several Todds were assembled to greet the small family. Ten-year-old Emilie, Mary's favorite stepsister, never forgot her initial glimpse of the tall sallow-faced man her sister had married. She was inclined to be frightened, but not after he looked around the circle and exclaimed, "And you must be Little Sister!" Then, her years notwithstanding, he swung her into the air.

The beloved Emilie would return the visit with long stays in Springfield and during the Civil War, when she was a Confederate, she added fuel to the fires burning around her embattled sister by showing up twice at the White House. Each time her brother-in-law begged her to take the oath of allegiance to the Union and stay. Later, in tears and some bitterness, she wrote articles on "Mary Todd Lincoln."

Humphreys' description of the Lincoln children, as Emilie remembered it, tallied perfectly with that given by all who knew the Lincolns. It was never a secret that they were fully permissive parents in an era long before that pattern was acceptable.

"The Lincolns belonged to that happily fatuous group of parents who think their children can do no wrong," wrote Ruth Painter Randall, who wrote the great work on their marriage.

Lincoln's law partner, William H. Herndon, who fostered many Lincoln untruths, was believed when he told how he dreaded visits of the boys to the office on Sundays. He dared not complain at the time but he longed to "wring their necks and throw them out the window." The flying objects and well-identified pencils which assaulted him were hard to take. He wrote about Lincoln:

"He worshipped his children and what they worshipped. He loved what they loved and hated what they hated."

During White House days a clerk in the telegraph office to which Lincoln, accompanied by his youngest son, Tad, often went at night to read latest dispatches from battlefields, felt the same way. Knowing the President to be the kindliest of men, he finally ventured to mention the chaos and misplaced files. Rather than receiving the expected apology, however, he was answered with, "Come, Tad. I don't believe we are wanted."

"It's my pleasure that my children are free, happy and un-restrained by parental tyranny," Mary Lincoln wrote that her husband always said. "Love is the chain whereby to bind a child to its parents." Anybody who failed to know this about Lincoln never began to know him very well. He was a doting father whose patience was never strained. "Father Abraham" summed him up in many more ways than one.

Some recognized the unswerving love he had for his boys as a fine thing. Others thought he did not know the meaning of discipline. Noah Brooks, a newspaperman who became a Lincoln intimate and later a Presidential secretary, belonged to the former group. He saw the sustenance which Lincoln gained from his children and how his love was so often re-turned. What could be lovelier than his description of how Tad would race into the office for some object, bestow a fierce hug upon the President and make his getaway before the ador-ing Chief Executive had time to ruffle his hair?

Secretary of War Stanton, never a dull man, quickly found a way to neutralize Tad's upsetting energy. He gave the lad a psuedo commission as a Union lieutenant, complete with uniform and sword, so that he could drill his own troops—thus throwing the scene of battle from his office back to the White House where he felt that it more rightly belonged.

Tad used this new authority to dismiss the regular White House guard and put the servants on safety patrol. The President found this hilarious but Robert, by then a much tameddown oldest brother, was outraged.

Mrs. Lincoln was only forty-two and her husband but fiftyone when he was elected President—which made them among the youngest of First Ladies and Presidents. Their children were unusually young, too.

Robert was seventeen and a freshman at Harvard. William Wallace (Willie) was only ten and Thomas (Tad) was but eight. Lincoln had given his youngest the permanent nickname at birth by exclaiming, "Why, he's like a little tadpole." (Little Eddie, the baby when his father went to Congress, died before Willie was born, but was never forgotten. His father spoke of leaving him behind when he left Springfield for Washington as President-elect.)

Robert was born at the Globe Tavern, where the newly wed Lincolns lived for monetary reasons, the board being but four dollars a week, and because Lincoln at times spent up to six months of the year riding his legal circuit—so as to pay off his debts and buy a home for his family.

He had his eye on a corner frame house with walnut floors, and bought it for $1,500. The other three sons were born there. It was one and a half stories tall until Mary had the roof raised during one of his absences. He loved the audacity of this and laughed heartily once he overcame his shock. They painted the house light brown and had dark green shutters.

Later Lincoln was able to buy Mary a carriage just like her

sisters had and was much pleased with this, saying, "Two things I won't loan, my carriage and my wife."

Mary was just as ambitious for his advancement and at times even more so than he was for himself, and was not afraid of the work which would speed the elevation. She did most of her own housework and all the family sewing, including making Lincoln's shirts. Her little boys dressed as well as any in town.

The brown house held much laughter and love. To view it otherwise is to deny Lincoln himself. Mary, like Lincoln, had an absorbing interest in literature, the classics and the poets. Next to politics, in which both were ardent Whigs, with Henry Clay their mutual hero, they liked "literature" best. Shakespeare was almost a daily diet. The little boys heard, memorized and often were called upon to give suitable quotations.

Willie, the son most like his father in disposition, began writing verses and small narratives quite early, was as eager to absorb anything the world held as were his parents. His father took him up to Chicago with him on one of his law cases, and Willie wrote a friend about life in a hotel room, describing the two pitchers, two towels, and two "little beds" with a novelist's eye.

Willie was easily his mother's favorite: a small Rock of Gibraltar in the uncertain sea of life, and a calming influence on effervescent Tad.

Robert was precocious as a child, so much so that Lincoln once wrote his friend, Joshua Speed, that he feared Bobby might be one of those "rare-ripes who are smarter at five than they ever will be again." Seven years older than Willie, he felt the age gap between himself and brothers. He developed into a polite youngster who could escort a lady from her carriage with the greatest finesse, just as his mother had taught him.

At age fourteen he went to study at Phillips Exeter in New

Hampshire, both Lincolns, especially Mary, being pleased that by then their finances would permit an Eastern education for him. Robert was more of a Todd than a Lincoln and during his years away at school a cultural gap developed between him and his family.

As for Tad, the youngest, perhaps the more said about him the better. Tad was a law unto himself, a wild one who resisted learning as if it had come from the Devil. His balance wheel was Willie, whom he adored. Tad had an impediment of speech, an odd sort of lisp caused by a defective palate. Springfield teachers gave up on him and so did a string of tutors brought to the White House. Tad in two minutes knew more about the tutors than they would ever know about him. He was smart but totally illiterate and, perhaps, the most engaging youngster who ever swaggered through White House halls.

His father, rather than worrying about him, enjoyed him to the utmost. "Let him romp," he said, "he will get 'pokey' soon enough." "Bobby used to be just like him," he said, "but look at him now." (There is reasonable doubt that Lincoln ever felt comfortable about Robert after the young man entered Harvard University.)

After his famous debates with Stephen A. Douglas, Lincoln was in demand as a speaker in the East. Robert's schoolmates were inclined to feel sorry for Robert when they glimpsed his Western father on the platform at Phillips Exeter, but not after the father began to speak.

Lincoln's mode of dress was rough by any standards, despite his wife's best efforts. His scrawny six-foot, four-inch frame was hard to fit and he never seemed to care one way or the other. When Mary bought him a new topcoat and hat en route to his inaugural as President the New York *Tribune* considered it worthy of an approving editorial.

Robert missed all the campaign fun, the bands and parades

and great crowds which made Springfield a scene of delight for Willie and Tad.

Lincoln was the nominee of the new Republican party. When the returns came in and the outcome seemed sure, he dashed from downtown headquarters to tell his wife, "Mary, Mary, we are elected!" It was a time of jubilation, and in Springfield all thoughts of a civil war seemed nonexistent.

Before the inaugural train left Illinois, however, news of fear for Lincoln's life came from the capital city and at one time it was decided that Mary and the smaller boys should travel on another train. This idea was canceled and most of the way the family traveled together.

Robert was in charge of his father's "grip sack" containing the inaugural speech, and managed to mislay it for a frightening spell. Willie and Tad had the time of their lives eating and sleeping on a train, waving at crowds and pointing out "Old Abe," whom ordinarily they called Pa. (Mrs. Lincoln was Ma to her sons and the pronunciations of both names were "Paw and Maw," although Robert later said Mother and Father.) The ride was triumphant until Gen. Winfield Scott sent word that a lynching mob awaited in Baltimore and Lincoln was put on another train.

Mrs. Lincoln and the little boys reached the Willard Hotel several hours after Lincoln and Robert did.

No other Presidential family has had to face such an angry city at inaugural time. War was not declared, but the nation was clearly divided North and South.

Mrs. Lincoln had invited relatives from both sides to attend the inaugural festivities and for the inaugural ball she wore a handsome gown of blue silk. Few Southern faces were noted, but an enormous crowd of Northerners and Westerners made the event a success. Mary Lincoln danced the quadrille with Senator Stephen A. Douglas, once her beau but now the husband of one of Dolley Madison's lovely nieces.

She knew that competition in dress was part of the Washington pattern and sent for Elizabeth Keckley, a mulatto dressmaker who had clothed the erstwhile social leaders of the city, and ordered an elaborate moiré dress made for her first White House levee on March 8.

Robert had returned to college before the levee, which was attended by a "monster crowd" and at which, a contemporary account noted, President and Mrs. Lincoln stood side by side in the Blue Room shaking hands to facilitate the procedure. At 10:30 the First Lady proceeded to the large East Parlor. She was followed by the President "attended by one of his younger sons." (Perhaps Willie, even though it is difficult to imagine that Tad had exhausted himself by a mere 10:30.)

Everybody wanted to see the new First Lady, and this is a contemporary description:

> She is neither tall nor slender in her figure, but rather below medium height, with the well-rounded proportions of a wholesome little Western matron of—yes, between thirty and forty summers of industry and the unobtrusive social life of the state capital of Illinois—dressed on this occasion in what the ladies call a Magenta, brilliant red, watered silk, with a lace cape, and with her hair tastefully relieved by a half dozen red and white japonicas in a wreath behind her ears.

Mary, the most maligned of all First Ladies and caught in the most cruel of all situations, would not have many happy days in the White House.

For Willie and Tad, however, the first year was a marvelous lark. On their first afternoon they explored the old mansion from cellar to roof, became acquainted with everybody in sight.

Mrs. Elizabeth Grimsley, Mary's cousin who stayed after the inaugural to help the First Lady get settled—and see the boys through a light case of measles—described Tad as "a gay, glad-some, merry spontaneous fellow, bubbling over with innocent fun, whose laugh rang through the house, when not moved to tears. Quick in mind and impulse, like his mother, with her naturally sunny temperament, he was the life, as also the worry of the household."

The boys soon made two wonderful friends about their own ages, "Bud" and "Holly" Taft, sons of Judge and Mrs. Horatio N. Taft—or one should say three wonderful friends, because sixteen-year-old Julia Taft always accompanied her brothers to the White House and monitored the lively activities.

As soon as the First Lady heard of the Taft boys she said to their mother, "Send them around tomorrow, please . . . Willie and Tad are so lonely and everything is so strange to them here in Washington. . . ."

The Lincoln and Taft boys staged theatricals in the unfin-ished attic, Tad swiping his father's spectacles on one occasion and Willie wearing his mother's lavender silk dress. "Tell Mr. President he will have to pay and see the show if he wants his specs back," Tad told the messenger who came looking for them.

The President came, and at times all four boys wrestled with him on a parlor floor. He was so tall, he presented a prob-lem. They could hold his arms and a leg each but that left the torso unattended. "Sit on him, Julia, sit on him!" they yelled to their shy chaperone who never could bring herself to do so.

Once the Taft boys were permitted to spend a night at the White House when a state dinner was scheduled. To the hor-ror of Mrs. Taft, a Victorian mother, the four youngsters were given seats near the end of the table: the only really young children, it appears, who ever attended a state dinner—but how like the Lincolns. No bedtime, no school time, but al-ways boytime for their adored children.

Soon after the inauguration Lincoln offered Ben Hardin Helm, "Little Sister" Emilie's husband, the coveted job of paymaster in the U. S. Army with the rank of major—but neither Helm nor "Little Sister" wanted any job connected with the Union. Mary's three full sisters married well-to-do men in the Springfield area and had objected to her marrying the poverty-stricken Lincoln. They were staunchly Unionist, but no closer to Mary than her Confederate half sister.

Throughout the Civil War the embattled First Lady withstood a barrage of comments and accusations which she was unable to combat. Her husband was just as viciously attacked but he was resilient under criticism and by his record neutralized many of the attacks on him.

If Mary gave several large dinners in a row there were cries of extravagance when "the boys are dying." If she had no entertainments for a while, there were cries of stinginess and of using household money to buy rich dresses. She was accused of spying for the South, the only First Lady accused of treason, and once a Congressional committee began to investigate her loyalty. Lincoln squelched the investigation by appearing before the committee to say, "I, Abraham Lincoln, of my own knowledge know that no member of my household is disloyal to the Union."

Her unfortunate and false image remained for almost a century. It was that of an erratic, perhaps partially insane, woman who was a weight around Lincoln's shoulders, a Confederate at heart and at best.

None of this, insofar as is known, touched Willie and Tad as they went their way and took great interest in the office-seekers and persons with problems who lined reception halls at the White House. They looked the visitors over, singled out what they thought to be the worthiest cases, rushed to the President with their recommendations.

They were staunch Union men. As military camps sprang

up around Washington they had their favorites. There were "Pa's camp," "Ma's camp," "Willie's camp" and "Tad's camp" an 1 each demanded special attention.

Their first actual brush with Civil War death came in the autumn of their first year in the White House when Col. E. D. Baker, the family friend for whom "little Eddie" of long ago was named, was killed in battle.

None will ever know whether Willie might have developed into a man of letters or into a man approaching his father in greatness. He celebrated his eleventh birthday in the White House, four days before Christmas, and was in evidence at the New Year's Day gala. But in January he fell ill with a fever variously diagnosed as typhoid and otherwise.

Doctors at first said that he would be up within a few days, but he died in the White House on February 1, 1862, young "Bud" Taft refusing to leave his bedside on grounds that "If I go he will call for me."

Willie's mother was inconsolable and there seems to be no reason to doubt Elizabeth Keckley's later words that the President at one time drew her to a window and pointed to the visible walls of the insane asylum, telling her, "Mother, you must pull yourself together; else you will land over there."

Tad was just as lost in his grief, and until his father assured him "Willie is in Heaven," was inconsolable, too. Neither Tad nor his mother was willing to accept the death of Willie.

Mrs. Lincoln never again entered the room where Willie died nor the Green Parlor in which he was embalmed. Her mind did not snap, perhaps, but her health did. For years a victim of migraine, the attacks now came more frequently.

Lincoln sent for her oldest sister, Mrs. Ninian Edwards, to come from Springfield to be with her. Mrs. Edwards wrote her daughters to be careful how they joined in gossip about their Aunt Mary, whose role was much more difficult than she had assumed.

Receptions were canceled for the remainder of the year, and also band concerts on the lawn. The latter action caused so much furore that the concerts were reinstituted, but in Lafayette Square where the noise was not so nerve-racking to Mary. In the autumn she and Tad went to New York and on to Boston to see Robert. "Dear little Taddie," she wrote her husband, "is well and enjoying himself very much."

The New Year's Day reception of 1863 was a great one, in celebration of the Emancipation Proclamation issued on that day. Mary stayed through most of it and in February the Lincolns had an impromptu reception for Tom Thumb and his bride. Robert, home for a holiday, refused to attend this, his lofty reply being, "No, Mother, I do not propose to assist in entertaining Tom Thumb. My notions of duty perhaps are somewhat different from yours."

Tad used the White House entrance hall as a lobby in which to sell refreshments and take up collections for war charities, catching his father's callers going and coming. Despite his lack of schooling, he was most adept at making change and pushing a bargain. Lincoln said he was going to be the kind of husband every wife liked: the good provider.

Criticism that Robert was not in the army grew each year. His mother wanted him to graduate and the thought of another death among her boys made her frantic. His father thought the troops could make out without him for a while longer.

In 1864, after his graduation, however, Lincoln decided that he could not in all conscience keep his son out of uniform any longer. He wrote General Grant, asking him to read the letter "as though I was not President," explaining his ideas about his son. "I do not wish him put in the ranks, nor yet given a commission to which those who have already served long are better entitled and qualified to hold. Could he without embarassment to you or detriment to the service be taken into your military family with some nominal rank, I, and not the public, furnishing his necessary means?" . . . Grant replied, "I will be most happy to have him in my military family in the manner you propose. . . ." He suggested the rank of captain, which Robert became.

Tad and his mother made several trips to the Virginia battlefronts with the President. Tad loved to ride with the cavalry and although his horsemanship was no match for that of the Grant boys he made a gallant try, "the tail of his coat flying in the breeze like the plumes of Henry of Navarre," wrote Noah Brooks. He saw some "graybacks" (Confederates) in camp at Fredericksburg and took delight in riding into Richmond with his father as the war neared its end.

Robert was in camp around Petersburg and, witnessing the surrender of General Lee at Appomattox, hurried to Washington with a firsthand account for his father. He was in Washington with General Grant on April 14, 1865, chatting at the White House with some friends, when the President was assassinated at Ford's Theater just seven blocks away. (By a strange course of events he also was near Presidents McKinley and Garfield when they were assassinated.)

As Lincoln lay unconscious in the house across from the theater his wife kept saying, "Send for Tad . . . I know he will talk to Taddie . . . He loves him so much. . . ." Tad's loud grief at his father's death was heartrending until he thought to ask a family friend, "Do you think Pa is in Heaven?" The reply, "I'm sure of it, my lad," consoled him and he in turn consoled his weeping mother, telling her, "Don't cry . . . don't cry . . You are breaking my heart. . . ." Only Tad could soothe her and this would remain true for many years, his tenderness and concern seeming to her "so much like his dear father."

As Lincoln's body traveled back to Springfield, a sad little footnote was that Willie's small coffin—which had been in a Georgetown vault—made the trip, too, the charge for its conveyance being listed as "removing the remains of Willie $10."

Robert went to Chicago where he entered a prominent law firm and was admitted to the Illinois bar two years later. Mrs. Lincoln purchased a home in Chicago for herself and sons.

Herndon began the lectures and writings in which he would say that Lincoln was not a Christian, was illegitimate and, anyway, had never loved his "terrible tempered" wife but only Ann Rutledge, a girl whose name the wife had not before heard. All this was salt in her open wounds and she had another great problem which she could not share with her sons. She was deeply in debt for clothing and bolts of material she had purchased on credit.

For years she had worried about money and now she was pursued by thoughts of poverty. She confessed her debts to Mrs. Keckley, the seamstress, and thought that with her help she could secretly dispose of some garments, some jewelry and the material in New York for enough to satisfy her creditors.

But the "old clothes scandal" broke in the newspapers and ended in a fiasco which made her wish the earth would open to swallow her. Mrs. Keckley's book, in which she estimated the debts at around $70,000, was a best seller and all the things ever said or thought about Mrs. Lincoln were reiterated.

Robert somehow settled his mother's debts and also cleared up his father's birth status. Perhaps during this embarrassing period he became the silent introvert he was to remain. Mrs. Lincoln urged Robert to hasten his marriage so that she could take Tad abroad to school and away from the headlines. He was engaged to pretty Mary Harlan, the daughter of Senator James Harlan, of Iowa, a romance which his mother had abetted.

The marriage was in Washington in September of 1868.

Mrs. Lincoln and Tad left immediately thereafter for Germany, where fifteen-year-old Tad began to make up for his lost time as a student.

They lived mostly in inadequate quarters and alone. Tad grew homesick and longed to see Robert's daughter, who was named Mary Todd for her grandmother. Congress gave Mary a pension of $3,000 a year in 1870 and next year she and Tad came home.

Tad was a charming young man of eighteen and the newspapers said he looked a great deal like his father. He spoke without any remnants of a lisp, but Robert said his perfect English had a German accent. He and his mother both were happy to be home and delighted to find Robert and family happy and prospering.

Tad developed a deep cold soon after his arrival in Chicago, however, and it turned into pneumonia. On July 15 of that year, home only a few weeks, he died. If his mother had been temperamentally unstable before, this was enough to push her into insanity and perhaps it did so, at least temporarily.

She wandered over the country with a companion, which Robert insisted that she have, found solace nowhere and sent her son aberrational telegrams when she dreamed that he was ill. In desperation Robert had her committed to the Cook County hospital for the insane. This required a public hearing, unfortunately, and her pride was lacerated. She attempted to take her life by an overdose of laudanum but even that was denied her.

But she was for the first time under the care of a good physician who specialized in mental diseases. Her sister, Mrs. Edwards, had Mary released into her custody, and as soon as she could be declared legally sane again Mrs. Lincoln, rather than face the American public, exiled herself to France and lived mostly at Pau—refusing to communicate with Robert—until

CHILDREN IN THE WHITE HOUSE—
a selected gallery of portraits

Martha Custis, granddaughter of Martha Washington. Painting by R. E. Pine. *Courtesy of Mount Vernon Ladies' Association.*

"Little Wash" Custis, grandson of Martha Washington. Painting by R. E. Pine. *Courtesy of Washington and Lee University.*

Elizabeth Parke Custis, granddaughter of Martha Washington. Painting by R. E. Pine. *Courtesy of Washington and Lee University.*

John Quincy Adams, oldest son of second President and Abigail Adams, at age 16. From pastel done at the Hague in 1783 and etched by Sidney L. Smith.

Charles Adams, middle son of President and Mrs. John Adams, from miniature done in his youth.

Thomas Boylston Adams, youngest son of President and Mrs. John Adams at age 23. From a miniature worn by his mother as a bracelet clasp.

Abigail (Nabby) Adams, only daughter of President and Mrs. John Adams. From painting by Brown done in London in 1786.

Martha Jefferson, older daughter of Thomas Jefferson, at age 17. Miniature by Joseph Boze done in Paris in 1789 and now in American embassy there. *Photo by U. S. Information Service.*

John Payne Todd, stepson of President James Madison, in miniature by J. Wood. *Photo courtesy of D. C. Public Library.*

President Monroe's elder daughter Eliza who was a White House hostess.

Charles Francis Adams, youngest son of President John Quincy Adams. Miniature done by Anson Dickinson in 1827. *Photo, courtesy of Smithsonian Institution.*

John Adams, the second, middle son of President John Quincy Adams. He married in the White House.

The painting by Earl of Andrew Jackson III, hung in Andrew Jackson's bedroom at the Hermitage.

Alice Tyler from painting done at White
House while her father was President.
Photo, courtesy of Library of Congress.

Betty Tyler Bliss, White House hostess
for her father, President Zachary Taylor.
Photo, courtesy of Smithsonian Institution.

Ann Mackall Taylor, oldest daughter of
President Zachary Taylor.

Talented Abigail Fillmore, only daughter of President Millard Fillmore. *Photo, courtesy of Buffalo and Erie County Historical Society.*

Millard Powers Fillmore was his father's secretary in the White House. *Photo, courtesy of Buffalo and Erie County Historical Society.*

Mrs. Franklin Pierce and her son Bennie. *Photo courtesy of Phelps Photo, Inc., Hillsboro, New Hampshire.*

Abraham Lincoln and his family. President and Mrs. Abraham Lincoln
with their children, Willie, Robert Todd, and Tad, at the White House.
Photo courtesy of Library of Congress.

"The Little Stovers," Andrew J., Lillie, and Sarah Drake, photographed in the White House in their everyday clothes during the term of their grandfather, President Andrew Johnson. *Photo courtesy of Mrs. Herbert Payne Richards, Bluff City, Tennessee.*

General and Mrs. Grant with their children: Nellie, Fred, U. S. Jr., and Jesse. Painting by W. Cogswell. *Courtesy of Smithsonian Institution.*

Fanny and Scott Hayes with their mother, Mrs. Rutherford B. Hayes, and a small visitor in the White House Conservatory. *Photo courtesy of Rutherford B. Hayes Library.*

President James A. Garfield and his family, including his mother, at the White House. *Photo courtesy of Library of Congress.*

Former President and Mrs. Grover Cleveland photographed at their Princeton University home with daughters Esther and Marion and their sons Richard and Francis. *Photo courtesy of Library of Congress.*

Four generations lived at the White House during President Benjamin Harrison's term. The First Lady is holding her grandson, Benjamin H. McKee, while her father, Dr. John W. Scott, holds his great granddaughter, Mary L. McKee. The children's mother, Mrs. R. B. McKee, helped her mother entertain. *Photo courtesy of Library of Congress.*

President and Mrs. Theodore Roosevelt and their children at Oyster Bay, New York, during his first term as President. The children, left to right: Quentin, Theodore, Jr., Archie, Alice, Kermit and Ethel. *Photo courtesy of Theodore Roosevelt Association.*

President and Mrs. William Howard Taft with their children Helen, Charles and Robert A., at the White House early in his administration. *Photo courtesy of Library of Congress.*

President and Mrs. Woodrow Wilson with their daughters Jessie, Eleanor and Margaret in 1912, the year he was elected. *Photo courtesy of Library of Congress.*

President Calvin Coolidge, Mrs. Coolidge, Calvin, Jr., and John at White House. *Photo courtesy of Library of Congress.*

President and Mrs. Hoover, Mr. and Mrs. Herbert Hoover, Jr., and Allan Hoover in the White House garden. *Photo courtesy of Library of Congress.*

President and Mrs. Franklin D. Roosevelt surrounded by their thirteen grandchildren in a White House study on January 4, 1945, the day he was inaugurated for his fourth term. *Credit, Harris and Ewing.*

President Harry S. Truman and family when they first went to live in the White House. *Photo by Fabian Bachrach.*

Easter Sunday 1956 in the White House garden with President and Mrs. Eisenhower, their son, Major John Eisenhower, his wife and four children: Barbara Anne, 6½, David, 8, Susan Elaine, 3, and Mary Jean, three months.

President and Mrs. John F. Kennedy with John, Jr., and Caroline at Palm Beach on their last Easter Sunday together. *Courtesy, The White House.*

President and Mrs. Lyndon B. Johnson with their daughters Luci and Lynda, at the White House. *Courtesy of The White House.*

near her death. She returned to her sister's home, forgave Robert, and died at Springfield in 1882, aged sixty-three.

Robert became Secretary of War in the Cabinet of President Garfield and later President Benjamin Harrison named him Minister to Great Britain. He had three daughters and a son named Abraham but always called Jack because, Robert told him, he must earn the name of Abraham. Jack died at seventeen while his father was serving in England, thus ending the possibility that Lincoln would have future descendants bearing his name.

Robert rounded out a successful career in law and finance by becoming president of the Pullman Company. During his later years he lived partly in Washington, where the Robert Todd Lincoln home still stands, and partly in Manchester, Vermont, where the golf courses were his delight. His name often was mentioned for the Presidency, a mention which he always quickly quelled.

When he died in 1926 at almost eighty-three, the Associated Press in its prepared obituary said in part:

> Robert Todd Lincoln, eldest son of Abraham Lincoln, was the last of the martyred President's immediate family and the last of the great emancipator's descendants to bear the family name.
>
> He will be remembered as an able lawyer, successful Cabinet officer and a dignified diplomat. But he was of a retiring disposition and preferred the practice of his profession to the activities of politics and the glamor of public office.
>
> He inherited almost none of the physical characteristics of his father and he was conservative in his position on nearly all public questions; reserved and even taciturn. He never appeared at public gatherings if he could avoid it. . . .

Robert destroyed some Lincoln memorabilia, but was persuaded to leave most of the family papers to the Library of

Congress, to be opened 21 years after his death. On the evening of July 25, 1947, a notable group of Lincoln scholars gathered at the library, worked all night so as to have an exhibit ready for the public next morning.

The new papers only confirmed the Lincoln verdict and made it richer—and, for the first time, they persuaded scholars to evaluate Lincoln's wife in other than the settings of Herndon's hatred and the Civil War animosity which beset her from both North and South.

Robert, despite some reservations, comes off quite well as a son. Not like his father and not remotely like his mother, he coped with the capitalistic world into which he was thrown, and kept a reserved balance. He attended the dedication of the beautiful Lincoln Memorial in Washington and always preserved a front of rectitude. Without Robert, the straitlaced son who lived on and on, the Lincoln story might have lost much.

Andrew Johnson's Family

SONS, DAUGHTERS AND GRANDCHILDREN

IN the second year of the Civil War a frustrated young colonel of the Union Army received what to him must have been a maddening telegram. It was from his father, Andrew Johnson, who less than three years later would become the nation's seventeenth President. It read, DO YOUR DUTY, AND ALL WILL COME OUT ALL RIGHT.

Col. Robert Johnson and his men were at Camp Spears, Ohio, having reached this Northern spot expecting to find supplies after 18 days of hard marching from Cumberland Gap on the Tennessee-Kentucky border—but no aid was forthcoming.

They were without tents, pay, uniforms or much of anything except their hunting rifles. Such had been their lot ever since Robert, an attractive twenty-six-year-old bachelor lawyer and an ardent "Southern Unionist," rushed to arms as soon as President Lincoln called for volunteers.

The War Department, happy to commission him, had been able to send him only congratulations and messages to carry on. One of several despairing pleas he had made to the government within the past year read:

> My men are exiles from home—and never received any pay. My official instructions have been intercepted from the Secre-

tary of War changing my regiment from Infantry to Cavalry. I have been in the mountains for three months. My men are naked, hatless and shoeless. In the name of Heaven can you not relieve them? Answer me at this or whatever point our Brigade may be ordered. . . .

> ROBERT JOHNSON,
> COL. COMDG.,
> *4th Regt. Tenn. Vols.*

When Lincoln made his father military governor of Tennessee, Robert felt that at last someone in authority might listen to him. His father could find no immediate way to send help, however, so he sent the reply which typified his tenacity —although it was hardly Robert's idea of loyalty.

Robert's plight was one of geography, and not of wanton disregard. His Union regiment was formed in a state which joined the Confederacy and its first headquarters at Greeneville, Tennessee, was on the route over which Rebels poured in great numbers to join General Lee's army in Virginia. The position was untenable, but Robert's beleaguered men did know the high mountains of East Tennessee and made a great name for themselves by swooping down on supply lines and harassing Rebel outposts.

Robert's brother-in-law, Col. David Stover, who married his younger sister Mary, was a slaveholder with a brother in the Confederate Army and carefully concealed his Unionist recruiting and bridge-burning activities. When recognized as he led his men from a burning bridge, he also took to the mountains for a winter of exposure and malnutrition.

All members of the Johnson family had prices on their heads. Andrew Johnson refused to leave his seat in the U. S. Senate when his state seceded from the Union and was wanted everywhere in the South as a spy and traitor.

Mrs. Johnson was in Greeneville when war came, having left Washington due to illness, and for two years heard only rumors of her husband's death by hanging and firing squad—but no direct word from him.

At first, three sons were at home with her: Robert and his older brother, Charles, a physician, and the baby of the family, Andrew Jr., who always, for reasons still unknown, was called Frank. Frank was a mere eight years of age. Charles was thirty and became a surgeon in the Union Army.

Ordered from her home with instructions to "go beyond the Confederate lines," Mrs. Johnson and Frank began a long period of wandering. She had many friends, but it was dangerous for any to shield her.

She and her daughters hid food and medicines for troops in the mountains as long as they could but news of her husband's arrival in Nashville—which fell to the Federals after General Grant and others seized river forts in the west—was the first good news she had heard in many a day. She, Frank, and the Stovers, who had three small children, decided to go there—if they could make it.

It was a long and hazardous trek without enough food and with nobody easy about giving them lodging. But they did make it—the last 30 miles on a pass from General Nathan Bedford Forrest under an exchange-of-prisoners agreement. Forrest, the noted Confederate cavalry leader, apologized to Mrs. Johnson because the wagon she had to use had no springs. Governor Johnson, the least sentimental of men, and perhaps of all the Presidents, wept when he saw his family.

There was another Johnson daughter, Martha, the oldest child. She was married to Judge David T. Patterson and they had two small children. The Pattersons joined the family in Nashville a few weeks later and by another route. They all lived together in one big house, and for the last two years of the war the Johnsons had a comparatively easy time, considering the spot they were in.

Robert's regiment finally made it back to Tennessee, received cavalry uniforms and fought in the Nashville area—where bloody battles were the order of the day. Charles, the surgeon, also was stationed in the area.

Mrs. Johnson was an invalid ever after her arrival in Nashville. Charles was killed when he fell from a spirited horse soon thereafter and in late 1864, Colonel Stover died of tuberculosis contracted during the winter in the mountains. But at least family members knew where the others were.

Nashville, its sympathies mostly Southern, was not the friendliest place to be, but Governor Johnson ruled with an iron hand and Mrs. James K. Polk, who remained neutral, occasionally came to visit.

None of Johnson's family went to Washington with him when he became Lincoln's second Vice-President. He was boarding in a hotel when the President was assassinated and did not move into the White House until after May 22, when prostrated Mary Lincoln finally left it.

The family—two daughters, two sons, and five grandchildren—came on in midsummer. One paper noted that Andy Jr., then going on thirteen, had arrived with his mother and was "expected to supply the place of frolicsome Tad [Lincoln]." But Frank, a quiet towhead, was not to be that sort of Presidential son.

He entered school in Georgetown and behaved himself. Like young Tazewell Tyler before him, Frank was rather lost between adults and grandchildren, and usually was considered by contemporary writers to be one of the latter.

Robert, now thirty-one, became his father's secretary. Martha Patterson, thirty-six, was the official White House hostess, assisted by her sister, Mary Stover, thirty-two. Mrs. Johnson remained in her rooms and made only one appearance in the downstairs parlors. That was near the end of the term and for a party in honor of the grandchildren on her husband's 60th birthday.

President Johnson received at receptions with both daughters beside him: Martha, a slender matron who photographed as a brunette but who had blue eyes and light brown hair, and Mary, a stately blonde with overtones of red in her hair.

Some of Washington's fashionables, noting Mary's beauty, commented that if she would dress more as they did she could become a belle. It took such women a while to note the quiet elegance and exquisite workmanship of the daughters' costumes, and to realize that they did not intend to enter the fashion swim.

Martha said right off, "We are plain people from the mountains of Tennessee, called here by a national calamity. I hope too much will not be expected of us." Mrs. Johnson, from her rooms, ordered plenty of soap and water plus disinfectant used on the White House, the parlors of which had been used unstintingly by troops stationed there after Lincoln's death.

Soon the windows and chandeliers gleamed and fresh linen was stretched over worn carpets. Martha went each morning in calico and apron to supervise the milk and butter operations.

At their first reception, for which Martha dressed in a pretty blue gown and Mary in black, the daughters made a good impression. Their press was good throughout the administration and whatever was said about President Johnson, his family became noted for sticking together and running a shipshape White House.

Names and ages of the grandchildren were: Lillie Stover, almost ten, Andrew Patterson, eight, Sarah Drake Stover, almost eight, Mary Belle Patterson, five plus, and Andrew Stover, five. No White House children ever received more compliments nor, apparently, had a nicer time in the old mansion.

During their more than three years there they all went to school, attended Marini's dancing establishment, and took music. The Stover girls began piano lessons when they were tiny and, along with their brother, learned to play the violin and guitar. Many entries for violin strings are in their mother's old account books.

The President found time to take walks and go on outings with the children, all of whom remembered their days in Washington as a most happy time.

The three granddaughters were learning to do fine needle-work and often took their sewing baskets—fitted out as the baskets of a good tailor's offspring should be—to stitch a while with their grandmother, always being cautioned beforehand to watch their noise and learn from an expert.

Early in 1866 Congress allowed $30,000 for White House renovations. Mrs. Patterson received estimates and realized that the whole amount would go on the downstairs parlors and dining room if contracts were let in the usual manner.

So she launched a do-it-yourself project to stretch the money by having old furniture mended, salvaging usable pieces of expensive old drapery and upholstery for re-use, and by shopping for bargains so that the President could have a new reception hall for official callers and other upstairs rooms could be made more pleasing.

The work continued all summer and much of the winter but was managed with such competence that some of the parlors were always usable.

For the New Year's Day reception of 1867 the large East Room still was shut off for completion, but guests were astonished at the pleasing changes made, the use of muted colors and paneling, the excellent effects. For this party Martha and her sister wore black dresses of matching design, both with basques, Mary's embroidered and braided in purple, Martha's in white. The sisters adopted the matching costume idea for use at later events.

Greatest news event of 1868 was the impeachment trial of Andrew Johnson, the only President to face removal from of-

fice on charges of overstepping his authority. The trial began
on Capitol Hill on March 13, lasted until May 26, with never
a vacant seat. Women flocked to the galleries, but not the Johnson daughters.

Mrs. Johnson, the invalid to whom they all turned in a crisis,
decreed that White House activities continue in the usual manner and that her family put on smiling faces. When a messenger reached her with news of her husband's acquittal she
said, "I knew he would be! Oh, thank you, thank you."

Johnson was a stubborn man, else he could not have
survived. Born into poverty, he as a child was apprenticed to a
tailor. He never went to school. He ran away from his bleak
situation, crossed the mountains from North Carolina with his
widowed mother and brother to seek a new life in the
new state of Tennessee. Their money gave out at Greeneville
and, anyway, it looked like a good place for a tailor shop.

At eighteen he married sixteen-year-old Eliza McArdle,
the shoemaker's daughter, who furthered his education. She
read to him while he worked and later he hired men to read
to him. His favorite reading matter was the Constitution and
it led to his interest in politics.

He helped organize a workingman's party, was elected alderman and at twenty-three was mayor. He went to the state
legislature, and twice was elected governor. Among the campaign songs which helped was one which went:

> If you want a brand new coat
> I'll tell you what to do
> Go down to Andrew Johnson's shop
> And get a long-tail blue.

When he went to the U. S. Senate his finances were in good
shape, his family living in a still-standing brick house, and
he had some investments.

As President he broke with Radicals in the Republican party. Congress overrode him to disfranchise white voters in the South and set up "carpetbag" governments under military rule. The full break came, however, over his determination to remove appointed officials who were disloyal to him. Congress passed the Tenure of Office Act forbidding such but he removed Secretary of War Stanton anyway—or tried to. Stanton barricaded his office and refused to leave.

Foreign diplomats and others were impressed by the manner in which the Johnsons kept up the correct front during the trial for impeachment. Their dinners were beautifully executed, the food, service and decorations meticulously prepared.

Johnson survived it all, and on December 29, his last birthday in office, it was decided to give a magnificent party for "the children." The *National Intelligencer* ran more than a column on this splendid event, which featured dancing under the direction of Mr. Marini, who ran a noted school, to music by the 15-piece Marine Band. Nearly 400 children came and adults lined the walls to watch. The program was most impressive.

Mrs. Johnson returned handshakes from her wheelchair and made the apology, "My dear, as you see, I am an invalid." "Only a good and noble woman could have been the mother of Mrs. Patterson and Mrs. Stover," it was said of her many times.

Robert, the solicitous colonel, was a family worry. He began to drink or probably only renewed a habit of earlier years. Rumors of this floated over Washington and Secretary of the Navy Gideon Welles noted in his diary that the President was much concerned about Robert.

White House physicians thought the drinking stemmed from conviviality and could be cured. Secretary Welles doubted it, but helped evolve a complicated plan for Robert to take a long sea voyage. To make this businesslike the State

Department was to assign him to study the slave trade on the coast of Africa. Delays in working out the scheme were so frustrating that Robert refused the offer when made.

Robert died quietly and unexpectedly, a month after his father left office. The Nashville *Banner* said of him, "He had his faults and weaknesses, like other men, but he always was a friend."

Johnson took his family back to Tennessee and immediately began to run for the U. S. Senate, so that he could work to vindicate his record. The state sent him back, the first and only ex-President to serve in the Senate, and he received a standing ovation

The Pattersons lived in the Greeneville home of the Johnsons, but Mary Stover moved her family to nearby Bluff City, where she could look after her father's interest in a cotton mill. There she built a brick mansion called Stover Hall and it was while visiting her that her father died. Mrs. Johnson outlived him by less than a year.

Lillie married Thomas Maloney, who with Frank started a newspaper called the Greeneville *Intelligencer*. The paper prospered moderately but did not last many years. Frank married a widow and died without children.

All the grandchildren married—except Andrew J. Stover, who resisted every opportunity.

His energetic and enterprising mother worried about his future. She went to Texas and bought Andrew a 1,000-acre ranch, had a house and barn built for him, stocked the ranch with cattle and thought she had him set for life. But Andrew remained a nonconformist.

He wandered back to Tennessee, decided to become a hermit and live high in the mountains. With only a brook and hunting dogs for company, he trapped and took it easy. At nighttime he played his violin and on still summer evenings people in the valley could hear his music. They explained to their children, "That's Andrew Johnson's grandson up there playing."

Sarah Drake Stover married William Bruce Bachman and had the only two Johnson great-grandsons. After her death Bachman remarried and a daughter of his, Mrs. Herbert Payne Richards, today treasures many Stover-Johnson mementos at her home, "Long Shadows," in Bluff City. Among them are schoolbooks used by the "little Stovers" in the White House.

Andrew J. Patterson's daughter, Mrs. Margaret Johnson Bartlett, has devoted much of her life to establishing and helping run the Johnson memorials, now under the National Park Service, at Greeneville, where the old tailor shop still stands.

General Grant's Four

"BEST AND SMARTEST CHILDREN IN THE WORLD"

TO young Jesse Root Grant (not quite eleven when his father became President) goes credit for discovering the White House roof as a desirable spot on which to spend an evening. He installed his small-but-powerful telescope there around 1870 and on many a night his father escaped from his burdens down below by helping his son chart the heavens. By the light of a lantern they pored over astronomical charts and tables until Mrs. Grant sent a messenger to bring them to bed.

Jesse, the youngest of four attractive children, also had a fine microscope and camera, gifts—as was the telescope—from an admiral who admired the general. Mrs. Grant interested herself in these, would sit patiently while Jesse called out the microscopic wonders. And occasionally would take a peek herself, although defective vision prevented her seeing much.

When Baine Dent, a cousin two years older than Jesse, came to live at the White House the boys developed a passion for stamp collecting. They squandered $5 on a batch before they thought of using status to cut costs. They wrote American ambassadors and ministers stationed abroad to send them samples. This worked fine until Mrs. Grant decreed that the diplomats should be thanked for their offerings. The thought of writing two letters for a few stamps was quite beyond Jesse's range of interest.

So the boys ordered some stamps from a bargain-promising mail order firm, but they did not come. Jesse thought this deserved attention from someone with real authority. The highest authority he could think of right off belonged to his friend Kelly, a policeman. Then he wondered whether the Secretary of War—with all those soldiers behind him—might not be better. He asked his father to have his Cabinet decide. After due discussion the Cabinet said that Kelly's intervention would carry more weight. Whereupon this letter went off:

"I am a Capitol policeman. I can arrest anybody, anywhere, at any time, for anything. I want you to send those stamps to Jesse Grant." It was signed "Kelly, Capitol policeman." And it worked.

Jesse was one of the busiest boys who ever lived in the White House. The Grant stables held two of his ponies, "Jeff Davis" and "Rebbie," both acquired for him during the Civil War. Gentler Rebbie was ridden by Tad Lincoln when he and his father went to the Virginia front. Jesse, much the better horseman, rode the wilder Jeff Davis, which was black. Jesse dashed about Washington on one or the other pony almost daily and the President howled with laughter when the black creature came back to the stables one day without its rider. Jesse had been thrown!

The lad's longest remembered White House deed, however, was his organization of the secret K.R.F. Society on Christmas Day, 1871, in the gardener's tool shed which had been assigned to him as extra play space. It had a membership of 12 which grew eventually to 76 and six years after its formation moved to the third floor of a nearby business building.

The K.R.F., which the President said stood for Kick Run Fight, had a circulating library of 200 volumes, became a debating society and put out its own newspaper. It was to hold a 50th reunion with 25 members, including Jesse, present.

The other Grant children were: Frederick Dent, almost nineteen at inaugural time; U. S. Jr., sixteen and called Buck because he was born at his father's old home in Ohio, the Buckeye state, and Ellen (Nellie) Wrenhall, a pretty thirteen and the mutual pet.

Each child believed himself to be the parental favorite for unique and specific reasons. Fred was oldest, Jesse youngest, Nellie the only girl and Buck the only one born in Ohio. Nellie also happened to have been born on July 4 and firmly believed her father's assertion that fireworks on that day were honoring her birthday.

The Grants believed and proudly declared their children to be the best and smartest in the world and treated them accordingly. A personal friend of Mrs. Grant said that she could not bear to discipline one of them, always found a suitable excuse for any action. And the children apparently responded with love and devotion. None was a boisterous rowdy. Taken together, the six Grants were one big mutual admiration society.

When his father came home from work each afternoon before the war, Jesse wrote in *In the Days of My Father,* he met him with the challenge, "Mister, do you want to fight?" The certain reply was, "I am a man of peace but I will not be hectored by a person of your size."

Wrestling with his sons was a top Grant pleasure. Once during the war a colonel entered his headquarters to find him pinned to the floor by the three of them. "Now you know my weaknesses," the general said, "my children—and my horses."

Fred, only eleven years old when war came, was with his father most of the time as an unpaid volunteer and, the general said, never gave him a minute's uneasiness. Mrs. Grant and the other three often visited the general and Fred. For these occasions pretty Nellie was dressed in laces and ribbons, which was the way her father liked to see her.

Mrs. Grant and the younger children were almost captured in northern Mississippi but that did not prevent their journey to Vicksburg when that city fell. It was there that Jesse found Rebbie awaiting him. When the general was transferred to Virginia the family was frequently with him, although Nellie was placed in boarding school in New Jersey.

Mrs. Grant had arranged for herself and the general to visit Nellie on the night President Lincoln was assassinated, and this was the reason Grant gave for not accepting Lincoln's invitation to attend the theater with him. News of the shooting reached them in Philadelphia, and the general rushed back by special train.

War's end found the heretofore almost homeless Grants with fine homes in various cities. Galena, Ohio, bought them the most handsome mansion in town, but they soon moved to Philadelphia where the Union Club gave them a home and furnished it for $30,000—but it proved to be too far from the center of gravity, which for Grant was Washington.

They acquired the fine residence at 205 I Street formerly occupied by Vice-President John C. Breckinridge and moved in for Christmas of 1865. A group of New Yorkers soon presented the general with $100,000 to pay off the mortgage. Then the "solid men of Boston" raised $75,000 and sent him a library to put in it.

This house was so rich and comfortable that Mrs. Grant wanted the family to continue living in it after her husband became President in 1869, using the White House only for parties. She was not to have her way this time, however.

The Grants lived richly in the White House and no Presidential family ever served so much food. State dinners of from twenty-three to twenty-nine courses were usual.

Fred, an outgoing and well-liked young man, was in West Point when his father became President and Buck was preparing for college at Phillips Exeter Academy. Buck, a good student, was a "modest, retiring lad, as sensitive and kindly as a girl, but not lacking whatever in virility or manly spirit. . . ." He was popular at school and admired there for his complete honesty and lack of airs.

As for Nellie and Jesse, their schooling lagged. Mrs. Grant had started Jesse to school with Nellie but he so strongly objected to all the girls that his father later let him go with Buck. But at the White House young Jesse was unable to crowd school into his schedule and Nellie neglected her homework so much that she was kept after school.

One afternoon the White House carriage came for her the third time before she was permitted to leave. Next morning the First Lady came to thank the headmistress. "Teach her she is plain Nellie Grant," she said, "entitled to no special privileges."

When Nellie was fifteen it was decided that for her own good she should go away to boarding school. Neither parent wanted to be separated from Nellie, however, nor did she care about going.

The President decided he would take her lest "Julia cry and bring her back." He delivered her at fashionable Miss Porter's in Connecticut but was not home again before Nellie was sending telegrams outlining her homesickness. He wired her to return home. After that she began to help her mother at receptions. Mostly, though, she dashed about town in her phaeton and attended young-set parties.

Jesse had an almost identical experience. He was sent to Cheltenham in Pennsylvania and immediately began bombarding his mother with letters saying he was not learning a thing. She assured him that he should give it a longer try. He wrote his father, "I want to come home." The President wired, WE WANT YOU, TOO. COME AT ONCE.

Grandfather Dent, the First Lady's father, who remained politically an unreconstructed Southerner, lived at the White House and Grandfather Grant, a taciturn Union man, visited frequently—but stayed in a hotel rather than to be too close to the Rebel.

The public loved newspaper stories about their differences. Grandfather Dent must have been a persuasive raconteur because his tales of how delightful it was to travel the National Turnpike westward influenced Buck and Jesse to undertake a walking tour of the route when Buck was home from school one summer.

Two other boys went with them—but the lads did not find conditions nearly so romantic as grandfather had remembered. Nonetheless, they had fun along the way and tales to tell when interviewed in Pittsburgh. One was of an innkeeper's daughter in Maryland who played for them while they sang loudly. She had no idea she had entertained Presidential sons, so they mailed her 50 copies of the paper with her name in it and all the sheet music they could find.

Mrs. Grant—a kindly little lady whose photographs show that each year she looked a little more like Queen Victoria in all her bustles, flounces, point lace, ribbons and bows—had strict ideas that Nellie must be accompanied to dances by a male member of the family.

This was tough on Jesse, who began begging her to leave by the second dance and who was so afraid of girls that it never occurred to him to dance himself. Once he took her to a Navy ball at Annapolis and she was so eager to get on the floor she forgot to take off her galoshes.

Fred graduated from West Point and was assigned to army duty out West. He invited Jesse to Fort Dodge for a buffalo hunt. They hunted over a wide area, saw few buffalo but had a good time.

Jesse saw the trip as the end of his boyhood. That autumn he entered Cornell to get an education. President Grant, immensely pleased, wrote an old friend, "Jesse entered Cornell University, without a condition, although he has never attended school but three years."

Nellie and Anna Barnes, her close friend, were given an informal debut into formal society at the White House. Nellie wore Paris muslin with a gracefully looped overskirt of Valenciennes lace, under which a dress of rose-colored silk blushed through. Anna wore black silk with a Roman sash.

One woman journalist, Mary Clemmer Ames, thoroughly disapproved of the all-night "Germans" Nellie attended. Mrs. Ames admitted that she forgave President Grant many things because he was so amiable at receptions and devoted to his wife and daughter. But the dances which began at 11 P.M. and lasted until 5 A.M. were too much. She felt that Nellie's youth was being wasted and conceivably her health undermined "in the wild, unhealthy excitement through which she whirls night after night."

Mrs. Grant was worried a bit about Nellie, too. She was far too popular with the boys. To get her mind off that subject, the First Lady permitted her to go abroad with Secretary of the Navy and Mrs. Adolph E. Borie. She was received by Queen Victoria and everywhere treated royally.

But on shipboard coming home the purpose of the trip was defeated. Nellie met and fell in love with a handsome Englishman, Algernon C. F. Sartoris, a nephew of Fanny Kemble, the popular actress.

To think of Nellie marrying and going to live in Europe was almost more than the Grants could endure. The President went around with tears in his eyes for days.

Nellie's wedding on May 12, 1874 was quite the most lavish and expensive in the White House to that date and by far the most publicized. All the world took an interest. It was in the East Room under a large wedding bell of white roses. The Brussels point lace on Nellie's white satin dress cost $5,000 and gifts displayed in the Oval Library were valued at nearly $75,000.

Twelve bridesmaids wore identical white dresses. Six carried pink flowers and six blue. Brother Fred, in the full uniform of a colonel, was best man. The President was in evening attire, like the bridegroom. Mrs. Grant, in mourning black (for her father), stood between Buck and Jesse.

The wedding feast was an extravaganza admired for its richness and "systematic arrangement." The newlyweds, accompanied by the Grant sons and several wedding guests, went to New York and had a spectacular sendoff as they sailed for England.

In October of the same year Fred was married in Chicago to Ida Honore, the beautiful Kentucky-born sister of Chicago's society queen, Mrs. Potter Palmer. The Palmers gave Ida $10,000 worth of diamonds and staged a wedding attended by President and Mrs. Grant and other notables.

Fred received a Washington assignment and took his bride to live in the White House, where their first child was born. He hoped for a son to name Ulysses S., but it was a girl and named Julia for the First Lady. (This White House baby eventually married a Russian prince and is still living.)

Scandals beset the administration, but not the order of their schedule, which moved with military precision. Mrs. Grant often asked several of her friends to lunch before her afternoon receptions and had them stand with her in the receiving line in the Blue Room, from which all hint of daylight was fashionably removed. She was not noted for remembering names, but was so glad to see everybody it made no difference.

She called her eight years in the White House the happiest of her life.

Fred assaulted a newspaper columnist who wrote disparagingly of his young wife, happily paying the $100 fine which the fight cost him.

Buck graduated from Harvard and was a Presidential secretary for a year before entering a New York law firm.

Jesse kept writing from Cornell that he and his classmates wanted the President to seek a third term—but the President wrote back to prepare for a trip around the world as soon as the second term ended. He had saved $15,000, he wrote. "We're going, Jesse. We're going."

And go they did—the ex-President and wife and Jesse. The Grant party steamed away from Philadelphia in May, 1877, arrived in San Francisco in September, 1879, both the send-off and the welcome-back calling for great pomp and ceremony.

They stopped first in England, where they visited Nellie at Southampton and spent a night with Queen Victoria at Windsor Castle.

Their trip about Europe was a zigzag from country to country, each one—including Russia—according the group the status of visiting royalty. Nineteen-year-old Buck was not a happy traveler, though. When they reached Rome he returned home and Fred joined his parents.

Upon their return the Grants lived in New York in a $95,-000 home bought by friends. They were financially solvent for life, they thought, with about $200,000 worth of real estate in different cities and an income of $15,000 a year from a gift trust fund.

But disaster was to overtake them when the brokerage firm of Grant & Ward collapsed in scandal. Names on its stationery included General U. S. Grant, and Ulysses S. Grant Jr. The ex-President had $100,000 in it and Buck, who married a rich wife, $50,000. Fred evidently had loaned the firm great amounts and Jesse, single and living at home, had deposited heavily.

Failure of the firm created a panic in 1884 and an unsavory aftermath in which the Grant sons were condemned without pity although the public felt sympathy for their father.

Congress restored the ex-President's rank as a general with pay of $17,500 a year and Mark Twain worked out a publishing deal whereby his *Memoirs* could provide a legacy for his family. Fighting cancer of the throat, Grant finished his monumental two volumes seven days before his death a year later. One of the last letters he wrote was to a future President asking an appointment to West Point for his grandson, Ulysses S. Grant III, Fred's son.

Buck and Jesse went West to live. Each had two marriages and engaged in financial enterprises. Jesse won a concession from the Mexican Government to colonize and develop land surrounding the hot springs of Tia Juana and set up a gambling casino. He became a Democrat in politics, like his Grandfather Dent, and lived until 1934, leaving an estate of about $2,000.

Buck prospered in San Diego as a respected businessman and became a leading Republican of his area. He aspired to the U. S. Senate but his chances collapsed in a bribery scandal involving the state legislature.

Beautiful Nellie's marriage to the Englishman was unsuccessful, due to his drinking. She returned to America with her three small children and later, in 1912, had a happy second marriage to one of her girlhood sweethearts, Franklin H. Jones of Canada.

Fred's career was the most illustrious. President Benjamin Harrison named him Minister to the Austro-Hungarian Empire and his family had four glamorous years in old Vienna, where young Julia—born in the White House—began to go to parties and learned the court manners which served her well when she married the Russian prince, Michael Cantacuzene, aide-de-camp to Grand Duke Nicholas.

Princess Cantacuzene celebrated her ninetieth birthday in Washington in 1966 and, although blind for a decade, still was one of the most delightfully charming women in the capital city, a great conversationalist with a gay sense of humor. She sent her three children, two daughters and a son, out of Russia during the Red Revolution and remained with her husband, who fought as long as it was possible to do so. Then they came to America.

She wrote her story for the *Saturday Evening Post*, lectured on the Chautauqua circuit and later wrote three books. Her proud boast is that in *My Life Here and There*, *Russian People* and *Revolutionary Days* there were no mistakes.

Her three children, six grandchildren and eighteen great-grandchildren keep in close communication with her, but she lives alone in a simple apartment, usually has dinner with her brother, Gen. U. S. Grant III, at least once a week. This General Grant was once Commissioner of the District of Columbia and for many years has been one of Washington's most devoted citizens.

Rutherford B. Hayes

FOUR SONS AND A YOUNG DAUGHTER

"WE originally called him Birchard, with no other Christian name. . . . I now offered him for his choice as a middle name Scott, Cook, Austin, Russell, etc., etc. He chose Austin, the maiden name of my grandmother. So Birchard Austin it shall be."

Thus Rutherford B. Hayes wrote in his diary when his oldest son came home for the Christmas holidays during his first year at Cornell University. Three years later his second son, by then in Cornell, too, also wanted to make some changes in his name. The father duly recorded:

"He was named James Webb. He is called Webb, and preferring another family name we agreed to drop the James and give him the middle letter C, for Cook. So Webb C. Hayes it shall be."

The other two sons were given two family names from the beginning. They were Rutherford Platt and Scott Russell. When the only daughter came along, though, the simple label of Fanny—very stylish at the time—was considered sufficient. Her sex alone made her more than welcome.

When Hayes, the Governor of Ohio who had been a major general of volunteers in the Civil War, was inaugurated President in 1877, ages of this proper group were: Birchard (at times Birch), twenty-three, Webb, twenty-one, Rutherford (Ruddy or Rud), almost seventeen, Fanny nine, and Scott, six.

Birch by then was almost ready to graduate from Harvard Law School and would be so busy establishing his legal practice in Ohio that he would see less of the White House than any other member of the family. Webb, a Cornell graduate, became the President's secretary. At one time the father had noted in his diary, "Webb is not scholarly" and one of his White House labels was "Webb, the Sportsman"—but he was an excellent and popular secretary.

Ruddy continued in school at the University of Michigan and Cornell, did not get to Washington too frequently and when he did he had a hard time finding a place to sleep. He claimed he considered himself fortunate to get the "soft side of the billiard table" at the White House. "Cots in the hall, couches in the reception room, billiard tables and even bathtubs had to serve as beds," he declared.

"Even Father had virtually no privacy. I have seen him retire to the bathroom, lock the door and prepare some important state papers."

One assumes that in this convention-like atmosphere young Fanny and Scott had regular beds of their own and slept well despite the number of guests and relatives revolving around them.

Reason for the overcrowding was that Lucy Webb Hayes, wife of the President, was just as wild about people in general as women of the press of her day were wild about her specifically.

Many of them stated firmly that she was the greatest First Lady the nation had known and perhaps the most beautiful. Some of them qualified it a bit by admitting that some of the first First Ladies were superior women, too, but insisted that only Mrs. Hayes had deserved accolades on all counts since the days of the first Mrs. Adams.

Reasons for the compliments were that Mrs. Hayes was the first First Lady to be a bona fide college graduate and espoused two causes dear to women reporters of the day: temperance and the right of women to vote. Also, she joined them in wanting a return to modesty in women's dress, helped create a backlash against the bare armed and exposed bosom décor of the Civil War era.

The new President and First Lady were teetotalers and devout, almost missionary type, Methodists who always had do-good projects under way. They served wine at the White House only once: at an already scheduled dinner for two grand dukes from Russia. Hayes was so new that the State Department had its way that time. However, he decreed that future guests, whether foreign or domestic, would find no wine at his table.

"Lemonade Lucy" became the First Lady's nickname. Many a Congressman groaned that "Lemonade will flow like wine at the White House tonight" as they set off for her at-homes.

It often fell to Webb to close the White House after his father and mother had departed for bed and guests still were entertaining other guests downstairs. He developed a system for having something heavy dropped on the floor above so that somebody present would look at the clock and start an exodus.

This son, in addition to being his father's secretary, was in charge of White House accounting and also supervisor of an expansion project at Spiegel Grove, the Hayes home in Ohio. Perhaps because bedrooms at the White House were at such a premium he kept adding them at Spiegel Grove until the rambling structure today has "no fewer than twenty." Webb may not have had enough sleep during his father's four years in Washington but he developed into an astute businessman.

Mrs. Hayes did not settle for one or two evenings at home

a week. Any evening when no large dinner was scheduled she was at home to the public from 8 until 10 P.M. Someone asked her, "Don't you get fearfully tired?" she replied in amazement, "Oh, no, I never tire of having a good time."

It was in the Hayes tradition that they should be the ones to save what is called the "oldest and oddest" Washington tradition: the egg rolling for children on Easter Monday.

Congressmen long since had tired of the lost children, ruined grass and trampled egg yolks, and during the Hayes administration threatened that any tot who showed up on Capitol Hill to roll even one egg would be thrown off the premises even if it took all the policemen in town to do it. "You are welcome on the White House lawn," said the President and in they flocked.

Fanny and Scott Hayes, dressed in their most stylish attire— white dress with colored sash and matching shoes for her, little tight-at-the-knees trousers and buttoned shoes for him—were there to play hostess and host.

The two youngsters had a gay time in the White House. Fanny played and sang for guests, telling some of them to remember her songs so they could tell their own little girls about them. Scott appears to have been more silent than Fanny was, but the President labeled him "Scott, the Adventurous" nonetheless.

He also wrote in his diary that Scott was "very interesting. Too honest to joke or to comprehend a joke readily. . . . He is fond of animals."

Scott wrote his very first letter in the White House. It said: "My Dear Mama: I am trying to write a letter and it shall be to you. Scott R. Hayes." Dated Nov. 14, 1877, it was labeled "Scott's first letter" and is in the Rutherfod B. Hayes Library at Fremont, Ohio.

Mrs. Hayes wrote her oldest son Birch, in December of 1877: "Scott and Fan are well and learning to ride beautifully. . . . I cannot say much of Scott's intellectual advancement, or—stop, that is not the word. The boy fortunately has sense and intellect, but his reading, writing and arithmetic does not develop as rapidly as desired. . . ."

Birch's father earlier had written him: "Webb has gone on a hunt down in Virginia. Rud had an attack of headache and vomitting and has remained here. He will return to Cornell tomorrow. Scott got a bruised forehead by his horse falling flat on the asphalt in front of the [White] house. He behaved like a little man, and his mother who was looking on, behaved still better."

When Marini's dancing school gave a costume ball for its pupils, Fanny and Scott, after much family discussion, went in costumes so pleasing to the President that he had an assortment of pictures made of them to send to his three older sons.

Fanny went as Martha Washington and Scott in the uniform of a sergeant of the 23rd Regiment of the Ohio Infantry—his father's old command.

In family letters of the administration are glimpsed facets of family life about which official documents are understandably silent. A few such glimpses are:

> Fan is feeling very important this morning as she has received a letter from Rud asking her to meet him at the Depot. The little damsel is suffering with a stiff neck and looks very firm and precise. She is doing beautifully in her Music and I look forward to real enjoyment in her attainments.

> Scott and your father are out walking . . . Scott is now engaged in recitation. The lesson is hard this morning—a new ball is the disturbing element, and the spelling lesson is correspondingly difficult.

> Scott's new goat is a success. He hauls Scott all about and is good natured. The two dogs suit him too. Your mother's

cat, the dogs, the goat and the mocking bird give a Robinson Crusoe touch to our mode of life.

Scott begins to learn at last [1879]. He is not especially bright [the understatement with which this President described all his children] but he is very much in earnest. His recitation of "Hottenlindren" would amuse you.

Scott and his bicycle are fast friends.

Fanny and Scott are doing nicely. Scott had a small encounter with a young comrade but came off victorious. He may possibly feel it encumbent upon himself to brag a little, knowing I am not in favor of fighting, but don't want him to be whipped.

You will take great delight in Fan and Scott. She is bright and keen and he is handsome, sensible and will be somebody some day.

We had a quiet but good Christmas yesterday [their last in the White House]. The presents were distributed to the little folks, servants and all, in our old way. Scott . . . was not demonstrative in his joy. But when the watch and chain with the little silver "bug" as a charm came to him, it was plainly to be seen that the boy's soul was touched with joy— Fanny weighs 100; Scott 97! Worth their weight in gold!

By almost any standards President and Mrs. Hayes were superior parents. She inculcated in all the children deep convictions of ethics and modesty. He was never too busy to write and counsel with them, and his diary showed how often he had them on his mind. Each was relished as an individual and enjoyed as a personality.

When Father was away during the war he wrote eight-year-old Birch: "I want you to resolve always to do what you know is right. No matter what you lose by it, no matter what danger there is, always do right. . . . Be kind to your brothers . . . and above all your mother."

He still was writing the same type advice to Scott, the youngest, when he went away to school after the Presidency ended: "First of all, keep your conscience at the helm. . . . Do not be uneasy for salary or promotion. . . . At all times have on hand some solid reading. Either history, biography or natural science. . . . Watch workmen, learn all facts, be practical as well as a man of theories."

The Hayes sons all became successful businessmen who interested themselves in public affairs. Webb started a modest business which grew into the huge Union Carbide Corporation.

Rud, who kept going to school so long his family wondered about him, began work in a small bank but became ever more interested in libraries. He was the first to think of reading rooms for children and traveling libraries.

Scott turned to business enterprises connected with railroad equipment.

Webb established a library and museum at Fremont, Ohio, to his father's memory. It was the first of the Presidential libraries, and still is expanding its work.

Garfield's Family

MOLLIE AND FOUR BROTHERS

JAMES A. Garfield was the third Ohio President to live in the White House in succession and, like Hayes before him, his children were a daughter and four sons.

Fanny Hayes and Mollie Garfield, each fourteen years of age, made a pretty picture as they sat together at his inaugural ceremonies on Capitol Hill. Fanny wore a dress of purple plush with yellow stripes in it and a white felt hat. Mollie, her successor, wore a little suit of plum-colored wool trimmed in plush. Her broad-brimmed "gypsy hat was tied over her ears."

Mollie's brothers were: Harry Augustus (Hal), seventeen, James Rudolph (Jim), sixteen, Irvin McDowell, ten, and Abram, eight.

Hal and Jim had been in the same class at St. Paul's School in New Hampshire, but persuaded their father to permit them to have a tutor at the White House so that they could live there until they entered Williams College the next autumn.

Garfield consented and the closely knit family remained together during most of his 199 days in office. Garfield's mother, the first mother to see her son sworn into the Presidency, was with them much of the time, too.

The same tutor also taught the younger boys. Irvin and Abram were more interested in trying their velocipedes and

bicycles in the lower White House halls, however, and in exploring the premises than in serious study. Mr. Hawkes, the
tutor, had to complain to their father about them. The President directed that their daily papers be sent to him, and their
grades began to pick up immediately.

Mollie, a vivacious young beauty who had been attending
Madame Burr's school in Washington during her father's
terms in Congress, continued to go there—walking the several
blocks daily, her arms full of books and her long brown
braids swinging behind her.

No Secret Service agent accompanied her nor had a guard
for Presidential children been thought of at the time. One
reporter wrote that seeing Mollie set off for school was "one
of the prettiest sights in town." She also attended dancing
classes at Marini's, where Hal and Jim joined her, and continued music lessons.

She had received a fine new piano for her thirteenth birthday and the family loved her playing. Hal was the natural
musician of the family, though, and had played the piano since
he was a very small boy. His father often slipped into the upstairs Oval Room to enjoy his playing at the White House.

The Garfields were by no means so straitlaced in their family life as the Hayes family had been. President Garfield, a
born giant of a man, was gregarious, outgoing and very popular. His wife Lucretia—called Crete by him—thought him
at times too outgoing, too trustful of people before he got to
know them. He liked a glass of wine or beer now and then. He
played billiards with his sons and enjoyed card games with
Congressmen.

Hal laid out a new lawn tennis court at the White House
and the President participated in fast games with him and
Jim and their friends. He was a rollicking father who kept the
nicknames and family jokes alive and loved to make up
tunes for favorite poems and sayings.

His favorite reading to them at New Year's time was Tennyson's poem about "Ring, happy bells, across the snow"—which is still sung to his tune by his descendants.

He called Irvin "Dutch Brig," depicting him as hard to get started but, once he moved, as pushing steadily ahead.

Nearly every mealtime was schooltime for his children during his White House days. A born educator, Garfield had worked hard for his own education and headed a small college before he added more hard work to his schedule to study law. He continued his teaching after elected to the state legislature and until he went off to the Civil War. He was promoted to brigadier general of volunteers and during the war was elected to Congress. His children frequently called him "the general."

He had enjoyed learning and fought so hard for a chance to go to school that he never could understand why a child of his could find any book uninteresting. He coined the much-quoted statement about "Mark Hopkins on one end of the log and a student on the other" being the best education possible. Mark Hopkins, a leading educator of the period whom he venerated, still was at St. Paul's when he sent his sons there.

Hal and Jim were good students, even by their tutor's high standard, and—like their father—they managed to edge in many a good time at the White House before disaster struck them.

But living in the White House is not like living at home, as the Garfields were neither the first nor last Presidential family to learn. When Hal fell head over heels in love with pretty Lulu Rockwell, daughter of Col. A. F. Rockwell, the President's classmate at Williams and his most intimate friend, the lad had to wait a month to be able to discuss it privately with his father.

Mollie gave a luncheon for ten young friends. Her mother

was too busy to guide her but was delighted to see that she automatically knew the right thing to do and had given Fanny Hayes the seat of honor.

The Garfields did not have so much company as the Hayes family did, but enough to prevent their sitting down to breakfast alone for 22 weeks. By that time the First Lady was ill from a malaria-type exhaustion. Her fever stayed far above normal for many days. Doctors were baffled, but the newspapers were certain that whatever it was she had was caused by living in that "pest house."

There must have been something to what they wrote. Her room was moved from the south to north side of the house to lessen sewer odors wafting in from swampy flats of the Potomac.

When Mrs. Garfield was able to come downstairs again on June 12, her husband and Hal made a "chair with their hands" and brought her to the dining room amid happy laughter. A week later she was able to go to Elberon, New Jersey, to recuperate in the sea breezes. She took Mollie and the two younger boys with her.

The entire family had great plans for the summer. The President and his older sons were to attend commencement exercises at Williams College, where he would speak and they would be enrolled for school that autumn. Then, the younger boys gone to their grandmother's in Ohio, Mollie and the First Lady were to meet the President and older boys in New York to embark on a cruise in New England waters.

On the morning of departure from the White House, July 2, the President was feeling so carefree he turned somersaults on his sons' beds and they all sang loudly before setting out in two carriages for the Old Baltimore and Potomac railroad station where several Cabinet friends, including Robert Todd Lincoln, were seeing them off.

Before the boys' carriage arrived at the station the President had been shot twice in the back by Charles J. Guiteau, who said the Lord directed him. One shot went through an arm and did little damage. The other lodged in a kidney.

Jim wrote that he was in tears and knew not what to do but that Hal kept his head and was a pillar of strength. The seriously wounded President was returned to the White House on a mattress and tried to calm the people around him. Mrs. Garfield and Mollie arrived that evening by special train.

All that long hot summer the President suffered at the White House. Miracle drugs and equipment of today could have saved him, and at times it was thought that he *would* recover.

In September he was thought strong enough to be moved to the New Jersey seacoast, and there he died on September 19.

One of the people Garfield had planned to visit during the cruise was Cyrus W. Field, who planned the laying of the first Atlantic Cable. Field took the lead in a public subscription so that Mrs. Garfield and the children need not suffer financially. The outpouring was great and $350,000 was subscribed.

The boys could continue in college and there was enough, too, for graduate study at Yale for Joseph Stanley Brown, the President's private secretary and a family mainstay following the President's assassination. Mollie was in love with "Mr. Brown," as she called him, although he was nine years her senior. Mrs. Garfield thought she would outgrow the attachment, but she didn't and when she was twenty-one her mother consented to their marriage.

Meantime Hal and Jim had graduated from Williams and begun the practice of law together in Cleveland. Hal was in love with Belle Mason, older sister of one of Mollie's best friends. So Hal and Mollie decided on a double wedding before the bay window of the Garfield home at Mentor. Mollie did not wear a veil, because her bridegroom did not like the idea, but Belle did.

It was Mrs. Garfield who suggested that her son-in-law hyphenate his name to Stanley-Brown so that the Stanley part of it would never be lost. His family had been Stanleys before they left England to escape debtors' prison—the reason many a family left the old country for America. So as Mr. and Mrs. Joseph Stanley-Brown the newlyweds went on a honeymoon to Germany, where he continued his studies.

Hal left his law firm to become the first professor of politics at Princeton under Woodrow Wilson, then became president of Williams College—from which he took leave during World War I to be fuel administrator for President Wilson.

James also had service in the government. President Theodore Roosevelt named him Secretary of the Interior and he had the double distinction of being a member also of Teddy's "tennis cabinet."

Irvin, the "Dutch Brig," also became a lawyer after he graduated from Williams but his practice was in Boston rather than Cleveland. Abram, to his mother's delight, became an architect. He followed his profession in Cleveland for many years. Mollie's son, Rudolph, also became an architect and her daughter, Ruth, wrote a charming book called *Mollie Garfield in the White House.*

Chester A. Arthur

A TALL SON AND PRETTY DAUGHTER

HANDSOME Chester A. Arthur, whose complexion was once described as being like strawberries and cream, was one politician who never slapped backs, hailed people by their first names nor went around kissing babies—unless they were his own or belonged to close relatives. He epitomized the rich New York clubman of his day in appearance and behavior. As Vice-President, it was said, he presided over the U. S. Senate as if posing for his portrait.

When President he wore Prince Albert coats in his office, always had a flower in his buttonhole and a colored silk handkerchief showing from his vest pocket. He ordered up to 25 pairs of trousers from his tailor at one time, and kept on pearl-tinted gloves at White House receptions. He had curly sideburns, rather than those thick whiskers which would have covered more of his face, and they only added to his 6-foot 2-inch elegance.

Reporters called him something new in Presidents: the complete metropolitan man. But they came to like him for his personal honesty, his impeccable politeness and the courage with which he tackled the job of being President with all the cards stacked against him.

When President Garfield was shot, Arthur hastened to call

on Mrs. Garfield to extend his sympathy. Members of the Garfield Cabinet who were present stared at him in open hostility.

"Chet Arthur President!" some of his club friends gasped. "God help us!" But when Garfield died on September 19, 1881, he became President nonetheless.

Elihu Root, his friend, wrote: "Surely no more lonely and pathetic figure was ever seen assuming the powers of government. He had no people behind him. He had no party behind him, for the dominant faction of his party hated his name. . . . He ascended the steps of the throne as one who is accused goes to trial."

He was a widower with two children: Chester Alan Jr. (Alan), a seventeen-year-old freshman at Princeton University, and Ellen (Nellie), not quite ten. His wife Ellen Herndon, a Virginia belle whose father was a naval hero, had died shortly before New Yorkers more or less forced his nomination for the Vice-Presidency on a deadlocked Republican convention.

Arthur, who had adored his wife, lived in affectionate concern for the welfare of his motherless children.

Alan was a tall, very handsome and very thin young man with piercing black eyes and a great deal of zest. When his father took the oath of office at his home in New York (the second oath being delivered in Washington two days later) Alan stepped forward, put his hand on his father's shoulder and kissed him.

Nellie, a dainty and endearing young miss, had a French governess at the White House and attended nearly all receptions given there by her father. She was in the personal charge of the President's sister, Mrs. Mary McElroy, of Albany, New York, who came with her own young daughters, May and Jessie, to care for Nellie and help with the entertaining.

The new President refused to live in the White House until

it was redecorated, declaring that he would foot the bill if Congress would not. He engaged Louis Comfort Tiffany, "a name which connoted rare jewels and lustrous glass," for the job.

An opalescent glass screen which reached from floor to ceiling was stretched across the front hall entrance—to shut off drafts which had bothered First Families since the shivering days of Abigail Adams. The screen's designs of eagles and flags were intricately interlaced in the "Arabian manner."

The Blue Parlor became a robin's-egg blue; in fact, for a while was called the Robin's Egg Room. The ceiling of the East Room became silver with touches of ivory. The State Dining Room received pomegranate-colored curtains at the windows, heavy gold paper on the walls and crimson lights near the big fireplace.

Arthur was so pleased with these and other changes that he decided to have a public auction and rid the place of a jumbled accumulation of furniture and furnishings in the attic. Almost 5,000 persons attended. Among the $6,000 worth of "antiques" sold were a globe from Nellie Grant's school days, high chairs bought by Mrs. Hayes for young visitors and—it was joked—the "trap which caught the rat which ate the suit which Lincoln wore."

Guests at his first New Year's Day reception in 1882 were impressed by the colorful new décor and by two new ways to leave a White House party. Heretofore guests had been forced to double back to the entrance or go out through a window. (Andrew Jackson's guests had used the windows in desperation, and since then a refined system of steps and canopies had made the window exit acceptable.) Now guests could leave through the conservatories, which received an outside door, or through doors of the Blue Parlor opening onto the south lawn.

Nellie Arthur and her cousins attended this first reception, the President greeting them with smiles and kisses. They wore white embroidery dresses with colored ribbon sashes: a favorite costume for little girls through several administrations. Alan also was there with several young friends.

Alan formed the habit of hopping a train from Princeton and showing up frequently. The President at times found him at the breakfast table without forewarning. He usually wanted to use the Presidential carriage, a magnificent dark green landau drawn by two fine bays, to go calling on some of the city's young ladies.

The President evidently worried about Alan's playboy tendencies. He received a letter from a woman in fashionable Newport who wrote: "I saw your dear little boy at the Casino the other evening—he was talking to the ladies in front of me for quite a while. . . . By the way, he did not seem silly and dudefied at all in spite of what you and some other men say about him."

The President took Nellie and Alan to Annapolis for an unveiling of a memorial to their maternal grandfather and the family often took cruises in the Presidential yacht, on which he was the first to fly the Presidential flag.

He never permitted his children to be photographed for the papers and anything resembling an interview with them would have curdled his blood.

Socially the administration grew in popularity and those watching Arthur's "moral firmness" in office, his insistence on doing something to eradicate the political spoils system on which so many government jobs had rested, came to respect him as a President. At one time it was thought that he might receive the nomination for a term of his own.

Mark Twain was one writer who thought he deserved it. He wrote, "I am but one of 55,000,000; still in the opinion of this one-fifty-five-millionth of the country's population it would be hard to better President Arthur's Administration. But don't decide till you hear from the rest."

The rest never had a chance to decide, really. He could not get his party's nomination. Before the next political convention exaggerated rumors about his elegant habits were used to crush thoughts that his record might be acceptable. The valet he had, the thought that he may have had a pedicure, the carriage lap robe of otter with embroidered initials, the 25 sets of trousers at one time, that he liked to stay up nights and to breakfast between 9 and 10 A.M.—all were used against him. Congressman Joe Cannon said, "Arthur was defeated by his trousers."

He left office in poor health and spirits, lived little more than a year after his term ended.

His will divided his considerable estate between his children, incomes from it to do them until they were thirty-one, when the principal could be paid if they so desired.

Alan graduated from Princeton the year his father went out of office and was studying law at Columbia University when he died. For several years afterward Alan was known in all the best places on both sides of the Atlantic—and particularly where polo games were popular. He married a wealthy California girl, Myra Townsend, in Switzerland in 1900.

After she divorced him he more or less settled in the Colorado Springs area of Colorado, where his horses and sportsmanship won wide acclaim. *The New York Times* in a piece about his second marriage, when he was sixty-nine, listed a lengthy string of clubs in which he was popular and called him a notable figure in the world of polo.

His son, Chester A. Arthur III, makes San Francisco his home. For years he was a professional writer and used the name Gavin Arthur. He worked on a book to be called *Full Circle*—or, as he said, it would go from the log cabin in which his grandfather was born in Vermont in 1829 to the one in which he himself lived on the California-Oregon border while panning gold in 1929. His career has held other adventures, too.

An interview in the San Francisco *Chronicle* in 1965 mentioned that he fought in the Irish Rebellion, had been a seaman and worked as an assistant psychologist in a prison, been warm friends with Gertrude Stein and Bernard Shaw, and was ready at the time to become official astrologer to President Lyndon B. Johnson if he could put across the idea that the White House needed such.

Herb Caen in his San Francisco column of late 1961 wrote that he had divorced his wife, Esther Murphy, "in Reno the other day on the perfectly reasonable grounds of desertion. She left him to go to Paris in 1947, and I guess he finally decided she wasn't coming back."

His Aunt Nellie married Charles Pinkerton and died in Mount Kisco, New York, several years before his father died in Colorado Springs in 1937.

Grover Cleveland

WHITE HOUSE MARRIAGE AND BABIES

WHEN ex-President Grover Cleveland became the ecstatic father of his first daughter he felt like a man "who has just entered the real world and sees in a small child more of value than I have ever called my own before, who puts aside as hardly worth a thought all that has gone before—fame, honor, place, everything."

He was fifty-four at the time (October, 1891) and his beautiful wife was twenty-seven. They had married in the White House more than five years earlier during his first term as President but in 1891, they were living on Madison Avenue in New York City and hoping to be returned to Washington in the next national election, as indeed they were. This gave Cleveland the unique distinction of being the President who was voted out of office and then voted back in again—and also the one who still causes some confusion among the nation's schoolchildren. Was he one President, or two?

The happy Clevelands named their first baby Ruth and in her father's second term as President, Ruth was a national personality who helped to make the Gay Nineties even more gay. She was only seventeen months of age when her parents returned to the White House, and she received so many gifts she could have opened her own toy emporium.

The President was so proud of her he scarcely could wait to show her to his callers. "Frank, bring Ruth in here," he would call down the White House hall to his wife. "Never mind the state of her frock, bring her on in."

The public saw her, too, dressed up and out on the lawn for her outings. White House gates were left open in those days, and anybody at all could saunter among the shrubbery and stroll on the grounds. "The White House belongs to the nation. The nation has a right to come in," Cleveland had said.

But what happened to little Ruth hastened an end to the open-gate policy. The public was not content to stand back and look at the child. Men and women wanted to pick her up. One morning Ruth's frantic mother and the nurse lost sight of her as she was passed from arms to arms amid clamor for a closer-up look. Ruth took it all quite placidly. Several persons said later that she never uttered a sound.

Mrs. Cleveland wanted the White House gates closed after that, and they were. This the public did not like. "The Clevelands don't want us to see the baby because she is dumb, and perhaps deaf, too," said some of Ruth's erstwhile admirers. "Else why would they want her hidden?" "You can't make me believe that baby is all right."

The rumors were untrue but they hurt, nonetheless, even though the Clevelands had been through rumors before and would hear more later. Rumors as much as anything had defeated Cleveland in his race to have a second term following immediately after his first one.

Among the rumors that time was one repeated over and over, preached from pulpits and shouted on street corners to the effect that Cleveland was not a family man who could be trusted, that he at times got roaring drunk, beat up his young wife, and shut her out of the White House.

That rumor grew to such size that Mrs. Cleveland was permitted to issue a most unusual statement in defense of her marital happiness. It said:

> I can wish the women of our country no greater blessing than that their homes and lives may be as happy, their husbands so kind, attentive, considerate and affectionate as mine.

Then there was the rumor which almost prevented his election the first time. This one could have been true. It was that in his youth he had fathered an illegitimate son by Maria Halpern, a comely widow.

Cleveland was the first Democrat elected President since before the Civil War and like Buchanan, the last one before him, he was a bachelor. When he went to the White House in 1885 certainly nobody expected to see children there during his stay.

He was a balding forty-seven years of age and weighed around 250 pounds. His reputation was that of a man who worked around the clock and was downright boring in his one-track pursuit of public duty. He at times worked all night on a message to Congress. Reporters—whom he detested as a prying breed—wrote that he was the only President ever who seemed to need no amusement whatsoever.

He did like to fish, insisting on absolute silence when he did so, but the church people never let up on him for traveling on Sunday to do so. Godly people did not travel on Sunday in those days. Cleveland probably had more sermons preached against him than any other President. That his father had been a Presbyterian minister, and a brother still was, only made him more of a target.

But Cleveland, the unsocial bachelor, had a dream on his mind and her name was Frances (Frank) Folsom, the daughter of his old law partner. After Oscar Folsom died in a carriage accident "Uncle Cleve" helped rear Frank and before that he had bought her first baby buggy. Frank and her mother attended his inauguration and left for Europe as part of Frank's education—and to shop in secret for a trousseau in Paris.

On May 29, 1886 the President himself wrote about 40 of these today very scarce wedding invitations:

DEAR MR. ————

I am to be married on Wednesday evening, at seven o'clock, at the White House to Miss Folsom. It will be a very quiet affair, and I will be extremely gratified at your attendance on the occasion.

Yours Sincerely,
GROVER CLEVELAND

Frank and her mother arrived on the overnight train of June 2 and the wedding was that evening in the Blue Parlor, with John Philip Sousa in charge of music. The President escorted twenty-one-year-old Frank in her lovely white wedding gown with long train and veil down the stairs, nodded to Sousa to stop the music, and the ceremony began.

Church bells rang throughout the city and guns boomed from the arsenal. The country was excited and happy about the Cleveland wedding, but he had blushed when bands a few weeks earlier began to play "He's going to marry Yum-Yum."

Frank was a beautiful First Lady, the youngest wife of a President ever yet to preside over the executive mansion, and was poised beyond her years. Reception crowds were so eager to see her that they came in great numbers and at one reception there was a near panic. Some women turned for a second look at her and found themselves going the wrong way—and soon everybody was.

The Marine Band was swept from its moorings in the front hall (where it still plays) and it took several policemen to put things right again. She inaugurated Saturday afternoon parties for workingwomen and went on an around-the-country speaking tour with her husband.

She cried when her husband was defeated for reelection, but told the doorkeeper to take good care of the White House because they would be back four years later—which they were, with Ruth.

Ruth had two little sisters born before the second term ended. The oldest one, Esther, was born in the White House —only child of a President to date who ever was—and Marion, the youngest, was born at Buzzards Bay, Massachusetts, at the Cleveland summer home.

Esther was a perfect White House baby, with just enough fuzz on the top of her head to be intriguing. A song called "Esther's Lullaby" was written for her and many a Gay Nineties baby was lulled to blissful sleep by lines which included:

> Swing, swing, baby swing
> Soft as a bird on the wing.
> Oh, you dear little thing,
> Swing, swing, swing.

Little Marion's pudgy finger was pressed to an electric button in the White House to open a cotton fair in faraway Atlanta and all the children were occasionally in the news.

Irwin Hood (Ike) Hoover, who came to the executive mansion to install electric lights during the Benjamin Harrison administration and stayed for 42 years, called the Cleveland daughters the most adored and best-behaved children who lived there during his stay.

The staff loved them and especially enjoyed their visits to the conservatories, where they ran about sniffing the flowers and petting the plants. Their mother gave them constant care, Hoover said, because she—like their father—always wanted them around. They learned not to be noisy when near Papa's office and at times tiptoed by his office door.

A newspaper now and then remarked how nice it would be if the President had a son and in 1897, the New York *Tribune* was able to run as a headline CLEVELAND HAS A SON. By then, however, Cleveland was a professor and lecturer at Princeton University and not in the White House. The son was named Richard Folsom and in 1903 Richard was joined by Francis Grover. Two sons and three daughters were not bad at all for the bachelor who married at forty-nine and was sixty-seven when his fifth and last child was born.

His family, it seemed to Cleveland, was one of his best proofs of a meaningful life.

At Princeton the little Cleveland girls were playmates of the three daughters of Woodrow Wilson, the youngest of whom, Eleanor, was about the age of Ruth.

Eleanor, in her book *The Woodrow Wilsons,* wrote that Ruth had a talent for writing plays, that Esther was a wild-eyed tomboy and that Marion was a dainty child who lisped.

Ruth died when she was twelve, a few months before her last brother was born. The other four are living today. Marion, now the widow of John Harlan Amen, a New York attorney, remembers only one thing from her White House baby days and it is more of a fragrance than a memory. When she visited Mrs. Herbert Hoover at the White House and Mrs. Hoover urged her to remember how things were in the Cleveland days she—to save her life—saw nothing which seemed familiar nor that she actually recalled.

"When we got to the second floor, though," she said later, "I was overwhelmed by a sense of nostalgia. . . . There was a smell of roses and also a subtle, musty scent, as in a house by the sea. I was so puzzled by the sensation that I said nothing about it to Mrs. Hoover. How I wish I had. . . .

"But the next time I saw my mother I put the question to her out of the blue. 'What did the second floor of the White House used to smell like?' I asked. 'Why, it was strange,' she replied. 'That one floor had the smell of an old house by the sea, a musty scent, overlaid with roses. I always put red roses in it.' So you see, it was true. I did have a kind of memory."

Esther Cleveland went to England to work during World War I, married William Bosanquet and went to live quietly in Yorkshire.

This quiet was broken when President John F. Kennedy moved into the White House with two small children and the papers mentioned that she, Esther Cleveland Bosanquet, was the youngest Presidential child ever to live there—because she was born there.

On a visit to her sister in 1963 she told the *New Yorker,* "Our life became a nightmare. Phones ringing day and night. Reporters rushing out to interview me. And they all wanted memories, memories. I find it remarkable that I remember anything at all. . . . It could be a *terrible* temptation to imagine White House memories."

She remembered a huge Christmas tree with great heaps of toys underneath, of rolling eggs on the lawn at Easter and "seeing Papa a good deal in the evenings. I'd be taken into his study. He'd be sitting behind an enormous desk and he would bounce me on his knee. I remember very vividly that he once let me dip my fingers in his inkwell and make big blobs on his papers.

"And I remember our last day there just before we went to the station. I was sitting all alone in the downstairs hall. I had on a pair of brown fleece-lined gloves, the kind with a little snap button near the wrist. How I remember buttoning and unbuttoning that little snap.

"Then somebody came along and asked me why I was leaving. 'Because McKinley's coming,' I said, 'and there can't be two Presidents.' I don't quite remember saying that, but I'm sure I did, because I do remember Papa telling guests about it later."

The two sons often are asked to recall their memories, too, and people keep urging them even after being reminded that they never lived in the White House. Richard, in Washington from his Baltimore home for a luncheon honoring Presidential descendants in 1959, told the Women's National Press Club, "It is disconcerting to be told, 'I remember seeing you and your brother playing on the White House lawn,' but one must try to understand the spirit in which it is said."

When Richard was born at Princeton a bulletin board notice was posted:

> Grover Cleveland, Jr., arrived today at 1 o'clock; will enter Princeton with the class of 1916; and will play center rush on the Championship football teams of '16, '17, '18 and '19.

His father explained that he was not named Grover Jr., "because so many people have been bothered by the name Grover and it has been so knocked about that I thought it ought to have a rest."

Princeton students nonetheless spoke of Richard as "Grover Jr." and he did play on the football team in his freshman year.

After two degrees from Princeton he studied law at Harvard, married Ellen Douglas Gailor, the daughter of a presiding bishop of the Episcopal Church, and moved to Maryland.

He never concerned himself much with elective politics but held some appointive state jobs and made a civic-leader name for himself by endeavors in behalf of child welfare, education and courts for juveniles.

When Francis Cleveland was born at Tamworth, New Hampshire, in 1903 his father inserted "Grover" as his middle name. Francis was interested in acting. He studied drama at Harvard and appeared on Broadway in *Dead End* and in *Our Town*. Then he organized a well-known summer theater group, The Barnstormers, based at Tamworth where he still lives.

Just as his brother, Richard, was anti-New Deal in the days of Franklin D. Roosevelt, Francis was—to use his expression —"violently anti-Vietnam War" in 1967.

Benjamin Harrison

SON, DAUGHTER AND GRANDCHILDREN

"YOUR grandmother, who thinks of everything and everybody, insists that I shall send the old crib. It is so ricketty I'm afraid it won't stand the journey," John Scott Harrison wrote from his farm at North Bend, Ohio, to his son Benjamin in Indianapolis early in 1858.

Benjamin, twenty-five years of age, was the father of a three-year-old son named Russell Benjamin and expecting to become a father again. He spent $2.50 to repair the crib and buy a mattress so that it was in readiness for his daughter, Mary Scott (Mamie), when she arrived in April.

The crib was not just any baby's crib, but the one in which William Henry Harrison, our ninth President, had slept at the family home in Berkeley, Virginia, when his father—Benjamin, who three years later would sign the Declaration of Independence—placed him in it in 1773. The Ohio and Indiana Harrisons were short on cash in 1858 but had an abundance of family and history behind them.

The grandmother who wanted the struggling lawyer to have the crib was Anna Symmes Harrison, who had been First Lady for a month in 1841 although, alone among First Ladies, she never lived in the President's House.

Benjamin was destined to become our twenty-third President although neither in looks nor disposition did he resemble his Presidential grandfather. "Old Tippecanoe" was a tall and swashbuckling type who enjoyed riding a white charger on his inaugural day and attending three balls that night. Benjamin was short and rotund and accused of having ice water in his veins. He could charm a crowd of 10,000 with his oratory, it was said, but was apt to make an enemy when he talked face to face.

His wife, Caroline Lavinia (Carrie), compensated for his unsocial traits by being the most outgoing woman in Indianapolis. She was a doer and a charmer and always had many projects under way. Among other things, she taught china painting (free to working girls) and a large Sunday school class for Presbyterian infants.

Also, Carrie knew that despite her husband's bluff exterior he was inwardly a sentimentalist. He sent her pressed flowers from Civil War battlefronts, urged her to write him every single thing which she and the children did every single day. "I love to know every little bit of it [your daily lives] to feed my love of home upon," he wrote her. When he was home on leave he insisted that she and the children accompany him to New York and be with him until he sailed to rejoin General Sherman's troops in South Carolina.

He came out of the war a breveted brigadier general, was the last of the Civil War generals to become President. After the war he lost a race for Governor of Indiana, but in 1881 was elected to the U. S. Senate. Carrie enjoyed Washington, entered into the life of the city and informed herself about Congressional duties and needs of the White House.

When her husband became President in 1889 she had three plans for getting the Presidential offices and the First Family's sleeping quarters forever separated—and presented them to Congress. She could do so in good faith, she said, because a solution would benefit future families and not hers.

One plan would have extended the White House with wings which formed a rectangle around a great courtyard with fountains. Another would have added wings at either end for offices. (This plan was followed in modified form later.) The third would have left the mansion for entertaining and offices and built a new residence for the President.

Meantime Carrie fitted four generations into the old mansion's "five sleeping quarters," which is what she said she found for her family—which, in addition to children and grandchildren, included Dr. John W. Scott, her father; Elizabeth S. Lord, her widowed sister; and Mary Lord Dimmick, the sister's widowed daughter.

Russell and Mamie were both married by then. Russell, thirty-four, married Mary Angeline Saunders, daughter of a Nebraska Senator, and they had a fifteen-month-old daughter named Marthena.

Mamie, thirty, married James Robert McKee, an Indianapolis merchant, and they had two children: Benjamin Harrison McKee (Baby McKee), eighteen months old, and Mary Lodge, an infant.

Mamie helped her mother with social duties and Mrs. Dimmick, the niece, became Aunt Carrie's secretary. Russell, interested in cattle and publishing, made his home in Helena, Montana, and was not a full-time White House resident although he became his father's secretary before the term ended.

The three grandchildren were as cute as buttons and ran away with the publicity of the administration, Baby McKee becoming as well known as the President. Photography was enjoying a heyday and the Harrisons were liberal about picture taking. Baby McKee was pictured leading a band, having tea, driving his goat, talking to his dog, and wearing a yachting cap.

Frank G. Carpenter, a Washington columnist, wrote lengthily about Baby McKee:

President Harrison and his family usually have prayers before breakfast, which is served at about nine o'clock. Baby McKee's high chair is pulled close to his grandfather, whose affection for his small namesake is the talk of the nation. This pretty little fellow and his place in the affections of the President have been so much commented upon in the press that word has gone out to let up lest the people of this country should come to believe the tales about this child's having more influence than members of the Cabinet.

Toys have been pouring into the White House for Baby McKee and his baby sister, Mary Lodge. His pony cart and his favorite French mechanical dog have lately been put aside for a miniature tennis set with which he plays, with a pretty, tasseled silk tennis cap on his head, often with his grandfather as a fascinated watcher.

When the Harrisons first moved into the White House, this child had not yet learned to walk well. He often crawled about like a crab. Many a visitor in the President's study has felt a warm little arm about his leg in the midst of his interview.

One day during a conference when Benny's presence was not noticed a roll of important papers disappeared. A frantic search was made by the President's secretary, who could not hold back a cry when he pulled the window draperies aside and found Baby McKee stirring the contents of a huge spittoon with the precious roll.

Grandpa for once lost his patience with the darling child, and sent him off with his nurse, while the secretary was sent to clean the brown stains off the documents.

The First Lady staged a party for Baby McKee's fourth birthday. Eighteen tots, most of them in high chairs, sat around a table heaped with goodies.

Marthena Harrison (still living) had her big day in the White House when she came down with scarlet fever and the premises were quarantined.

Congress never approved the First Lady's plans for adding

to the White House but gave her a sum with which to do the old place over and to have electric lights added. In removing walls and floors, at times six layers of them, to stop dampness in the basement she found old cupboards and shelves with remnants of china and crystal from former administrations.

She became so fascinated with the former that she began the White House china collection, which finally was completed by Mamie Eisenhower.

She also continued her china painting, took French, started orchids growing in the greenhouses and kept up her water-color paintings of flowers, some of which are in the White House today.

Also, she became the first president general of a new group called the Daughters of the American Revolution and through her love of orchids made them "the" flowers still most seen at DAR conventions.

The Harrisons were so timid about their new electric lights that Ike Hoover turned them on at dusk and found most of them still going when he came to work next morning. They also were afraid to push the electric bells which called the servants. Hoover said of the administration:

> The one term of President Harrison was most simple and homelike all the way through. . . . The family group was always large. More often than not, both a son and a daughter would have their families in the White House. Then there were nieces and nephews, even their husbands and wives, staying great lengths of time . . . doubling up in the sleeping quarters was the rule. . . . The President was, judging from everyday observation, a very indifferent and distant person. . . . Very seldom did he work after lunch.

Politically, the administration was marked by strong rivalry between the President and Secretary of State James G. Blaine, an elder statesman who wanted to be President. Secretary

Blaine blamed the Harrison son for editorials in *Leslie's Weekly* and *Judge,* both magazines partly owned by the son. It became evident early that Harrison might not be reelected —and before the administration ended, the Harrison clan was glad of it.

The First Lady died of cancer in October of 1892 after a brief illness, the second wife of a President to die in the White House. Her father had died there earlier and also her sister.

The President lost the election to Cleveland, and the old mansion was a sad scene for the final Christmas there. The New Year's Day reception was canceled, but on January 23 Mrs. McKee resumed the entertaining schedule and finished out the social season. It was always said that the Harrisons were more happy to leave Washington than the Clevelands were to get back.

The ex-President three years later married Mary Dimmick, the widowed niece, causing a rift between himself and his children.

He and his new wife had a daughter, whom they named Elizabeth. She was born in 1897, a year after Russell had fathered a son named William Henry. The new baby girl thus was younger than her father's four grandchildren.

When Harrison died he left most of his estate to the second wife and in his will, drawn two years before his death, he expressed hopes of fathering another son. "If a boy shall be born to me he shall bear my name, and my sword and sash shall be given to him instead of to my son Russell," he wrote.

Russell served in the Spanish-American War and reestablished himself in Indiana as an attorney. He was in Indiana's Senate at the time his son William Henry was elected to the Indiana House of Representatives. The latter afterward moved to Wyoming and came to Washington from there in 1945 as a member of the U. S. House of Representatives where he served intermittently until 1964.

Marthena, who caused the quarantine, married Harry Williams, a Washington real estate man, and continues to live in the capital city.

At age seventy-three she drives her own car, plays a fast game of bridge and describes herself as "indestructible." "I am always on the go," she says, "although that siege of scarlet fever in the White House left after effects and I was considered a weakly child."

Baby McKee studied law but never was a practicing attorney. During World War I he organized an ambulance corps and took it to England, where he married an English girl. He then went with the Corn Exchange Bank in New York and for several years made his home in Greenwich, Connecticut. He died in France while living on the Riviera.

Teddy Roosevelt's Children

"MADDEST SCRAMBLE IN WHITE HOUSE HISTORY"

➤➤➤➤➤➤❮❮❮❮❮❮

WHEN President William McKinley died in Buffalo on September 14, 1901, from gun wounds received while shaking hands at the Pan-American Exposition, Vice-President Theodore Roosevelt was on a mountain camping trip with his wife and five children. He rushed from the hills in his roughing-it clothes but his wife, the lovely Edith, saw by the papers that he somehow managed to have on more suitable attire when he was sworn in as the new President.

Edith hurried the children and their camping gear to their home, Sagamore Hill, in Oyster Bay, New York. Then, taking the oldest one, Theodore (Ted) Jr., fourteen, with her, she set out for Washington, stopping only long enough to buy a black dress for herself and a mourning band for Ted as they went through New York City.

Her stepdaughter, Alice, a truly beautiful and precocious seventeen years of age, was attending a house party with friends of her own age, and was so interested in being newly grown-up she failed to take in the situation and rather resented it when one of the friends talked about the change it would mean for her family.

"I was not merely an egotist," she wrote of herself in

Crowded Hours, "I was a solopist. . . . I neither telegraphed nor wrote to either Father or Mother which I think hurt their feelings."

During the McKinley years there had been no children in the White House, although pictures of their two little daughters, Katie and Ida—dead many years—hung on the bedroom wall and Mrs. McKinley often spoke of them with tears in her eyes. Ida had lived only a few months but Katie was a sturdy four-year-old when she died after a brief illness. Mrs. McKinley, a victim of epilepsy, was in a way the "child" of the administration and tenderly cared for by her husband. Her nieces visited from Ohio and she loved it when mothers brought their children to see her.

Edith Roosevelt thought the White House dark and gloomy indeed during the McKinley funeral, wondered what effect living in it would have on her happy brood of boisterous children. Most of all she worried about her outgoing husband. Could he endure the confinement? He was so young! Only forty-two: our youngest President ever.

He departed with the funeral train for Ohio and she thought of the only thing which might lift her spirits, and that was to have more of the children around her. SEND DOWN AS MANY OF THE CHILDREN AS POSSIBLE, she wired home. Then she quickly canceled that with a decision to go move them all down herself—all except the adolescent Alice, who was still visiting friends.

And what a movement it was. Special railroad cars were needed for the family pets, horses, and sports equipment. Each child was permitted to bring in his hands and pockets all the toys and pets he could handle without disrupting the caravan.

Edith was great on the logistics of moving her household and probably was glad her husband was not along. She claimed he could not get the children anywhere without having a volatile influence on them and losing a child or so. "Now don't tell Theo," she often said when some project which needed a steadying influence was brought up. "I'd only have another child on my hands."

In addition to Ted and Alice, the other children were: Kermit, almost thirteen, Ethel, ten, Archibald, seven, and Quentin, who lisped and would not be four until November.

When Ted was born, Alice had claimed him as her very own and they had been devoted companions, and had their own "gypsy" language.

Kermit and Ethel were inseparables for many years, Ethel being by far the greatest tomboy who ever lived in the White House and well able to hold her own in the "manly" sports which her father fostered.

Archie and Quentin were individuals, each a fireball on his own.

Moving to the White House along with this galaxy of personalities were bicycles, stilts, tricycles, tennis rackets, tents, boxing gloves, wading boots, books unending, dogs, cats, parrots, horses, ponies, lizards, frogs, snakes, colonies of white mice and guinea pigs. Ike Hoover, the head usher, said their oncoming "set off the wildest scramble in White House history," that rooms which had not heard a human voice in years began to ring with excited laughter, that not only the rooftop but the flagpole on it was well explored the first day.

The downstairs hall was perfect for stilts. The kangaroo rat found the White House breakfast table much to its liking, especially when the President fed it sugar. Algonquin, the calico pony, could be fitted into the elevator and run up to see a child with measles. Ethel and Kermit saw right off what fun it could be to follow the lamplighter around Lafayette Square, shinnying up the poles and putting lights out once he turned the corner. If the 18 acres of White House lawn became confining, these two always had their bicycles on which to explore the city.

The old family stairs, which then came steeply down to the State Dining Room door, were ideal for tobogganing, if one could borrow a large cookie tin from the kitchens. "It was quite dangerous, you know, sailing down the stairs that way," recently said a stately Washington dowager, Mrs. Robert Low Bacon, who once joined the fun.

The First Lady need not have worried. The White House was not the least bit confining to her husband and children, and the nation loved it when they let loose with all the fierce energy at their command. They made the country feel young again.

In Washington the President led his children and often their friends, too, on "scrambles" up and down the hills along Rock Creek. He took them out on the Potomac River to an island (now Theodore Roosevelt Island) on picnics and nature treks, and he liked nothing better than 3-hour horseback rides with them and their mother. Mother was as good at sports as any of them. Her children admired her abilities so much that Baby Quentin said once in admiration, "I'll bet Mother was a boy when she was little."

The President's first wife was pretty Alice Hathaway Lee of Boston, with whom he fell in love when he was attending Harvard. She died when her daughter, Alice, was born and Alice lived with his sister until he remarried almost three years later. Alice never liked it when anybody spoke of Edith as her stepmother. Of Edith she said: "She was the only mother I ever knew or ever wanted."

Alice, however, spent six weeks of the year, three in spring and three in autumn, with her Lee grandparents, aunts and uncle in Boston—and was adored by them all. As she grew up she often was a trial to her parents. Smart beyond her years and self-centered, no amount of persuasion could change her mind.

When she came to the White House she sensed the emoluments that could go with her father's office. She was the first girl her age to live there since Nellie Grant and she quickly became the national sensation.

She was great on visiting and house partying and there was a long period during which she was not at the White House for more than a week at a time. She bought herself a cool green snake named Emily Spinach and took it with her, to the distress of hostesses. She learned to smoke and later she and friends were noted for speeding in automobiles.

A friend asked the President why he did not make Alice behave. The reply was that he could be President or the full-time supervisor of Alice, that nobody could be both.

Her parents gave her a debut party in the East Parlor of the White House on New Year's Eve, 1902, with about 1,000 guests present from Boston, New York, Washington and sundry other cities. Everybody else thought it magnificent, but Alice thought it childish because her parents did not serve champagne.

She was called "Princess Alice," and was the rage. She christened ships, went to the Mardi Gras, made a trip to Cuba. She went to Chicago for a horseshow: her appearance there leading to a cartoon showing all the crowd, and even the horses, more interested in Alice than in the race.

Alice had refused to go to boarding school, promising to do something so terrible that she would get in jail if her parents made her. Not doubting her, the parents gave up and let her go her merry way. Her three older brothers one by one went off from the White House to school at Groton, and little Quentin, when old enough, went to a public school.

Ethel attended a Washington boarding school so as to be near her mother and, forsaking her tomboy ways, grew up most sedately. When the First Lady was away during their early White House years the President became Vice-Mother, as he called it, doing the bedtime reading and keeping track of the children. As Edith grew older she became Vice-Mother. During the summers at Sagamore Hill she taught a Sunday school class.

When the children were away at school or visiting, the President wrote them many letters filled with affection and advice, but not orders. Ted wanted to enter either West Point or Annapolis. His father urged him to consider all sides of the question. He did not recommend the choice, but would not stand in its way. He wished Ted and Kermit to enjoy school sports but urged them not to sacrifice grades to them.

This family really obtained the "new" enlarged White House for which other First Families had waited. A wing for offices was extended on the west side and a new entrance for tourists on the east. The State Dining Room was enlarged to its present size; the columns and rafters which General Grant had added to the East Parlor were removed in a return to original simplicity.

The additions were hastened when a German prince came to go horseback riding with the President and no place could be found in which he could change into riding togs. He was asked to return to the German Embassy and come back changed.

On St. Patrick's Day in 1905 President Teddy went to New York to give his orphaned niece Eleanor Roosevelt in marriage to her cousin, Franklin D. Roosevelt. Between the Irish parades and the fame of her uncle, the twenty-year-old bride received scant attention.

In June of that same year Alice went with Secretary of War Taft and a huge Congressional party, including Representative Nicholas Longworth of Ohio—whom she would marry—on a trip to the Orient. It was on this trip that she jumped into the ship's swimming pool with her clothes on and made worldwide headlines.

One headline with subheads about the trip read in part:

ALICE IN WONDERLAND How First Maiden of Land Will
Travel to the Orient—To cross Pacific in floating palace
—Will have her own suite of rooms aboard—Her father
will pay her expenses—What she will see in the wonder-
lands across the Pacific—Reception in Japan—Will she
make speech to Empress as Mrs. Grant had to? . . . Representative Longworth to go along—Tropical romance
anticipated.

She came home loaded with gifts, and newspaper editors
badgered their Washington correspondents to know: "Is Alice
engaged?" The head of the Chicago *Tribune* office in Washington wired back one day: SHE WENT OUT DRIVING WITH NICK
LONGWORTH THIS AFTERNOON WITHOUT A CHAPERONE. IF THEY
ARE NOT ENGAGED, THEY OUGHT TO BE. The paper announced
the engagement next morning, and the parents followed suit
that afternoon.

The wedding on February 17, 1906, was in the East Parlor
at high noon and eclipsed Nellie Grant's in elegance and cov-
erage. The Washington *Post* next morning had on its front
page not a word about anything else. Its three-line streamer
read:

ON A SUN-KISSED DAY IN BLOOM, THE EYES
OF THE WORLD BEHOLDING, ALICE ROOSE-
VELT, THE PRESIDENT'S FAIR DAUGHTER, BE-
COMES MRS. NICHOLAS LONGWORTH.

Even the weather smiled on Alice.

Alice-like, she had no attendants, shared the spotlight only
with her father and the bridegroom: an urbane and charming
man of distinguished lineage who would become Speaker of
the House of Representatives.

Alice enjoyed her wedding and received lavish gifts. She
enjoyed most a necklace of 62 matched pearls sent by the government of Cuba and eight rolls of never-tarnish gold-

threaded brocade by the Empress of China, who also sent a white fox coat, an ermine coat, two rings, some white jade and a pair of earrings.

One guest at the wedding, incidentally, was Nellie Grant Sartoris, the White House bride of 32 years earlier.

Quentin was eight years of age at the time of his sister's wedding, and having trouble at school. His teacher wrote the President suggesting the lad needed some Presidential disciplining. She received an interesting reply which in part read:

> DEAR MISS ARNOLD:
> I thank you for your note about Quentin. Don't you think it would be well to subject him to stricter discipline—that is, to punish him yourself, or send him to Mr. Murch for punishment that you are not able to give? Mrs. Roosevelt and I have no scruples against corporal punishment. We will stand behind you entirely in doing whatever you decide is necessary.
> I do not think I ought to be called in merely for such offences as dancing when coming into the classroom, for singing higher than the other boys, or for failure to work as he should at his examples, or for drawing pictures instead of doing his sums. . . .
> If you find him defying your authority or committing any serious misdeed, then let me know and I will whip him; but it hardly seems wise to me to start in whipping him for everyday offenses which in point of seriousness look as if they could be met by discipline in school and not by extreme measures taken at home.

When Archie went to Groton the President kept him informed of Quentin's doings. He was proud that Quentin was on his school baseball team. "I like to see Quentin practising baseball. It gives me hopes one of my boys will not take after his father in this respect, and will prove able to play the national game." Charlie Taft, whose father would be President

next, was on the same team as Quentin. He and three or four
other boys often spent the night with Quentin.

They were at the spitball age and one night tried the art on
some White House portraits, including that of Andrew Jackson. The President pulled Quentin out of bed to undo the
work and next morning lectured all the boys on their boorish
manners.

All the while Ethel was the delight of the household. Major
Archie Butt, military aide, wrote his mother about her:

> She looks very grown up since she put on her young lady
> clothes and when she went out this afternoon I thought she
> looked lovely. [She was 16 years of age.] I never thought her
> pretty before. She was always dainty and sweet looking, but
> she will develop into a splendid looking woman. She has
> a tremendous amount of dignity which she gets from her
> mother, and yet there is nothing snippy about her.

The parents wished to give Ethel a debut party before they
left the White House and the party was on December 28, 1908,
although she would not be seventeen until next August. Major
Butt determined to make it the best party ever. He kept the
main floor rooms cleared for dancing, had two orchestras so
that the music would never stop, and had the food served at
small tables in what he called "the crypt": the ground floor
rooms under the Green, Blue and Red Parlors and along the
wide hall outside them.

"We served 400 guests at tables with a course supper in less
than an hour," the major wrote his mother. "It was the first
time that I had ever seen that many people entertained at the
White House and yet have plenty of room. The old place
never seemed so beautiful. . . . Miss Ethel looked lovely in
white. Mrs. Roosevelt wore a beautiful gown of blue brocade,
which matched admirably the Blue Room in which they received."

For their last Christmas "family" dinner in the White House all the Roosevelt children were there, including the son-in-law and enough friends of all of them to make the number sixty.

President Teddy, although he enjoyed being President and ventured to say that his family was the happiest which ever lived in the White House, did not want a third term. He was eager to take Kermit with him and go hunting in Africa.

He wrote "Blessed Ethel" how he worried because Kermit seemed too reckless, killing leopards right and left with never a thought for safety. Kermit, who kept a book of Kipling's poems in his pocket, also thought his father a "little soft," the father wrote Ethel.

None of his children let him down, yet Ted's wife, the former Eleanor Butler Alexander, in 1959 wrote a book, *Day Before Yesterday,* in which she expressed the thought that her husband would have been better off had his father never been President. "All his life," she said, "Ted was overshadowed by the fame of his father, the President. There was no escape from it. No matter what Ted did somebody said he was imitating his father."

When World War I came all four sons were in training camp at the same time. Quentin, twenty, engaged but not yet married, lost his life in aerial combat over France.

Ted, who served with conspicuous bravery, was gassed. He, like his remaining two brothers, was back in uniform during World War II and participated in the Normandy invasion. He died in Normandy in 1944.

Archie came out of World War I seriously wounded, with a paralyzed arm, but this did not prevent his going into World War II and serving in the Pacific. He came out of both wars with disabilities each time rated "100 percent."

Kermit, the great game hunter who lost only a thumb in

World War I, died in the Aleutian Islands during World War II.

Ethel and her husband, Dr. Richard Derby, went to the front with the American Ambulance Corps during World War I and Ted's wife went, too, the first woman sent to the front by the YMCA. As Quentin said, "Well, as you know, it's rather up to us to practice what Father preaches."

Mrs. Longworth was still the grand dame of Washington in 1967 and still her unorthodox self. She turned night into day, played a stiff game of poker and read far into the morning, would not accept telephone calls before 1:30 P.M. Any party was more sparkling if she was there.

Her only child, Paulina, born when she was in her forties, married Alexander McCormick Strum, a writer, who died at age twenty-eight after a lingering illness. Paulina committed suicide a few years later, leaving her daughter, Joanna, to the care of her mother.

Taft's Two Sons and Daughter
HE ACCEPTED THE PRESIDENCY FOR THEM

WILLIAM Howard Taft was our most jovial President and our largest one. He had a chuckle which endeared all 300 pounds of him—up to 340 pounds when he was under pressure—to everybody around him. Despite his weight he was light on his feet and had a reputation as an excellent dancer.

When Teddy Roosevelt became President the two already were dear friends. With Elihu Root, Secretary of War and later Secretary of State under Roosevelt, they called themselves the Three Musketeers. Roosevelt was D'Artagnan, of course. Root was Athos and Taft was Porthos. They often wrote notes to each other using these names.

Taft was a born lawyer whose dream in life was to be Chief Justice of the United States, but he was so good natured that he always was being sidetracked into political jobs.

President McKinley talked him into heading a commission to form a civil government in the Philippines and become the first Governor General of the islands. Roosevelt, shortly after he became President, offered to name him to the Supreme Court, but he declined because his work in the Philippines was then at a crucial stage.

His wife, Helen (Nellie to him), never minded his political

assignments because her dream for him was and always had been the Presidency.

When the Tafts set sail for the Philippines in 1900 the ages of their three children were: Robert A., eleven, Helen, nine, and Charles P., not yet three.

Robert was a serious-minded lad and something of a mathematical genius. In his seventh year he kept a log for the fire department located across the street from the Taft home in Cincinnati, added up the number of miles each engine went, number and location of the fires—and presented the department with an annual report. He taught himself to play chess and was adept at all card games.

Helen was quiet and studious, and her joy in life was reading. She had a weak back which called for corrective exercises but prevented strenuous games. Mrs. Taft, who loved parties, thought Helen too shy socially but her husband said, "Don't worry about Helen. She'll be all right because she has a head on her shoulders."

Charlie, a beautiful child who grew into the best-looking member of the family, was as mischievous and given to fun as the other two were silent and retiring.

Taft was a sentimental family man, deeply in love with his wife and children. Anything Nellie wanted carried enormous weight with him.

Nellie loved to travel. She took her children all over the Orient and by the time Charles was eight he had rounded the globe twice. When Robert was fourteen he crossed the Pacific alone to enter Taft School, founded by his Uncle Horace Taft in Connecticut.

He donned long pants for this trip and his father wrote Uncle Horace that he had no bad habits except that he at times breathed through his mouth and was averse to cleaning his fingernails. He also explained his son's bent for mathematics, and said he already had studied algebra and geometry.

He also wrote his hopes that Robert could finish Taft School in three years and enter Yale in time to graduate in 1910, "which I prophesied on the day of his birth."

Roosevelt called Taft home to be his Secretary of War— and to have him near him. Helen entered the National Cathedral School for Girls in Washington and Charlie went to public school in the same class with Quentin Roosevelt. He became an ardent member of Quentin's White House "gang" and was as outgoing as any Roosevelt.

Secretary of War Taft was always on the go for Roosevelt. He electioneered for him in 1904 and wished to do so again in 1908, believing that he should run for another term on his own. Teddy decided that 7 years and 171 days in office would be enough at the time, however.

Roosevelt told Taft at a dinner party one night that he saw a gift in his future. He could be Chief Justice or he could be President. "Make it Chief Justice," Taft said. "Make it the Presidency," Nellie said.

Taft later said that he made the decision on the basis of what being President would mean to his children and their children. He thought they would benefit more if he became President. He never liked being President, however, and early faced grueling problems. He counted on Nellie to help pull him through, always admitting that she was the politician in the family.

Immediately after Taft's nomination Roosevelt invited him and Mrs. Taft to have dinner and spend the night before his inaugural at the White House. In the following months he may have regretted the invitation, because even before the inauguration the well-known friendship between the two had begun to unravel, and Mrs. Taft felt that Mrs. Roosevelt would have preferred not to have company her last night in the old mansion.

The President and President-elect tried to keep the conversation spirited at the dinner party, but were not wholly successful. Taft went off to a smoker the Yale Club was giving for him and Mrs. Taft went to her room—but not to sleep. The worst sleet storm in years hit the Eastern Seaboard that night. Trains could not get through. Telegraph and telephone lines were broken.

Mrs. Taft breathed a sigh of relief when she saw her three children in the gallery for their father's inaugural in the House of Representatives next morning. Charlie had brought along *Treasure Island* to read if Pop's speech bored him. The new President always considered it a great compliment that his youngest son did not use the book.

Helen and Robert, the latter home from Yale, watched and listened carefully, and Helen later said that she believed it was at that time Robert decided he would like to be President some day.

Quentin Roosevelt skipped school in Alexandria to be with Charlie during the slippery parade. Inside the White House, luncheon guests and tea guests overlapped and when the last one left, the huge new President said, "Let's go upstairs, my dears, and sit down." Charlie ran the elevator for them. Also, through his friendship with Quentin, he knew how to operate the White House switchboard and at times was permitted to do so.

Mrs. Taft, who had so much looked forward to being First Lady, collapsed before she had been in the White House three months. She was accompanying a large party to Mount Vernon on the Presidential yacht *Mayflower*, having seen Charlie through a tonsillectomy at the hospital that morning, when she suffered a paralytic stroke, the severity of which was kept secret for several weeks. She had to learn to talk again.

She had plunged into her new job with whirlwind energy, given six large dinners in a row, held two enormous tea parties, put the doormen into uniforms, hired a housekeeper to replace the traditional steward, changed outside lighting so as to have more lawn parties, and launched the drive which would bring the Japanese cherry trees to Washington.

Helen, who had enrolled at Bryn Mawr College, came home to hostess for her ill mother, and Mrs. Taft's sisters came in relays from Cincinnati to help—and the cherry trees did get planted, although not without difficulties.

In the Orient Mrs. Taft had fallen in love with Japanese cherry blossoms and with Manila's luneta: a promenade where citizens rich and poor mingled at dusk to the strains of lovely music. She wanted a luneta rimmed with cherry trees along the Potomac River, a band playing at either end.

The Japanese government sent her 3,000 trees, but the Department of Agriculture was afraid they would spread germs among native trees—so 3,000 more were grown for her in sterile soil. It would be difficult to imagine the capital city today without its cherry trees, and the luneta idea flourished briefly, President Taft at times riding a horse down or going in the carriage with Mrs. Taft to join in the mingling.

Americans, however, were discovering the automobile. Taft was the first President to have a fleet of automobiles (four) at his disposal . . . and also the last one to keep a cow (Pauline Wayne) on the south lawn. Times were moving on and the luneta could not compete with the car.

Helen, who became a White House hostess before she had a debut, was given a coming-out tea attended by 1,208 guests in December, 1910, when she was nineteen. This was followed by an exclusive ball for 200 on New Year's Eve and Ethel Roosevelt attended, to the joy of Major Butt who still was military aide at the White House and who grieved that the Tafts and Roosevelts were no longer close friends.

Taft did not win a second term because former President Teddy formed his own Bull Moose party and split the Republican votes. A Democrat named Woodrow Wilson was elected.

Taft then went to teach at Yale and in 1921, President Harding named him Chief Justice, a job he held happily for almost 9 years or until his death.

Daughter Helen, the delight of her father, took a master's degree at Yale and became dean of Bryn Mawr. She married Dr. Frederick J. Manning, was—and still is—a much respected educator.

Both Robert and Charles became lawyers and practiced together in Cincinnati. Charles was more outgoing and liberal in his outlook than his brother was.

Elected Mayor of Cincinnati, Charles was active in community affairs. He became president of the Federal Council of the Churches of Christ in America. He taught Sunday school, settled strikes, organized campaigns for the Community Chest, built low-cost housing.

Ex-President Taft described the difference between his sons as being "ideally good"—Charles, and "practically good" —Robert.

During World War II, Charles accepted several wartime jobs in Washington. In one of these he worked to get Congressional renewal of the Reciprocal Trade Agreements Act. His brother Robert, then in the Senate, was strictly opposed but absented himself from the hearing when Charles was testifying.

"I'm still the little brother," Charles said. "He doesn't pay any attention to me." "The trouble with Charlie," Robert said, "is that he takes the opinions of any group of people with whom he is thrown." Yet the two managed to avoid political haggling and remained good friends.

Robert's career was the more remarkable, and it seemed for many years that he might become President. He became known as "Mr. Republican," but the Republicans never let him win their nomination for the Presidency.

He was elected to the U. S. Senate in 1938 and remained

there until his death in 1953, the ominous foe of all things New Deal and Democratic—or almost all. He was for low-cost public housing and government help for education.

He married Martha Bowers, who was politically astute and a remarkable campaigner. BOB AND MARTHA TAFT ELECTED TO THE SENATE, an Ohio paper headlined after the first such election. Some people compared Martha Taft's political sophistication with that of Eleanor Roosevelt—a comparison her husband did not favor.

Senator Robert Taft had the respect of all his Senatorial colleagues. In a poll they chose him as the most outstanding man ever to serve in the Senate and at his death erected a marble monument topped by a bell tower to his memory on Capitol Hill.

Helen and Charles are still active, and also there are plenty of Tafts around who give promise of holding public offices for years to come. One of them is U. S. Representative Robert A. Taft, Jr., now serving his second term in Congress from Ohio.

Wilson's Daughters

A TRIO DEVOTED COMPLETELY TO HIM

"IT was fun to wake up in the White House, to jump out of bed, bathe in the gorgeous big tub, and laugh with Jessie because we didn't know where the family dining room was," wrote twenty-three-year-old Eleanor Wilson, the new President's youngest daughter, in her book, *The Woodrow Wilsons.*

This was on March 6, 1913, the morning after Wilson's inauguration. March 4 fell on Sunday that year and he was not sworn into office until Monday, the 5th. He had canceled the inaugural ball as not at all suited to the dignity of the occasion and both things probably were all to the good, despite the fact that daughter Eleanor already had purchased a dazzling blue satin ball gown and was eager to use it. The delay gave the Wilsons a chance to get a little rest.

The campaign had been hard on all of them and particularly on the wife and three daughters, none of whom had enjoyed his previous political job as Governor of New Jersey. The daughters were campus born and bred and the wife was at once an exceedingly shy and brave person.

Wilson was our first President from a university campus— a popular professor of government at Princeton. He was lifted into the national political spotlight by the admiration of his students and all who heard him speak.

He might not have been elected except for the split in the Republican party, with Teddy Roosevelt forming his own Bull Moose party to run against his old friend Taft.

Wilson was a reformer in a new sense of the word. He was such an idealist that he had hoped to do away with fraternities at Princeton and, for his efforts, was accused of trying to "ruin the best country club in America." All his life he had studied history and political science. He believed that the things taught in schools could be carried over into actual government and was a veritable Don Quixote, willing to tilt with hundreds of windmills to prove his theories true.

He and his family entered Washington a few days before his inaugural rather the worse for wear. They were elated but too tired at the moment to savor the full joys of victory. He had borrowed $5,000 for the move.

They stopped at the old Shoreman Hotel and the Tafts invited the President-elect and his wife to tea. Taft already had written Wilson a warm letter and told him ways by which he could save a little money out of his salary, which by then was $75,000—an unheard-of sum for Professor Wilson.

Daughter Eleanor helped her mother dress for the tea but after her parents left for it she crawled under her bed, face down on the carpet to deaden the sound, and cried her heart out, sobbing all the while, "It will kill them. It will kill them both." In a way Eleanor's sobs were prophetic. The Wilsons had less than two completely happy years in the White House, despite his tenure of two full terms, eight eventful years.

But in the few days after their arrival and the breakfast on March 6, the mood of the Wilson women was joyful. Mother knew she was going to love the White House the minute she saw all the garden space. On the afternoon of the inaugural she called her daughters to an upstairs window to say, "Look, children. Isn't it beautiful?"

Eleanor's sisters were Jessie, who was twenty-five, and Margaret, twenty-six. They adored each other and yet each was completely different. Margaret and Jessie had graduated from Goucher College in Baltimore and Jessie had a Phi Beta Kappa key.

Since a little girl, Jessie had wanted only to be a missionary, and the Wilsons never interfered with their daughters' deepest wishes. Both the father's and mother's fathers for several generations back were Presbyterian ministers and the Presbyterians believed in foreign missions. But there was "unholy glee" in the Wilson household when the Missions Board decided that Jessie was too frail for a foreign assignment. She consoled herself by doing settlement work in Philadelphia and coming home each weekend.

Margaret had a lovely mezzo-soprano voice and wanted to give concerts. She commuted to music classes in New York and was the most independent of the girls.

Eleanor did not want a college education. She wanted only to be an artist and to attend the Art Students' League in New York, just as her mother had. Mother by then, however, thought the Pennsylvania Academy a much better place for Eleanor and Eleanor commuted there daily from Princeton.

Eleanor received her first political shock when Father was nominated for the Presidency and her commuting friends began to avoid her lest they be accused of currying her favor. She found such behavior hard to understand; it was uncharacteristic of a friend, but it was a fact of life to which she and other Presidential daughters have had to become accustomed.

Her feeling was that some friends shunned her because she was the President's daughter and others, not so near to begin with, began to cultivate her for the same reason.

The sad fact perhaps is that *no one* is capable of treating the members of a President's family as mere human beings.

The Wilson girls were the most watched-after children on the Princeton campus, but they did not grow up disassociated from campus activities. They cried when Princeton lost football and baseball games; and they never lacked for escorts when they went to parties.

Eleanor thought her escorts became tongue-tied in the presence of Father and complained to them. "It's not that I'm afraid of your father," one said, "but that I respect him so much I do not wish him to know what a moron I am."

Wilson was the first President to hold regular press conferences, but he did not share with the press the big secret that both Jessie and Eleanor were engaged to be married. The press kept getting it wrong and insisting that Margaret was engaged—to so many men, some of whom she never had heard —that he threatened to deal with the press man to man rather than as President if its members continued to run such stories.

Jessie was engaged to Francis B. Sayre, who stayed away from the inaugural festivities lest someone suspect the alliance, and who looked so much like a relative that he passed for a cousin when he did visit from New York, where he was an assistant to the district attorney. He and Jessie courted undiscovered while walking along the old Chesapeake and Ohio Canal and canoeing on the Potomac.

Eleanor had become engaged on a trip to Mexico to a Western lad unknown to her parents. They sent Mrs. Wilson's brother, Stockton Axson, to investigate him and he was accepted as suitable.

In the White House, however, Eleanor found herself in a quandary. She fell in love with her father's Secretary of the Treasury, William Gibbs McAdoo, a much older man—a widower with grown children. He was a Californian and a noted builder, and was so rich and sophisticated and sought after that, it was said, almost every widow in Washington had her cap set for him.

Not one of the Wilson daughters was photogenic and they loathed the sight of themselves in the newspapers. Margaret was the tiniest but photographed the largest because her largish face was almost the duplicate of her father's, and she wore glasses. Eleanor said that in their news pictures they all looked "like middle-aged ladies." They were publicized as highbrows, which was not true, despite their upbringing. A White House aide assigned to escort Eleanor was astonished to learn that she could dance. "Oh, do you dance?" he asked her.

Well, naturally she did, because all the Wilson girls had attended proms at Princeton from the age of fifteen and their father had delighted the politicians of New Jersey by demonstrating his cakewalk for them.

Eleanor and her father were inveterate theatergoers. At times at summer performances when other family members had chosen not to go he said to her, "Nell, why don't you and I run away and go on the stage?"

Belle Hagner, the White House social secretary, decreed that the daughters should go to separate parties. Why waste three girls on just one affair? Eleanor was shy about this until she learned to make the grand entrance as an actress would. She enjoyed the parties and dances. She also learned to slip away from her mother's receptions, take the younger people upstairs for dancing to the Victrola. She taught McAdoo to one-step and fox-trot.

Jessie did YWCA work in Washington and Margaret continued her music with regular lessons in New York. The First Lady worried because Eleanor seemed only pleasure bent, so for a while her youngest attempted day nursery work. She was not the missionary type, though, as Mother soon admitted.

The First Lady saved enough out of her White House accounts to fix a studio for herself on the third floor. She also developed a series of gardens—one of them with a telephone so that her husband could enjoy fresh air and still be in constant touch with his office—and she interested herself in housing conditions among Washington's poor.

In June of their first year the President and Mrs. Wilson announced Jessie's engagement to Francis Sayre. They were married in the East Room on November 25. Next day the Washington *Post* carried a three-line streamer:

NATIONS OF ALL THE WORLD DO HOMAGE TO WHITE HOUSE BRIDE AS SHE TAKES SOL-EMN VOWS AMID SCENE OF UNEQUALLED SPLENDOR.

Margaret was maid of honor and Eleanor one of four brides-maids, all of whom dressed in varying shades of pink. More than 700 persons attended the afternoon ceremony. Eleanor wanted the bridesmaids to wear "Tiaras" of rose velvet trimmed in silver lace. When they came, made to her design, they looked rather awful. She sat up all night redoing them.

Jessie's wedding presents were magnificent but she considered some of them much too elaborate for the life she would lead as a professor's wife. The Senate sent a silver service, the House of Representatives a diamond pendant. Frank had a new job awaiting him as assistant to Dr. Harry Garfield, son of former President Garfield, who was president of Williams College.

Eleanor's wedding next May 7 was a much simpler affair, held in the Blue Room. Mrs. Wilson had injured her spine in a fall and the pomp was cut to save her health. Jessie was matron of honor and Margaret maid of honor. There were two flower girls, one of them McAdoo's youngest child, twelve-year-old Sallie.

Wilson was the only President who gave two daughters in marriage at the White House. He approved of both of his sons-in-law, although the affection between him and McAdoo was not to be permanent.

For their honeymoon the McAdoos drove to the Wilson summer place. To her husband's dismay Eleanor was in tears when they left the White House and for many miles thereafter.

She was worried about her mother, and with cause. When she returned two weeks later the First Lady was seriously ill and would not recover. She held Eleanor's hand and said, "I needed only to see your face, as I did Jessie's, to know that you are happy."

The First Lady worried about "my bill" on slum clearance for Washington, and Congress speeded it through for her. The President forbade anyone to tell her about the oncoming of World War I in Europe. She died August 7, the third First Lady to die in the old mansion.

Deep gloom settled over the White House and enveloped the President. Margaret, not remotely interested in social doings, refused to discuss an entertainment schedule, turned increasingly to her music. Belle Hagner left to get married. Helen Bones, the President's cousin who had helped the First Lady as secretary, was pale and depressed. Dr. Cary T. Grayson, the White House physician, was worried about the President and Helen.

Eleanor and "Mac" were in and out of the White House and a cheerful influence, but Eleanor's days as a Cabinet wife were filled with an unavoidable social routine.

Jessie and Francis came for Christmas and Jessie stayed on for the birth of their first child, Francis B. Sayre Jr., on January 17, 1915. He was the last child born in the White House and is now dean of the Washington Cathedral.

Before the next Christmas the President was married to a

stunning Washington widow, Edith Bolling Galt, after a summer romance which rocked the capital city. They met via Dr. Grayson, who sought to interest Mrs. Galt in taking Helen Bones on some of her walking and motor trips. Mrs. Galt was forty-two years of age and had lived in Washington half her life but had never been in the White House nor was she vitally concerned with the welfare of its inhabitants. She was not cooperative.

But the doctor telephoned one day and wanted to take her motoring. When he showed up he had Miss Bones and the President's daughter, Eleanor McAdoo, with him. The women got along well, just as he expected, and the walks which he hoped would improve Miss Bones' health began. They stopped by the White House for tea one afternoon in the spring just as the President and the doctor were coming in from golf, and the romance was on.

Mrs. Galt was a Virginian, like the President, had innumerable relatives, like him, and—in addition to being beautiful—was gay and witty. The family approved of Mrs. Galt, but son-in-law McAdoo was among the Presidential advisers who did not think the marriage should take place until after the 1916 elections.

They ignored the advice and were married at her small home on Twentieth Street on December 18, with the Wilson daughters and sons-in-law present, and went on a Christmas honeymoon.

Public reaction was good. One editorial said that no man ever should be alone in the White House. World War I was raging in Europe and the President's duties were arduous. His second wife assumed many burdens of assistance and did much to make the White House a more cheerful abode. Edith Benham Helm, who became social secretary, wrote in *The Captains and the Kings* that she became the "best wife in the world" to a man who needed loving and constant attention more than most men ever do.

Francis Sayre, the son-in-law, wrote in *Glad Adventure,* "All of us were supremely happy that his days of grief and utter loneliness were over. Without her, I often wonder whether he could have faced the loneliness and carried on his work."

In the 1916 elections it appeared certain that Wilson had lost the Presidency to Charles Evans Hughes. Margaret's friends telephoned to sympathize, but she sat up for the late returns and at 4 A.M. knew he had won.

The second Wilson term was filled with Red Cross work, heatless and meatless days, American troops singing "Over There" as they embarked for the trenches of Europe. Margaret gave concerts for the Red Cross, making more than $10,-000 for it on her first one.

She was eager to go sing for the troops overseas. Her father at first said her presence would be a burden on the French, but eventually consented.

Margaret was a great morale booster. She sang in all sorts of weather—often outside—and her program was mostly one of nostalgia with many Irish songs scattered through it. She was still in Europe when her father and Mrs. Wilson went to Paris for the Peace Conference and to visit battlefields. Mrs. Wilson took some court dresses and a fresh wardrobe to her and she accompanied them on much of their triumphal tour. When she met them at Brest she was very thin and had laryngitis, but was in great spirits.

Francis Sayre went overseas for the YMCA, leaving Jessie, Frank Jr., and the baby Eleanor in Williamstown. The Sayres had a third child in 1919 and named him Woodrow Wilson. All three Sayre children visited in the White House and delighted their grandfather. He attended their christenings and the Sayres often spent part of the summer with him.

The McAdoos had two children, Eleanor and Mary Faith, who also saw and charmed their grandfather frequently.

Margaret came home from the war with no singing voice left, but she did not want anything said about it. Soon afterwards she was vacationing in North Carolina and attended a dinner in Asheville for Gen. John J. Pershing. There were insistent calls for her to sing. She rose to explain that she no longer could. General Pershing lauded her war work, said people like her deserved medals just as much as soldiers did. She received a standing ovation.

The President's peace program ran into unyielding opposition in Congress. He took his plea for the League of Nations and ratification of the Peace Treaty as it had evolved in the European conferences to the people in a cross-country speaking tour.

He made headway, but was not to finish the crusade. One night he was stricken by partial paralysis as his train sped from Denver to Wichita. Other speeches were canceled and his train headed back to Washington while a stunned country read of their President's illness.

Mrs. Wilson stood between him and the public, working around the clock to do his bidding. She was widely criticized for it, but never apologized. Although the President's health was gone, his mind was not. Some Congressmen doubted that he was sound mentally, however, and wanted a bipartisan committee to call on him to see. A Senator who was a special foe headed it. His greeting to the invalid was, "Well, Mr. President, we've been praying for you." "Which way, Senator?" the President shot back.

When Harding became President the Wilsons moved to the house on S Street in Washington which is now open to the public under supervision of the National Historic Trust and Council. Wilson died there February 3, 1924. Margaret and Eleanor were with him but Jessie and family were in Siam, where Francis Sayre—who had been teaching at Harvard before then—was adviser to the royal family. The McAdoos were by then living in California, and he had unsuccessfully sought nomination for the Presidency.

Jessie was the first Wilson daughter to die—in 1933, when she was only forty-five. Her husband continued his public service career. President Franklin D. Roosevelt named him High Commissioner to the Philippines and he was serving there when the Japanese attacked the island at the beginning of World War II.

Margaret's last days were the most unusual of any White House daughter. She lived in New York after her father's death and became deeply interested in the religious philosophy of India. In 1938 she decided that she must go live there to be nearer Sri Aurobindo, the philosopher whose work she found so meaningful while reading it in the New York Public Library on 42nd Street.

From Pondicherry, India, in 1939 she wrote a friend:

> One cannot live with immortals and escape their influence, even if one would, so here I am in the asram of Sri Aurobindo who belongs to the unending line of Indian Immortals. His Essays on the Gita which I discovered in 1932 were for me one of those unforgettable revelations that reorient the whole thought and life of a man or woman.

In the asram, which means merely an abode or residence in which a collection of people with similar interests live, Margaret apparently led a full and contented life of study and work but the torrid climate was hard on her health. In 1942 a friend of hers wrote Francis Sayre to say, "Frank, I do not think Margaret can survive a fourth hot season on the hottest coast of India. . . . The Swami here in New York with whom she worked thinks she should by all means return. I begged her to do so a year ago, but you know Miss Wilson's 'fanatical loyalty to a cause.' "

She wrote her brother-in-law that same year:

> Yes, I was ill for a long time, but now I am well again and getting acclimated to the tropics at last. . . . There are about 200 disciples here, men and women from all parts of India and a few from Europe. I am the only American. The life here consists of work and meditation. Much of the work is manual or superintending labor, for there is much of that kind of work necessary to the running of a big asram like this.
>
> Before my illness I was active as a gardener, superintending the planting in the compound in which I live. Since my illness, the Mother is not giving me active work to do, so I spend my days quietly, studying Sri Aurobindo's works, meditating, and studying French—also running my servants. As I say, and I am telling the literal truth, I am well again, but have not gained back quite enough energy for running around in this heat. . . . You wanted me to tell you about my life here, and that is the reason I have written so at length about myself.

The above was a long handwritten letter, the first of it filled with her happiness at hearing that the Sayres had safely escaped from Corregidor in the Philippines. It was the last letter her brother-in-law received from her. He wrote her in December of 1943 and it was returned the next March with DECEASED stamped on the envelope.

On the marble stone which marks her grave in the Protestant Cemetery at Pondicherry is cut:

LA DÉPOUILLE MORTELLE
DE NISHTA
MARGARET WOODROW WILSON
16 April 1886———12 Feb. 1944

Nishta is the Moslem name given her in the asram and the fact that she is buried in the Protestant Cemetery shows she did not have to forsake her religion to experience the Indian ways which brought her peace. "Margaret was a most unusual person," Francis Sayre says, "and always felt very deeply about everything."

Eleanor's marriage to McAdoo did not end happily and they were divorced in 1934. One of her daughters committed suicide and the other one made a marriage which did not go well. Eleanor wrote two books about her parents and continues to live in California.

Wilson's three Sayre grandchildren have interesting careers. The granddaughter, who never married, is with the Boston Museum of Fine Arts and a leading expert on the works of Goya. Also, as a hobby, she made a noted collection of Christmas carols.

Woodrow, now teaching classes in history and government at Springfield College in Massachusetts, has exploring as a hobby. He turned his experiences climbing Mt. Everest into a book. Francis Jr. is a distinguished churchman who takes a lively interest in politics. His grandfather and the second Mrs. Wilson, who lived to be almost ninety, are buried in the Washington Cathedral of which he is Dean.

The Coolidge Boys
BOTH WERE BRIGHT AND GOOD-LOOKING

>>>->>>)((-(((

WHEN Vice-President Calvin Coolidge was aroused from sleep in the middle of the night to take the oath of office as President by lamplight at 2:47 A.M. on August 3, 1923—in his father's farmhouse at Plymouth, Vermont—it was typical of him that as soon as it all was made legal he would blow out the lamp and go back to bed.

Nor did it occur to him to get messages to his two teen-age sons. One was at a military training camp and the other had a job on a tobacco farm. They would hear soon enough, their father reasoned, and would know without being told that they were to stay right where they were. John, who would be seventeen the next month, was at Fort Devens, Massachusetts, while fifteen-year-old Calvin Jr. was making $3.50 a day harvesting tobacco in the same state.

Their father would repeat with pride the story of how young Calvin reacted when he heard the news. "Isn't it great, your father being President?" the lad's supervisor asked him next morning. "Yes, sir," the lad replied. "Where do you want this tobacco put?" One of Calvin's co-workers said that if *his* father were President *he* would not be bundling tobacco. "If my father were your father you would," Calvin said.

Reporters rushed to John's camp with questions, the main

one being, "How do you feel now that your father is President?" "Just as I did when he was Governor of Massachusetts," John replied.

Reason for the unusual Coolidge "inauguration" was that President Warren G. Harding, who had been in office only two years and 151 days, had died unexpectedly in San Francisco after a trip to Alaska.

The message informing the Vice-President of Harding's death arrived about midnight. "Father, are you still a notary?" Coolidge asked Col. John Coolidge. When the answer was affirmative he continued, "Then you will swear me in."

The colonel shaved and put on his best suit while Mrs. Coolidge found more lamps and put the family Bible on a center table. Only a few neighbors, a congressman and a reporter witnessed the unique ceremony.

All was so quietly done that Aurora, the family cook, knew nothing about it. She had to pass through the Coolidge bedroom to get to the kitchen that morning and noted that Calvin and Grace (President and First Lady by then) were sleeping peacefully. Grace, the most adaptable First Lady before Lady Bird Johnson, who followed her forty years later, naturally was asleep since her husband had suggested it.

The jovial Hardings, who had no children, had lived richly in the White House—but the Coolidges would live there frugally and establish a record for penny-watching, although the country itself was on a wild prosperity spree.

It was the President who pinched the pennies. The housekeeper soon learned to send him a copy of the daily menus.

Just one for the First Lady was no longer enough. He was able to cut $1,000 a month from the household budget and soon changed housekeepers so as to make it $2,000.

The first one never made him believe that even the White House needed six hams to serve sixty people. (As ex-President he wrote that one of his irritations in office was that he could not determine what happened to the leftovers.)

The Coolidges had few personal guests and often ate alone —in complete silence. They gave all the official parties, however, and during their years entertained some exciting official guests, including the young Prince of Wales, now the Duke of Windsor; Queen Marie of Roumania, who outwitted President Coolidge and brought photographers to his reception for her; and young Charles A. Lindberg after his Atlantic flight.

Charming and friendly, Mrs. Coolidge became a most popular First Lady—and her husband's idiosyncrasies made lively conversation.

In the Roaring Twenties it amused Flappers and their Boy Friends that the President wished to be in bed by 10 o'clock, but it comforted their parents. He was called "as sound as the American dollar." William Allen White, the Kansas editor, said he believed in "one God, one country, one wife, and never more than three words on any occasion." Appropriately, White called his Coolidge biography *Puritan in Babylon*.

Sons John and Calvin came to the White House when their summer assignments ended and had a chance to learn its procedures before they departed for school at Mercersburg Academy in Pennsylvania, less than 100 miles away. It had been chosen because Mrs. Coolidge could get up to see them easily and they could have some weekends at home.

Mrs. Coolidge always had been a companion to her boys and was closer to them than their father was. But they, like her, always considered Father's words only slightly below the Ten Commandments in importance and ever sought his favor.

Calvin was blondish and more mischievous than his older brother. He looked like the Coolidges and especially like the President's mother, or so Father liked to think. He had a sunny disposition and could fend for himself when his father poked verbal sarcasm at him. He appreciated Father's odd sense of humor. Also he was a nature lover and endeared himself to Father by loving the Plymouth farm. He had taught his mother to swim there, holding her chin and shouting encouragement.

John was more like his attractive brunette mother. He was musical, as she was, played the violin and loved to dance and sing, but was as silent—almost—as his father. He found Father's ways mysterious and was not wholly at ease with him. He had a mechanical bent and once had made a recognizable automobile.

The boys had a happy childhood at Northampton, Massachusetts, and over the living room mantel they daily saw this prominent quotation:

> A wise old owl sat on an oak,
> The more he saw the less he spoke;
> The less he spoke, the more he heard.
> Why can't we be like that old bird?

Father took this motto literally but he was a proud loving husband and father despite his austere exterior. He was in public office most of his life but his family never heard his jobs discussed at the dinner table. Politics was not for women and children!

As First Lady, Mrs. Coolidge never knew when nor whether she was supposed to accompany her husband to some event. "Are you going, Mrs. Coolidge?" a staff member would ask. Her reply was, "I don't know, but I'm ready."

When the family moved to Washington Mrs. Coolidge wanted the boys to take dancing lessons so they would enjoy the city more. "Did my father take dancing?" Calvin asked and, when told he had not, said, "Then I don't need to." But Father overruled him and he trudged to classes with John, who enjoyed them very much.

John and Calvin had only one Christmas together at the White House. Mrs. Coolidge had a large Vermont spruce in the Blue Room when they arrived from Mercersburg and scheduled a dance for them. They were hosts to 60 young couples. They also went to several parties and had their friends in to visit.

For the summer of 1924 John returned to Fort Devens to complete his training, but Calvin—released from a paying job—was free to enjoy the grounds of the old mansion to the fullest. He adored the tennis court where young friends or White House aides played with him or where he at times practiced alone.

He was so eager to get onto the court each day that one morning, not finding his socks nearby, he put on his sneakers without them and streaked to the net. He raised a blister on a toe, put a little iodine on it and thought nothing about it.

He had shot up like a reed during the school year, was 5 feet, 11 inches tall, frail of build and weighed only 115 pounds. Doctors said later that he had "grown beyond his strength." At any rate, he did not tell his parents of the blister until he had pains shooting up his leg and could not go out to play. The President was not uneasy until the White House physician pronounced Calvin "a very sick boy."

Knowing Calvin's fondness for animals, the President captured a rabbit on the White House grounds and took it to him. It won a smile, but blood poisoning had set in and the lad was too ill to play with it. He was taken to Walter Reed Hospital and died there July 7, his body too weak to combat the infection.

The nation expressed its sympathy for the bereaved parents. At the Democratic National Convention, then in session, reports on the sixteen-year-old's condition were read twice daily and his death was announced by Delegate Franklin D. Roosevelt.

Calvin's father was nominated for a term of his own by the Republicans, but campaigning was forgotten in the national sorrow following his death. Not since Lincoln's young son Willie died in the White House, editorial writers pointed out, had there been such a bereavement.

John arrived from camp too late to see his young brother alive. The funeral was in Northampton at the church Calvin attended in his earlier childhood and burial was at Plymouth alongside his ancestors.

The President, following his pattern of rigid attention to set duties, thought John should return immediately to camp but Mrs. Coolidge objected. She needed to be with her remaining son and was sure from the look of hurt and loneliness in his eyes that he needed to be with his family. So they lingered at Plymouth a few days and before they left dug a 5-foot spruce to plant on the White House grounds near the tennis court as a memorial to the lad who lived there so briefly.

Before the family left Plymouth the President put John against the doorjamb on the back porch and marked his height, as he had for his sons every year for a long time. At a 6-foot mark he wrote, "J.C. 1924." "How tall was Calvin?" he asked. "Just an inch shorter than I," said John, and the father wrote an inch below, "C.C. 1924, if he had lived."

The autumn after Calvin's death John entered Amherst College where his father had gone, and became a popular student who engaged in several extracurricular activities. He had to watch himself however, because his father was not enthusiastic about extracurricular "frills."

For the 1925 inaugural of his father John was permitted only one day away from classes. The newspapers reported, "John Coolidge, the President's son, arrived in Washington at 8 A.M. and left at 7 P.M. John wanted to stay on but it was felt he could not spare the time from college."

On the train coming to Washington for the inauguration, however, he met Florence Trumbull, daughter of the Governor of Connecticut and a student at Mount Holyoke College, just a short trolley ride from Amherst, and this made the brief trip very much worth while. After that his Saturday nights were well booked.

In his junior yearbook his classmates had this to say about John:

> Coolidge came to college with a second-hand pea jacket, a perfect complexion, and an air of perfect boredom. These possessions he guarded jealously and has augmented them in his three years here with a very slight knowledge of the saxophone, a slighter acquaintance with the art of pugilism, some seven thousand scented letters from admiring school girls, and a scrapbook bulging with newspaper clippings arranged alphabetically from "Elopement" to "Secret Service." John is really a darn good gent but so reserved it's hard to get acquainted with him.

"Elopement" referred to the standing Amherst joke that the only way John ever could get married was to elope from the Secret Service man assigned to him.

JOHN COOLIDGE A PEACH read a headline in *The New York Times* about this time over a short column which quoted an unidentified Mount Holyoke girl as saying, "John is a perfect peach. He is so very polished and smooth and he dances divinely. They talk about him being shy and reserved—well, he certainly is a peach."

Florence was a popular girl: tall, slender and with reddish-blond hair, a quick bright manner and a wholesome zest for life. Mrs. Coolidge liked her and always saw that John had White House orchids for her corsages. She at first was afraid of the President—but not after she sat beside him at dinner and spilled a piece of fish in her lap. "Mam-ma," called the

President across the table to his wife, "Miss Connecticut has ruined her lovely gown."

Florence, who didn't even know that the President knew who she was, thought it fun to be called "Miss Connecticut" and became very fond of her future father-in-law.

The Coolidges always ate in the State Dining Room and dressed for dinner, even when there were just two of them— and often in silence, even when John was there on holidays. The First Lady would attempt to get the conversation bubbling, but usually had to give up. John just was unable to unbend in the presence of his father.

One holiday he took a house guest to a tea dance and they arrived back just at dinnertime. John asked to be excused from dressing, there was so little time. His father said, "This is the President's House. You dress for dinner and arrive promptly." They dressed in four minutes and were in the dining room on time.

For his son's senior year at Amherst the President decided that his grades should be better and assigned Colonel Edward Starling, head of the Secret Service and in his fifties, to go to Amherst, live in John's room with him and make him study more.

Colonel Starling wrote, "John was embarrassed and so was I. He was a thoroughly decent chap, however, and had inherited his father's sense of humor. He decided to make the best of it and I made him realize that I had no intention of sticking his nose into a book and holding it there."

Every Saturday night the two took the trolley to Mount Holyoke and the colonel killed time as best he could while John courted Miss Trumbull. At Christmastime the colonel was able to shake off the assignment by persuading the President that John was doing fine and needed a younger companion.

Florence avoided all mention of an engagement and wore

her diamond ring on her right hand when she went abroad for the summer of 1929. John made the headlines that graduation year by saying he would consult his father before deciding what to do about his future. He admitted, however, that he probably would not enter Harvard Law School, as had been expected, but was interested in a business connection.

He took a job in the statistical division of the New York, New Haven and Hartford Railroad and Governor and Mrs. Trumbull announced their daughter's engagement to him.

The marriage was in September. He was twenty-three, she was twenty-four, and the Coolidges were no longer in the White House. They could have been, doubtlessly, except that two summers before Coolidge had said—from his vacation spot in the Black Hills of South Dakota—without telling his wife or anybody else in advance, "I do not choose to run." The phrase became a classic.

John's wedding was a great social event of which "talkies" were made. When the former President, looking very pleased and dapper with a carnation in his buttonhole, discovered a microphone under his feet at the reception he demanded that it be taken away.

When reporters asked if he cared to say what he gave the young couple for a wedding gift, he replied with self-aware humor, "I do not choose to say." Part of the gift was colonial furniture for a bedroom in the couple's 4-room apartment in New Haven.

John remained with the railroad for a decade and then became president and treasurer of a small manufacturing company. Mrs. Coolidge, who lived into her seventy-eighth year in 1957, was proud of John's business career and happy home life and was especially fond of her two granddaughters, Lydia and Cynthia.

Before her death she had plans for giving the Coolidge

birthplace at Plymouth to the State of Vermont so that it could be opened to the public. In her will she asked Florence and John to complete the plans and to restore the house to what it had been during her husband's youth, and this they did.

And John also decided to reactivate his grandfather's old cheese factory to make the place an authentic replica of what a self-contained farm was like when his father was a Vermont schoolboy and this they did.

Hoover's Two Sons

WORLD TRAVELERS AT BIRTH

NEITHER son of the thirty-first President, Herbert Hoover, could qualify for the Presidency in his own right even if such an unlikely thought ever should occur to him —because both of them were born abroad: Herbert Jr. in London in 1903 and Allan Henry in the same city in 1907. England was home base for them throughout their early years but they literally grew up everywhere.

Five weeks after his birth, Herbert Jr.'s parents set out with him on a mining expedition to Australia and proved to their delight that babies make good traveling companions. By the time this baby was four he had rounded the globe three times, and soon Allan would join him as a globe-trotter.

No other White House family has lived in so many different countries—nor has another First Lady begun to speak and work in so many foreign languages as Lou Hoover did. She was versatile in four, including Chinese, and had a working knowledge of some others, including German and Latin: two she forced herself to master so she could help her husband translate Agricola's *De re Metallica,* the world's first treatise on mining.

The five years the Hoovers spent on this work, taking it and the children with them on his assignments, formed a most unusual background for the Presidency—but then no other First Family was like these reserved Quakers who avoided emotions and shunned personal references.

Only once in his memoirs did Hoover permit himself the luxury of sentiment—and he apologized for it. He included a letter to his wife telling of a pilgrimage he made to Red House, the home in London where they and the boys had been so happy. It reveals a great deal about the warm family life they had. In part it said:

> On the way my mind travelled over the thousands of times we had driven along Pall Mall, Knightsbridge and High Street to take the second turning to the left beyond the church. And the church was the same as when the boys used to attend all weddings as doorstep observers—returning to tell us if the red carpet and awning were up—that service being five shillings extra—and how many bridesmaids and how many peals of the bells there were—those being two shillings six pence each.
>
> I came to the door of the Red House, flooded with memories of the months we lived there, alternately with our New York and California homes, for nearly twenty years. How we had first come, as a couple, from stays in Australia or China or Russia or Burma or New York or the Continent: then when we had brought the babies; then when I would return from long journeys to meet you all again. . . .
>
> I imagined again sitting on the opposite side of the desk from you, with the manuscripts and reference books of Agricola piled between us as we worked over the translation of "De re Metallica." Again I saw "Pete" [Herbert Jr.] at the little table in the corner making marks and announcing that he was writing a book, too; and "Bub" [Allan] clambering into his mother's lap and demanding to know what the book said. . . .

When the boys grew to school age the nomadic life had its drawbacks, especially since the parents wished them to be educated in America. So Hoover relinquished his British-based job and began a free-lancing engineering career with his base at Stanford, California, and Mrs. Hoover began to build her dream house there.

This house was not finished when the family went to England in 1914 to give the sons, then eleven and seven, a vacation and also to promote interest in San Francisco's proposed Panama-Pacific Exposition, for which Hoover was a commissioner.

That was the summer World War I broke over Europe and more than 100,000 Americans poured into London, all eager to get the first boat home, but many of them without money or possessions enough to last them until transportation could be found.

President Wilson asked Hoover to form the American Relief Committee to assist the stranded and find ways to get them home. This job was managed with tireless engineering efficiency, and was the beginning of Hoover's renown as a humanitarian.

He by then had amassed a fortune of more than six million dollars—an astonishing amount for the day and for the orphaned son of an Iowa blacksmith—and ever after his interest would be public service.

Mrs. Hoover, who always helped with whatever he was doing, organized activities for the stranded women and children. Her committee sent them on excursions to the Lake Country, to cathedrals and elsewhere, to make the waiting more bearable.

In the autumn she took the boys home to California to school and came back without them, promising to return to take them camping next summer. She kept her promise and, England seeming relatively safe, let them return with her to London, where they attended a private school near the Hoover home.

One night an air raid warning sounded and Mrs. Hoover rushed to take Herbert Jr. and Allan to the cellar. She found their beds empty. They were on the roof watching a German Zeppelin being destroyed over the northern part of the city. Their parents joined them and next day all four drove to view the wreckage.

When America entered the war in 1917, Mrs. Hoover and the boys returned to California and in the nationwide influenza epidemic which took so many lives the next year all three were ill. Herbert Jr. forever afterward would be deaf in his left ear and have to wear a hearing aid.

President Wilson called Hoover home to become U. S. Food Administrator. He instituted meatless and wheatless days, urged expanded farming efforts and home gardens, and issued lists of ways to save food. His name became known in every household and everybody tried to "Hooverize" to help feed others.

His family saw little of him during these busy years. The boys grew into handsome young men who did uncommonly well in their studies and had likable although reserved personalities. Both attended Stanford University.

Herbert Jr. graduated in mining engineering in June of 1925 and that same month married Margaret Watson, his childhood sweetheart. Three years later, when his father was elected President, he was the father of two children, Margaret Ann (Peggy) and Herbert III (Peter), had earned a master's degree in business administration from Harvard, and was surveying air routes on the West Coast under a grant from the Guggenheim Foundation.

An amateur radio operator since the age of twelve and also excited about aviation, he was interested in working out ways for flyers to keep in touch with stations on the ground.

Allan, who displayed some of the same interests, was a senior at Stanford and getting his degree in economics. Both were following in their father's footsteps in that they planned to enter the business world.

Neither son was in the White House much during their parents' four years there. Allan, who came for the inauguration, found life in the mansion boring and was widely quoted for saying, "If I don't get out of here soon I'll have the willies."

That autumn he entered Harvard Business School, where he remained two years.

During his first Christmas holidays his parents scheduled a White House dance for him and a hundred young couples. He was charming and popular but seemed to have no romantic interests, although newspapers had said that he was engaged and reproduced a not-too-new group photograph of him standing near a girl to prove it.

Allan one holiday hosted a young people's dinner in honor of the children of President-elect Rubio of Mexico who was visiting in Washington. Most of the guests were in their teens or younger. He sat at the head of the table and kept the young people chattering with gaiety. Mrs. Rubio called him most *simpatico*.

Meantime Herbert Jr. was making scientific history. He had a $200-a-month job with Western Air Express as communications engineer and when the airship *Graf Zepplin* was on its round-the-world cruise he spoke over a radio network on "Roads of the Sky." In his speech he daringly predicted that commercial planes soon would be equipped with two-way telephones by which pilots could be in constant touch with landing fields.

A week later he was engaged to describe the *Graf Zepplin*'s visit to Los Angeles. The Associated Press reported, "Nearly all of the United States was linked yesterday morning by radio when a word-picture of the arrival of the *Graf Zeppelin* at the Pacific Coast was told by Herbert Hoover, Jr. . . ."

The family received a shock in the summer of 1930.

Herbert Jr. was taking a physical before two weeks' training at an Air Corps camp when the doctors found that he had tuberculosis and ordered him to bed for complete rest for at least a year.

He went to a sanitarium in Asheville, North Carolina, and his family—wife and three children—moved to the White House. A baby named Joan Leslie had by then joined Peggy and Peter. The three stayed with their grandparents for a year while their mother spent as much time with her husband as was permitted, and always was with him during the holidays.

Peggy was a pretty little girl aged four. Alice Roosevelt Longworth described her as looking "absurdly like her grandfather in a miniature feminine edition" and as being "particularly engaging." President Hoover was noted for drawing doodles at his desk, and one manufacturer made up some "doodle" cloth in blue and white so that Peggy could have a dress of the material. She called it her curlicue outfit.

The White House Christmas of 1930 revolved around Peggy and the babies. Peggy was permitted to eat at the dinner table with her grandparents and guests and afterward they all lit candles and, led by the President and Peggy, went to see the tree and gifts.

Peter was so small and well-behaved that he made no headlines although he did astonish the staff one morning by eluding his nurse and wandering through the upstairs rooms with no clothes on. He was found standing at a front bedroom window waving at passersby on Pennsylvania Avenue.

Their White House years were not happy ones for the Hoovers. Rightly or wrongly, he was blamed for the Great Depression which followed the stock market crash of 1929. Economic conditions went from bad to worse during his term in office and, it seemed to the millions of unemployed, he did nothing to better them.

Defeated for reelection in the landslide vote which elected Franklin D. Roosevelt, Hoover and his wife returned to California, where their sons had established residence, and lived at last in the dream house which she had designed. (This house is now the home of Stanford University's presidents.)

After his Harvard graduation Allan returned to California to try banking, but soon resigned his position. He became a rancher, orchardist and grower and, with associates, purchased extensive agricultural acreage in the fertile San Joaquin Valley.

He and Margaret Coberly, a Los Angeles socialite, married in 1937, went to live on the Hoover ranch near Bakersville and the next year became the parents of a son, the Hoovers' fourth grandchild.

After a decade of horticulture Allan sold part of his holdings for $432,000 but retained substantial agricultural interests and held directorships in several business enterprises.

When Mrs. Hoover died in 1944 she left the properties in her name to her sons and also left them a touching letter in which she wrote, "You have been lucky boys to have had such a father and I am a lucky woman to have had my life's trail alongside the paths of three such men and boys." Her husband called it "the sweetest compliment ever given to men."

Herbert Jr. through the years made headlines in the scientific press as he discovered new ways to find oil and perfected mining techniques. At forty he was president of two large engineering companies and special consultant to several foreign governments, including Venezuela, Iran, Brazil and Peru, on oil explorations and production.

In 1963 President Eisenhower asked him to become consultant on oil to the State Department and help settle the British-Iranian oil controversy which was threatening to wreck international relationships.

The former President's son worked behind the scenes for

ten months, shuttling between London, Teheran and Washington and effected a settlement to which the British, Dutch, French, Americans and Iranians all agreed. Iranian oil began to flow again.

He was asked to stay on in government as Undersecretary of State. He accepted, saying, "Public service runs in my family." During his four years he became known as a skillful diplomat.

The Associated Press said of him: "An engineer like his father, Hoover sidestepped publicity and the limelight. He took no part in politics. The result was that the general public hardly knew this quiet, self-effacing son of a President even after he had gained wide recognition in engineering circles."

The son did not like government work, however. It kept him tied to a desk for long hours and, he said, interfered with his family life—to which he was happy to return. His children were married by then and he was several times a proud grandfather. Herbert III, following in his father's and grandfather's footsteps, already was a member of the Society of Petroleum Engineers of the American Institute of Mining, Metallurgical and Petroleum Engineers.

The former President outlived most of the stigma attached to his Presidential days and served his country in several unpaid jobs under both a Democratic and a Republican President. He died in 1964 at the age of ninety and the next year, when his birthplace at West Branch, Iowa, was made a national historic site, his son Allan represented the family in ceremonies at the White House.

Franklin D. Roosevelt's Five

A DAUGHTER AND FOUR STRAPPING SONS

FOR ceremonies marking his fourth inaugural as President on January 20, 1945, Franklin Delano Roosevelt wanted all thirteen of his grandchildren present. His wife Eleanor Roosevelt demurred, not only because of logistics involved in getting them to the White House from so many different places but also on grounds that they might catch childhood diseases from each other.

Eight households would be involved, due to divorces and remarriages among the five Roosevelt children. To the First Lady it sounded most complicated and she would have preferred to skip it.

The President insisted, however, and so on that memorable and snowy day the thirteen were there, most of them towheads, all watching Grandfather take the oath of office which he had taken each four years since March 4, 1933, with a regularity that had become a national habit. Three were teenagers, the others small fry and toddlers.

That year the inaugural, like the children, had come to the President and for the first and only time the ceremonies were staged on the south portico of the White House rather than at the Capitol. World War II still was raging not only across the Atlantic but throughout the Pacific, and rituals were simplified.

A small but distinguished group of spectators stood on the south lawn on canvas stretched over the snow and, looking upward, heard again the magic Roosevelt voice.

He looked thin and ill as he reached the rostrum on the arm of his military aide, and locked the heavy leg braces which enabled him to stand alone—but when he threw back his head and flipped an edge of his admiral's cape so that its red lining showed on a broad shoulder he seemed as indestructible as ever. All thoughts of him as a crippled weary man disappeared quickly.

His four sons—James (Jimmy), Elliott, Franklin Jr., and John—were serving with the Marines, the Air Corps, and the last two with the Navy. None was present. Anna, the daughter, four daughters-in-law, and the grandchildren represented his farflung family. Three of the grandchildren—Eleanor (Sistie) and Curtis Jr. (Buzzie) Dall and little Johnny Boettinger—were Anna's by two husbands.

Pretty Sara and Kate Roosevelt were Jimmy's daughters by Betsey Cushing. As yet he had no children by his second wife. Elliott's third wife, Faye Emerson, the actress, was present as were William Donner, Elliott Jr., Chandler and David Boynton, his children by two former wives. Franklin D. III, and Christopher, sons of Franklin Jr., were there with their mother, the former Ethel Du Pont, and John's wife Anne had brought their two, Haven Clark and Anne Sturgis.

On April 12 of that year President Roosevelt died of a brain hemorrhage in Warm Springs, Georgia, where he went every year to swim in the medicinal waters as therapy for his crippled legs, which had withered under an attack of infantile paralysis in 1921.

The world scarcely could believe his death. Soldiers fighting overseas read about it and wept and so did hard-bitten city editors as the news came over the tickers. He had been in office 12 years and 39 days, and was a way of life to Americans.

Not long after his death, however, Congress passed a law limiting to two the number of times one person may be elected President.

FDR, as he was often called, was the second magnetic member of New York's old and noted Roosevelt family to become President. He was a fifth cousin to President Theodore Roosevelt and his wife Eleanor, the most incredible First Lady the nation has had, was Teddy's niece.

The first President Roosevelt had invited his niece and her fiancé FDR to his inaugural in 1905 and in return the second one invited Teddy's children to his own festivities in 1933, although by then scant political love existed between the two families. Most members of the Theodore Roosevelt family were strictly anti-FDR.

Sprightly Alice Roosevelt Longworth felt so strongly that FDR would be bad for the country that she broke her lifelong rule and campaigned against him, and when he was running for reelection the first time, Teddy's widow Edith came out of retirement to declare his policies un-American.

The second Roosevelt was elected in a landslide victory to end the economic depression which by then had lasted more than three years and affected every family in the country. It is trite by now to say that people who have not lived through a real depression never can know what one is like—but it is probably true.

Ten million people were unemployed in 1933, and they were not what were later to be called the unemployables. (An expression FDR would have deplored.) They were the man next door, the banker whose bank had closed, the white collar workers who no longer had customers to serve. "There but for the grace of God go I," said troubled men as they saw acquaintances selling apples on the street.

FDR restored hope and in doing so he changed the social fabric of the nation. In 100 days of unprecedentedly swift legislation and through countrywide radio hookups, themselves new for Presidents, he set the country singing "Happy Days Are Here Again."

FDR's programs struck sensitive nerves, however, and it seemed that everybody at times had something bad to say against one or more of them. An American coming home from a long stay abroad during his third term was amazed at the amount of criticism. "Who likes Roosevelt?" she asked. "Nobody," her relatives assured her. "Then who votes for him?" "Why we all do," she was told. Again, again and again "that man in the White House" was reelected.

Criticism only made him jauntier and when the critics could not get at him they criticized his family. The First Lady was to many people just as "dangerous" and as bad for the country as he was, and no other set of White House children has been criticized as much as his were.

Mrs. Roosevelt, or Mrs. R as members of her press conference group called her, was an unbelievable sort of First Lady in that she was here, there and everywhere inspecting living conditions, making speeches, writing a daily column, doing a weekly broadcast, holding conferences and promoting her husband's New Deal. She was more political than all the other First Ladies put together, and much more intimately concerned with social welfare problems.

Her speaking voice was unfortunate at first, her sentences often ending at a high nervous pitch. So she hired a speech teacher. Mrs. R drove her own car and refused Secret Service protection, but was made to keep a pistol in a car pocket. Clothes meant less to her than to most women, and neither cooking nor housekeeping interested her much.

One irate woman wrote that she had ruined her white gloves on the White House stair railing and asked why Mrs.

R did not dust more. New York's Mayor Fiorello La Guardia, who came to lunch with her once, said his wife was always interested in what he ate at lunchtime. "This time," he said, "I can truthfully report that I didn't have much."

Mrs. R was great cartoon material and also, to the delight of audiences, was easily mimicked on the stage. Her code name was Rover and she always suspected that her husband had given it to her.

In England during the war her driver could not find the camp at which her son Elliott was stationed, and called back to the U. S. Embassy, "Rover has lost her pup." Not even her husband, who sent her on most of her trips, always knew where she was. One morning he rang from his office to speak to Eleanor. "Why, Mrs. Roosevelt is in prison this morning, Mr. President." "I'm not surprised," he quipped. "What has she done now?"

When he ran for reelection the first time his advisers thought Mrs. R so controversial that she should not make speeches. A Gallup poll taken that year, however, showed that a good majority of Americans approved of her and her activities. A cabdriver summed up his beliefs about why she was unpopular by saying, "The wives don't like her because she makes all of them seem lazy."

She learned to take criticism of herself, but never became hardened to criticism of her children and always defended their right to make their own decisions and mistakes. With the frankness for which she was noted she probed into their upbringing and analyzed for her readers the errors which she felt had been made.

In essence her findings were : 1) That her mother-in-law, Mrs. James Roosevelt, who considered all the children her own, spoiled them with rich gifts and undermined such discipline as was laid down for them, 2) That her husband, resenting having to be too dependent on his mother, went to extremes in seeing to it that his sons were on their own financially and otherwise as soon as they graduated from college, and 3) That she herself had not been as strong a mother as, in retrospect, she would have liked to have been.

Mrs. R did not need to make all this explanation, perhaps. Her family seemed a happy one and few Presidential children escape criticism. The things most criticized about hers were their divorces, the alacrity with which they took jobs with their father's political enemies, the amount of money some of the boys made and the way they made it.

When Franklin Roosevelt became President the ages of his children were: Anna, almost twenty-seven, James, twenty-five, Elliott, twenty-two, Franklin Jr., eighteen, and John had been seventeen for only two days. His nicknames for them were Sis, Jimmy, Bunny, Brud, and Johnny, respectively. Among these Roosevelts rarely anybody was called by his real name.

Three of the five children—Anna, Jimmy, and Elliott— were married. Franklin and John still were in Groton and had been since they were twelve. Anna was married to Curtis Dall, a Philadelphia stockbroker; Elliott to Elizabeth Donner of the same city; and Jimmy to Betsey Cushing of Boston.

When Anna, the only and much loved daughter, married, her grandmother gave her an allowance and her father continued the one she had from him. Mrs. R thought that a similar system should have been followed for the sons, that the allowances for Jimmy and Elliott should not have been stopped the moment they graduated from college. She felt that this would have eliminated their urgency to find jobs immediately and made them more careful about the jobs they accepted.

Anna and her two children Sistie and Buzzie moved into the

White House at the beginning of the Roosevelt administration because her six-year marriage to Dall already was ending.

During her more than a year in the White House Anna, for the entertainment of her children, and because she wished to become an editor and writer, wrote *Scamper, the Bunny Who Went to the White House* and *Scamper's Christmas, More About the White House Bunny*. At parties given for Sistie and Buzzie their grandmother often could be found with her lap full of tots and toddlers reading them chapters from Anna's books. A magician who pulled purple eggs from Sistie's mouth brightened the Easter Egg rollings; Punch and Judy shows enlivened the scene.

In 1934 Anna divorced Dall and married handsome John Boettinger, White House correspondent for the Chicago *Tribune*. The Boettingers, plus Sistie and Buzzie, then moved to Seattle where the new husband became publisher of the *Post Intelligencer*, a Hearst newspaper; Anna edited the woman's page.

Elliott had the first divorce among the children, however, having dissolved his one-year marriage in 1933. He then married beautiful Ruth Googins, a Texas heiress, and became Texas representative for the radio interests of William Randolph Hearst, a vitriolic critic of his father. He wrote an aviation column, too, and became active in state politics.

How much the sons saw of their father after he was President is a moot question. It was a family joke that they had to make an appointment to get his attention. Their mother at times interceded to get them on his schedule. Once when a son needed to see his father about a personal matter he thought to be of desperate importance, the President kept reading during the "interview." When the son finished the father handed him the document asking, "Have you seen this? I would like your opinion on it."

A most irate son returned to his mother to declare that never again would he consult his father on a personal matter.

John had an irritating experience when he showed up from Groton in a jalopy for a visit and could not get by guards at the gates. He telephoned from a drugstore, "How do I get into the place?"

Franklin Jr., upon graduation from Groton, was given a small automobile by his parents. He took it to Harvard with him and received many headlines for speeding. The first time he was arrested his parents hoped that he would be treated severely and thus receive a lasting lesson in the democratic application of laws. To their unhappiness he was not even fined.

He soon wrecked that car and talked his grandmother into giving him a better one. Of her mother-in-law Mrs. R wrote, "She never heard anything she did not wish to hear, and pretended ignorance of our wishes when told that she should not have done it."

Meantime Jimmy was in public hot water because he was selling insurance in Boston. He was hired fresh from Harvard for $15,000 a year—during the depression—and it was reported in the *Saturday Evening Post* that after his father became President his income zoomed to more than $250,000 a year. And, also, that he considered himself to be the political clearinghouse for administration jobs in the Boston area.

Jimmy, for a rebuttal article in *Collier's*, produced tax returns to show that in five years his income had totaled only $170,000. As for the starting salary, he said, "I wasn't kidding myself. I knew they wanted my name, but I have had disappointments just like everybody else in insurance." The public still thought $170,000 quite a bit of money and other agents still worked on policies which went to Jimmy, often thinking they had the contract until news ran through the insurance world, "Jimmy's Got It!"

There was talk of Jimmy's running for Governor of Massachusetts, but his father called him to the White House to be his aide. His salary there was $10,000, or the prevailing one for that job. Mrs. R did not think he should be on the government payroll and objected to the move, but the public took this one in stride. Through the years sons have been secretaries and aides to their Presidential fathers without adverse comment and FDR in his crippled condition needed the strong arm of his oldest son—or somebody—to lean upon when he was out of a wheelchair. (All the Roosevelt sons were six feet or more and John, the youngest, became the tallest of all.)

In 1941, before our entry into World War II, Jimmy had ulcers and went to the Mayo Clinic for treatment. News leaked back that he was in love with his nurse. Whether his marriage to Betsey, the President's favorite daughter-in-law, was in trouble before then was not known. The President sent Harry Hopkins, his favorite troubleshooter, to the clinic to advise against a divorce, but to no avail. The son married Romelle Schneider.

After his graduation from Harvard young Franklin married Ethel DuPont, a pretty daughter in Wilmington's famous family of "economic royalists." It was the sensational wedding of the year and likened to a marriage between the Capulets and Montagues. Indeed Ethel in gossamer white made a lovely Juliet and Franklin, the son most like his father in looks and manner, was a handsome Romeo.

The young couple went to live in Charlottesville, Virginia, where Franklin studied law at the University of Virginia. His father continued his allowance because he would be in school, and he did the same for John when, the next year, he married Anne Clark of Nahant, Massachusetts. John was unlike his brothers in that he wanted to learn merchandising from the ground up and was taking a job as stock boy at Filene's in

Boston at $18.50 a week. John was unlike them, also, in that he became a Republican.

With the oncoming of World War II Jimmy, who had had Marine training, became a colonel in the Marine Corps. Elliott chose the Air Force and his entry as a captain maddened many people. "Watch carefully during the enlistment period," wrote William Allen White, the Kansas editor, "and see whether any other citizen of the United States, without military training, goes in as a captain."

Franklin and John chose the Navy, the former serving on a destroyer and John in the supply section.

Anna returned to the White House when her husband went into the army, bringing their small son Johnny Boettinger with her. (Both Sistie and Buzzie were by then in boarding school.)

Little Johnny was a lonely child in the White House. After Pearl Harbor all except necessary entertaining was discontinued. He had no parties given for him and no playmates; at times he went up and down the stairs running a ruler along the posts to make a little noise. Once he grew so bored he crawled into a White House limousine and mumbled something about an errand for his grandmother. Never surprised at anything Mrs. R said, the driver went several blocks before he realized Johnny had no address in mind, was only hitching a ride.

Elliott, who had been on photographic reconnaissance flights over Europe and Africa, was on leave during the latter days of 1944 and spent Christmas with the family at Hyde Park. During this leave he and his second wife were divorced and five days later he married Faye Emerson, the actress. He was the last son to see his father alive.

After the war Elliott began to grow Christmas trees for sale at Hyde Park but did not prosper. Anna and her husband started a newspaper, the *Arizona Times,* in Phoenix and it went bankrupt. Jimmy mixed in California politics and was defeated when he ran for governor against Earl Warren. There was a Roosevelt backlash running over the country.

Jimmy did come to Congress from California later and Franklin won a Congressional seat from New York. He gave it up, however, to run for Governor of New York but lost the nomination to Averill Harriman. Some people still felt that the Roosevelt boys should be more willing to start nearer the bottom and climb up more slowly.

Franklin then became a Washington-based distributor for Fiat automobiles and served as a representative for Dictator Trujillo of the Dominican Republic. He reentered politics to campaign in West Virginia for John F. Kennedy, who as President made him an Assistant Secretary of Commerce. Later President Lyndon B. Johnson named him to head the new office of Equal Employment Opportunity set up after the Civil Rights Act was passed. He resigned that post, however, to run for Governor of New York on the Liberal ticket in 1966 and lost.

Elliott, married to his fifth wife, is Mayor of Miami Beach, Florida. Anna lives with her third husband, Dr. James Halsted, in Washington, where he is with the Veterans' Administration. Her daughter Sistie, happily married to Van H. Seagraves, who is in the Department of Commerce, is librarian and teacher at a school for the handicapped and lives near her mother. Buzzie, who changed his name from Dall to Roosevelt, works in New York with the American Association for the U.N. John Boettinger, Anna's other son, is married and working on a graduate degree in California. His mother calls him "the intellectual in the family."

Jimmy, married the third time, is with the U. S. delegation at the United Nations. John is a successful New York businessman and not interested in running for any office, although President Eisenhower named him to some committees. He and Franklin, each divorced only once, have three and four children, respectively. Jimmy has six, including a son adopted by him and his third wife. Elliott has four and Anna three— making twenty Roosevelt grandchildren in all.

President Truman's Margaret
ANOTHER "SWEET MISSOURI ROSE"

MARY Margaret Truman was a scant twenty-one years of age, a junior in college and getting ready to go to a birthday party, for which she had both a new dress and a new beau, when a telephone call from her father changed her life forever.

Vice-President Harry S. Truman wished to speak to his wife but his daughter wished to chat with him. "Are you coming home to dinner?" she asked. "*I'm* going out." With an unusual note of impatience in his voice he repeated, "Margaret, *will* you let me speak to your mother?" Offended, she yelled "Mother!" and went back to fixing her hair.

The next thing she knew her mother, with tears streaming down her face, was saying, "President Roosevelt is dead. You'd better change your dress."

Margaret wrote in *Souvenir*, the book about her White House years, "I did not analyze her emotions at the time. I was too busy with my own. . . . Along with her grief for a great man and good friend, she must have looked down the unknowable future and shuddered. If I had had any perception, I might have been a comfort to her but I couldn't collect myself."

She found a brown suit which seemed to be the best pressed

garment in her closet and was about to put it on when the apartment doorbell rang. Distractedly, she opened the door in her slip and found a woman reporter outside. "I can't possibly talk to you now," she cried as she pushed the door closed and resumed dressing.

"That was the beginning," she wrote. "It was at that time I ceased to be a free agent. . . . Never again would I open a door without knowing who was outside."

The unexpected news of President Roosevelt's death was as much of a blow to Vice-President Truman as to his family. He had received a call to come to the White House and gone expecting to see the President—only to learn that he himself was President. For the first time in his life, he wrote his mother, "I felt that I experienced real shock."

He delayed taking the oath of office until Mrs. Truman and Margaret arrived in the White House car sent for them, and would not have thought of doing otherwise. All who knew him knew that his womenfolk had a front place in his thoughts. Mrs. Truman, a shy and reserved woman, was his mentor and disciplinarian, and the only one, except his mother, who could call him down for his peppery language. Margaret was the apple of his eye and they had great times together. As often as not he called her Baby. They were a devoted family and long ago had adopted the motto of "one for all and all for one."

President Truman inherited some sizable problems, not the least of which was the immediate national tendency to underestimate him because he was *not* Roosevelt and had no intention of trying to be. He's the President who had to decide whether to drop the atom bomb on Japan, and to fight in Korea. He formulated the Truman Doctrine for the containment of Russia and sponsored the Marshall Plan for the economic recovery of Europe. World War II was by no means over when he took office on April 22, 1945, and the cold war with Russia was already building. It was not a "safe" time in which to be President.

When the Trumans moved into the White House, Margaret's baby grand piano had to be swung by block and tackle into her second floor sitting room. It was a gift from her father on her eighth birthday and very important to her happiness for, although she was majoring in history at George Washington University, her serious mission in life was to become a singer. She had promised her parents to graduate from college before she devoted full time to music, however, and she was a good student.

She adjusted to her new life by refusing to think about either the prerogatives or penalties which go with being the President's daughter. She found riding to school in a limousine much better than taking the bus and did not mind being shadowed by the Secret Service, except when on dates. Telling a boy good night under a floodlight at the White House door with a Secret Service agent present was not her idea of romance. One of the first promises she made herself was that, come what might, she would not become engaged while her father was President.

The Hatchet, GW's student newspaper, embarrassed her and irritated her father by plastering a story full of romantic speculations on its front page and headlining it *Boss' Daughter Great Catch for Anyone.* When she reported on world affairs in class her comments at times made the papers, with implications that this must be White House policy. When she turned in papers fellow students sometimes whispered, "Which Under Secretary of State do you suppose prepared it?" It was not pleasant, but it did not turn her bitter.

However much Margaret's life had changed, she herself did not change. She managed to remain active in Phi Beta Phi, her sorority, and to have hamburgers and chocolate malteds with her schoolmates, and she always remembered the Truman code, which was: "Do the right thing. Do it the best you can. Never complain and never take advantage."

There could have been real headlines in one of her night classes, but Dr. Lowell J. Ragatz, her professor, outwitted the reporters who were determined to be there when Margaret gave her report. The class was studying European alliances and alignments since 1873 and Margaret had chosen Russia as her field of research.

Relations with that country had deteriorated markedly since she began her study. As Dr. Ragatz said, "Such a subject had become educational dynamite in the hands of the President's daughter. However, she had spent months on the project and, in fairness to her, no change could be made."

He decided to hold the session at which she would report in his own home and telephoned Mrs. Truman for approval. The First Lady said that it would be easier for him to hold it at the White House. "The President and I will be upstairs and you can have the downstairs," she said. "Just prepare a list of who will be along so the guards will let them all in."

So the group met in the State Dining Room around a large table. Margaret had put up maps and a blackboard and was there to greet her guests. "We started on the dot of eight, as usual," Dr. Ragatz recalled, "and she gave an excellent report just as she normally would have done on the campus. It was one of the most able presentations of the year." At 10 o'clock two tea carts of Cokes and cakes were rolled in. The class sat around "eating and coking just as in any student's home," and then Margaret gave them a private tour of rooms on that floor.

Margaret at that time was not a real beauty—is more so now than then—but she was lovely. She had large gray-blue eyes, a flawless complexion, pale golden hair worn almost shoulder length and which she rolled up every night to make the ends turn under. Most of all, she had unusual naturalness.

When helping her mother entertain she had the charm of a little girl and the poise of an adult. She was accustomed to meeting people; she liked people and long since she had learned ease of speech as part of her training for going on the stage. She admitted to being stagestruck and "something of a ham."

Her joy was unbounded when she learned that at the White House she could see almost any American movie ever made. ·*The Scarlet Pimpernel*, with Leslie Howard, was her all-time favorite and was run for her 17 times on different occasions. Howard was her favorite hero until Great Britain's Anthony Eden showed up at the White House. "Now I've seen my dream man!" she told the staff.

The first time she met Bob Hope was at the White House. She gasped and said, "If I had known *you* were coming I would have . . ." "Baked a cake?" he broke in. "No, I would have asked my sorority," she replied. Once she attended the theater in New York with her mother and when she saw the crowds lined up she "began to gawk for the celebrities," not realizing that the crowd was there to see her and Mrs. Truman. Celebrities to her were people who made good on the stage after years of effort—the entertainers of the world.

Margaret thought what fun it would be to have her three best friends—Jane Lingo, Annette Davis and Drucie Snyder—spend a night with her in the Lincoln bed. It's traditional that Lincoln's ghost wanders the White House halls at night. The President decided to have his tallest aide don a stovepipe hat and whiskers and knock on the door at midnight.

Fortunately for the girls and perhaps the reluctant aide, too, he was ill and not on duty. Anyway, the girls did not sleep a wink. The mattress was so old and lumpy they could not arrange themselves comfortably, and spent most of the night on the floor laughing and talking.

The President made the commencement address when his

daughter graduated in 1947 and was permitted to present her diploma. He also gave her a big kiss and they enjoyed their own private jokes as the flashbulbs went off. Then Margaret went home to Independence, Missouri, alone, to study music under Mrs. Thomas J. Strickler, the teacher who had told her she had a soprano voice of top concert quality. And that summer while she lived in the family's enormous Victorian home —where both she and her mother were born—she also reread all of Shakespeare.

Already she had auditioned before some experts as Margaret Wallace, which was her mother's maiden name and the one she at the age of twelve decided would be her stage name. "You have a lovely soprano, but you definitely must put time and work on it," the experts said. Lawrence Tibbett of the Metropolitan heard her sing, too, with some misgivings. When she finished he said, "Thank God, you've got a voice. Now all you need is more work!" So Margaret worked, and in the autumn she went to live in an apartment in New York with the First Lady's personal secretary, Reathal Odom, to keep an eye on her.

She came to Washington nearly every weekend and always for special White House events when her presence was needed. It was a crowded and uncertain schedule and whether, as the President's daughter, she had a fair chance at her career is doubtful.

Her first concert was scheduled for March of 1947. She would sing with the Detroit Symphony Orchestra. After arriving in that city for rehearsals she went to bed with bronchial pneumonia and the concert was postponed. When she went on the stage a week later the backs of both legs were painfully burned from sun lamps. She wore a beautiful billowing dress of blue chiffon and sang the songs she knew best, beginning with "Cielito Linda" and ending with "The Last Rose of Summer."

"Perhaps sheer naïveté saw me through," she wrote. "I was

probably the first unevaluated singer to make a debut with a major symphony to an audience of 20 millions, a gamble which would have turned a more sophisticated singer gray." But Margaret had reached the outskirts of her dream in this appearance. Her press was mostly friendly, although a Chicago critic said she had a small voice which was "immature, unremarkable and unobjectionable."

After that she sang to enormous audiences throughout the nation, making $1,500 to $3,000 a concert, but during the election year of 1948 she dropped everything to go on a whistle-stop campaign tour with her father and mother. Nobody thought Truman could win a term of his own but, win or lose, Margaret thought the whistle-stop fun and loved it when in almost every crowd someone would call, "Give 'em hell, Harry!" The President introduced Mrs. Truman as "my boss" and then Margaret as "her boss." At 4 A.M. the morning after the election he was 2 million votes ahead. Nonetheless, Commentator H. V. Kaltenborn went on the air to say he would not win. Both Margaret and her father loved to imitate this broadcast.

Back at the White House the legs of Margaret's piano had begun to go through the ceiling and, with the election won, the family moved across the street to Blair House while the President launched a $5-million renovation job for the old mansion. There was nothing slapdash nor hurried about this reconstruction project. The Trumans lived at Blair House three years while the job was thoroughly done. Air conditioning and two levels under the ground floor were added, the latter being for storage and bomb shelter purposes, and every unworthy beam was removed.

Everybody assumed Mrs. Truman was happy to be living in the much smaller house, but it made her life ever so much more complicated. Major dinners were held in hotels and receptions were staggered, it now taking three days to entertain the diplomatic corps while at the White House it could have been done in one.

Truman crowds were enormous and foreign visitors were numerous. Fitting Princess Elizabeth and Prince Philip plus their retinue into Blair House was not easy, and they were not the only royal couple to grace the crowded premises. Margaret spaced her concerts so that she could be home on such occasions.

Her father fumed when she received bad notices and did not care who knew it. His wife was forever after him about his language and Margaret called from New York once to complain. "Now see here, Margaret," he told her, "I've just had an hour of that from your mother and have no intention of taking it from you." She thought her press overall fair enough and was able to laugh at the bad reviews.

Probably her worst press notice was in Sweden. She spent her own money to go to Europe on a vacation and was warmly received in England and France, but in Sweden the press taunted her Secret Service agents because they were armed and, it said, protected her more closely than the Swedish royal family ever was. One columnist wrote, "Since Miss Truman is not scheduled to sing, there's no need for her to be afraid in Sweden.!"

The President's daughter was popular with other entertainers and relished knowing them just as much as she had thought she would. When she mugged too much on some of her shows with Jimmy Durante and others, she heard from her father, who reminded her that her mother had brought her up to be a lady.

One television show for which she had a vast audience was on a Sunday night when she substituted for Edward R. Murrow and interviewed her parents, by then living back in Independence, on his popular *Person-to-Person* program.

She did not marry until she was thirty-two years of age and three years out of the White House. Her choice was Clifton

Daniel of *The New York Times*. Lillian Parks, the seamstress who wrote *My Thirty Years Backstairs at the White House*, said the staff was not surprised. "Remembering how she had liked Leslie Howard and Anthony Eden, we always knew she would select a thin-faced man with gray at the temples and who was an intellectual."

When Lyndon B. Johnson was elected President, he invited Mr. and Mrs. Daniel to bring their children and stay at Blair House during the inauguration. Margaret was then the mother of three sons named and aged: Clifton Jr. (Kiffie), seven and a half, William Wallace, five and a half and Harrison (Harry) Gates, two. The youngest remained in New York with his nurse but dark-blond Clifton and towhaired William were intrigued to visit "Mother's old home" and sleep in the room she once had. Since then another baby boy has joined the family and is named Thomas Washington.

About being a mother Margaret has said, "My main feeling is that I have more and more sympathy for my own parents every day!" She wants her children to be individuals. "Being grandchildren of a United States President may make hanging on to that individualism tougher," she said, "but if they're made of the right stuff, it won't make any difference. If they decide to follow politics, all well and good, but I certainly won't point them toward it."

In addition to being a mother and the wife of a busy executive Margaret has managed to keep her career going with TV shows and a regular radio program.

The Eisenhowers' Son

AND FOUR GRANDCHILDREN

-->>>->>)<<<-<<<-

ON the election night of 1952, Maj. John Eisenhower, only child of the Republican candidate for President, sat in a drafty tent in Korea listening to the returns on a small portable radio, sounds of which at times were inaudible because of artillery rumblings a few miles away. When the results at last became obvious the thirty-year-old major hit his fists together and shouted gleefully, "That does it! It's a real landslide!"

A short while later a fellow officer called: "Johnny, your father's going to speak." John's eyes misted over as he listened to the newly elected President. Correspondents crowded in wishing to know what he thought of the speech and he was unable to get out the sentence. "I guess I've said enough," he finally managed.

John Sheldon Doud Eisenhower, West Point, 1944, was as unassuming and reticent as any son whose father ever lived in the White House, and a distinct change from the outgoing Democratic children who had been "in office" for the twenty years before him. He was proud of his father but never enjoyed the public spotlight into which the fame of Gen. Dwight D. Eisenhower, and then the Presidency, drew him. He admitted that his father's positions brought him advantages, but he also felt they at times shackled his effort to be himself—and hampered his attempts to be a good soldier.

As soon as his father was elected, for instance, he was ordered out of the front lines and assigned a job at Korean headquarters, his commanding officer insisting the Communists willingly would sacrifice many troops to capture the son of the American President and that by staying in the lines he would jeopardize the lives of his men. John saw the wisdom of this, but did not like it.

He graduated from West Point the week in which his father, the Supreme Allied Commander in Europe, was launching the D-Day invasion of Normandy and when he reached Europe as a lieutenant, with an infantry division, he resisted all offers of desk jobs, thinking some had been offered because of his name.

It never occurred to him to ask leave for his father's inauguration and when the offer to attend came he turned it down, not knowing that President Truman had initiated it. So President Truman, who thought he should be present, commanded, "Send him anyway." John, thinking his father had asked for him, was angry when he arrived in Washington. The President-elect, innocent of the accusation but delighted his son was coming, had ordered a blue dress uniform—John's first—for him to wear to the inaugural ball.

"It was a very kind thing for President Truman to do," Major Eisenhower admitted when he learned the truth. He stayed three nights in the White House, called it much more comfortable than Korea, and then escorted his wife and three children back to the home he had rented for them in Highland Falls, New York. Almost anyone else would conceivably have welcomed a chance for his family to live in the White House during his absence, and the parents would have loved it. But that was not John's way. He did not want his children spoiled.

John had met his wife, Barbara Jean Thompson, the daughter of a career Army colonel, when he was stationed in Vienna in 1946, and they were married less than a year later. She was a gay and charming brunette who held the same down-to-earth views about living one's own life and rearing children on a no-nonsense basis as John had. Their children were: Dwight David 2nd, almost five when his grandfather became President; Barbara Anne, three, and Susan Elaine, one. They would be joined later by Mary Jean, whose coming was announced by the President five months in advance at his press conference.

Prouder grandparents than Ike and Mamie Eisenhower never lived and these four children were a bright feature of their eight White House years. They called him "Ike" and her "Mimi" and although their father never permitted them to live in the White House they visited frequently and when he was assigned to the Washington area they often were in and out daily. Their swing was kept ready for them, their tricycles filled the downstairs hall and "Mimi" kept an abundance of toys for them on the third floor. Also, she played war games with them on the south lawn.

The Presidential yacht was renamed the *Barbara Anne* and the weekend camp in Virginia became Camp David. When the President bought his Gettysburg farm the caretaker's cottage was made into a home for the young family. The Eisenhowers were sentimental about birthdays and all other anniversaries. Birthdays of the grandchildren were celebrated by White House parties, to which the child being honored could ask about twenty friends to see movies and eat mountains of ice cream. One year David selected *War and Peace*, which ran three hours. He loved movies and the longer they were the better.

Between the President and his only grandson there was a special rapport. David was a cute youngster who looked more like his grandfather than his father did and was not above "swaggering" when he had pictures made. He and Ike made a ritual of bowing most formally to each other when they met. They played at golf together on the White House putting green, and often shared a steak Ike cooked just for them in his third floor kitchen.

It became questionable whether the American public thought of John, the introvert, as a celebrity because he was the son of the President or because he was the father of David, the extrovert everybody enjoyed watching grow up.

The young Eisenhowers lived modestly in a three-bedroom rambler in nearby Alexandria, Virginia and were strict about household chores for the children, all of whom early learned to make their own beds. Their grandmother liked to tell about five-year-old Susan having so much trouble with hospital corners that her mother finally bought contour sheets for her bed. Other chores included setting the table, mowing the lawn, tending the baby and running errands.

David and Barbara Anne attended St. Agnes Episcopal School and Susan went to the Fort Belvoir kindergarten. Their best school drawings were kept for Ike. When he was in the hospital over one Father's Day the children took him ivy and philodendron in pots decorated by themselves and samples of their latest schoolwork.

John was musical like his mother, who had gone to endless trouble to find a harmonica for him when he started off to World War II. She kept a small electric organ in the White House and played for family songfests at which everybody, including the President and baby, joined. "Don't screech, Ike," Mamie frequently had to say to her husband, whose hobby was painting and not music. Barbara Anne pleased him by deciding to paint, too.

David at the age of eleven went off to summer camp in Colorado accompanied by Secret Service men. He told reporters in Denver that he and his camp buddies had stayed up most of

the night on the train from Chicago and "played real poker."
Barbara Anne also went to camp in Virginia that summer accompanied by two Secret Service agents, who were resented
by the camp's director. She made them pitch their tent 500
yards away.

As the children's activities and party invitations expanded
their father feared that the simple life he wanted for them was
in total jeopardy. As grandchildren of the President, if they
went to one friend's birthday party they felt obliged to go to
all others. Their freedom of choice was limited by protocol.
One week his daughters had thirty-four invitations to birthday
parties and John, by now a lieutenant colonel, decided to
move his family to his home in Gettysburg and become a
long-distance commuter to his job in the White House. He put
his children in public school and ushered in a more pastoral
life for them.

His job at the White House was as assistant to Brig. Gen.
Andrew J. Goodpaster, military staff director, his pay was that
of his army rank. He granted few interviews, but was friendly,
well liked, and repected for shunning the headlines. General
Goodpaster stressed how invaluable John was to him because
he not only understood the work involved but wrote such good
and concise reports.

John was an English student and writer at heart and had been
for several years. In *The Howitzer*, West Point yearbook, it
was said of him the year he graduated:

> Nothing at West Point ever worried Ike much. [He was
> then called Ike, too, and even in Korea was known as "Major
> Ike."] A natural "hive," he generously gave much of his time
> to coaching deficient plebes. Quiet, easy-going and unassum-
> ing, Ike has the enviable quality of winning the sincere friend-
> ship of everyone with whom he comes in contact. Another
> 4-star general? Maybe. But he wants to be a writer. He'll
> make a good one.

After his European duty and before he went to Korea he was instructor and then assistant professor in English at the Point, fitting a postgraduate course in English at Columbia University into his schedule. His thesis for the course was on the life of a soldier in Elizabethan days. Many of the ideas for this came from Shakespeare, his favorite author. Perhaps always he liked either teaching or writing better than being a soldier although he was an excellent one.

His chance to write came in 1961 when his father, his Presidency ending, began a two-volume work on his administration to be called *The White House Years*. John took leave without pay from the Army to get it started and two years later resigned from the Army, forfeiting the pension which would have been automatic had he stayed in little more than a year longer. He joined the publishing firm of Doubleday and Company to be a nonfiction editor in the field of history and biography and continued to work on his father's books.

This President had what some of our Presidents have lacked and wished for: a son willing and able to get his papers together and write coherently about his record as chief executive. John continued living in the Gettysburg area and in the 1964 elections interested himself enough in politics to write letters to a hundred key people in his father's administration telling why Gov. William Scranton was his choice for President and asking their support. His daughters won horse show trophies and all the Eisenhowers live in close proximity, still celebrating together on special occasions and remaining one family. David graduated with honors from Phillips Exeter in June, 1966, and chose to go, not to West Point, but to Amherst College.

The Kennedy Two

LEGENDS IN THEIR BABYHOODS

WHEN John Fitzgerald Kennedy was elected President
in November, 1960, his pixy daughter Caroline was
the first to call him by the title he had won. Her nurse suggested it to her. "Will Daddy like it?" Caroline asked. Told
that he would like it very much the almost three-year-old raced
to his room, pounced on the bed to awaken him, waited for her
usual kiss and cried, "Good morning, Mr. President!" As usual, her timing was superb. Daddy had gone to bed not at all
sure what his status would be next morning.

John-John, the brother with whom Caroline would share
a national adulation unheard of for White House children
since the days of Teddy Roosevelt's bevy and the little Cleveland girls, was not born yet—and not expected before Christmas.

No sooner was the President-elect on his way to Palm Beach
for a post-election rest in the sun than he had to turn back in
transit. His son was born November 25, two days before Caroline's third birthday. The public came to know her under most
engaging circumstances: wearing her mother's shoes and peering between her father's legs at a press conference, calling on
her cousins with a small purse in one hand and a toy six-shooter

in the other, trying Daddy's patience at church, and presiding over her birthday party.

For the party, dining room furniture of the Kennedy home in Washington was replaced by child-sized chairs and tables. Caroline was so intrigued by her small chair that she did not wish to leave it to greet her guests and she kept calling, "Oh, do it again," to the clown who entertained them all. Nothing she did or said was too small to notice. Accustomed to crowds, she knew no strangers, found reporters and photographers fascinating.

When Daddy took her and her big rag doll to a grown-up church she was immediately down inspecting the shoes of worshippers and peering up to see who was in the next pew. Retrieved and held firmly by Daddy, she sought friendly faces in the audience and waved a paper to all who turned to look. It happened that the paper was a page of type headed "Let Us Pray" which the church was distributing that morning.

It amused and delighted readers and viewers to see pictures of and think about the forty-three-year-old President-elect in charge of irrepressible Caroline, a storybook child with fluffy honey-blond hair and a great gift for communication.

So much public exposure did not delight Caroline's mother, Jacqueline Kennedy, however, and shortly thereafter Daddy said of his daughter, "I think it's time we retire her." Jacqueline did not want the spotlight on her children, but wished them to grow up naturally without realizing that their father was a man set apart.

She succeeded remarkably well in achieving this desire during almost three years in the White House. When anyone said to Caroline, "Your Daddy is President," she corrected this with, "Oh, no. My Daddy is my Daddy." Her Secret Service agent was instructed to stay merely within reasonable distance and not interfere with her games such as running to kiss the wind. She looked upon him as just another adult playmate.

It was impossible to keep Caroline completely out of the news, though, once the public had experienced her charm. In keeping with her upbringing, she had the run of the White House—after being banished to Palm Beach to get her away from the excitement of inaugural festivities. She explored all 132 rooms. Her father had been President only a few days when she walked into the map room, part of the business side at the mansion, to announce one afternoon, "Daddy's sitting upstairs with his shoes and socks off doing nothing."

With a child like that loose in the White House the new President scarcely needed a press secretary. Caroline alone could have kept him on the front page. She was a breath of fresh air for editors weary of the cold war and other insolubles. One of them snapped at his Washington correspondent, "Never mind that stuff about Laos. What did Caroline say today?"

When former President Truman came to see Caroline's father she was ensconced under the President's desk waiting to greet him with, "How are you? You used to live here." When former First Lady Eleanor Roosevelt came to a meeting Caroline helped show her over the premises to see the changes made since her own tenancy. Then, entering the room where the meeting was to be, they found several participants already gathered. Thinking to brighten the atmosphere, the President asked, "Does anyone want a drink?" Caroline, who had been on an inspection tour, called, "They've already had drinks, Daddy. I saw the glasses."

Any VIP who came and failed to see Caroline felt he had missed something. "Why won't hair grow for you?" she wonderingly asked bald-headed Speaker Sam Rayburn. Scarlet-coated members of the Marine Band who loved her friendliness began to play "Old MacDonald Had a Farm" or other nursery tunes when she popped in for White House social events, which she was likely to do, and they created as much of a stir as when "Hail to the Chief" announced the President's arrival. Guests stopped talking and craned to see Caroline.

Republicans enjoyed her, too, and laughingly called her an unfair political weapon. The First Lady seemed to be the only one *not* happy about her daughter's universally favorable publicity. She began to fill Caroline's days with play school and ballet lessons outside the mansion and would not consent when photographers wished pictures of her in her white leotards or with playmates at school. Reporters did not relish being shut out, because their editors were pressuring them daily; but the First Lady's whims could be iron when it came to spacing and timing the type of stories she would permit about her daughter. She feared what would happen as Caroline grew older and began to recognize her "importance."

Oddly enough, life in the White House drew the Kennedy family closer together. Heretofore John F. Kennedy, although deeply attached to his family, all his married life had been in political campaigns or spending long hours on Capitol Hill as a senator. Now he had much more time with his wife and children, could eat more of his meals with them and be home at night. Rather than taking his after-lunch nap on an office sofa, as he did on the Hill, he took it in his own bed—with Caroline and later John-John, too, on hand to greet his awakening with screams of "Daddy, Daddy, Daddy!" His hours were just as long or longer but, however many late hours he spent on crises occurring in one part of the world or another, he made time for his family.

From his office he could see Caroline and John-John at play on the south lawn and at times when burdens pushed too much he would step to the veranda and clap his hands to bring them running. A few minutes with them and his tensions seemed to ease away. Always he kept the strains of office separate from his family life.

Jackie, as the world called her, was not the type of wife who

greeted him with, "What's new in Cuba?" That was his job not
hers. He took great pride in her self-selected job of forming a
committee of experts to help her fill the White House with
furniture and art worthy of the structure and its traditions.
She made him, and the nation too, freshly aware of the beauty
of excellence and elegance. Before, he had seemed immune to
his surroundings, but now he would say proudly to friends,
"Look at those rugs and these colors." Caroline became aware
of fine furniture and French kings, too. "Oh, that's Louis
Quatorze!" she once cried delightedly at a picture in a book.

And Mrs. Kennedy did something to improve living conditions in the White House. One marvels that earlier First Families had not thought of it. She turned a bedroom and living
room suite on the second floor, where the family lives, into a
kitchen and dining room thus making the second floor a self-
contained home.

For more than 150 years White House families had dressed
and gone downstairs to eat their meals in a "family dining
room" which did not seem like one because all the other
rooms on the floor were completely formal. As for cooking a
meal, being able to snack easily, etc., that was impossible—until President Eisenhower, who cooked for relaxation, had a
small kitchen put on the third floor.

The family dining room now is a lovely place where up to
fourteen guests can be accommodated and where children
such as Caroline and John-John, or older or younger, could
have their meals in privacy and where their parents could entertain guests at dinner.

Also, Mrs. Kennedy filled the broad center hall of the living floor with furniture, bookshelves, lights, rugs and flowers.
She did it for her family as well as for beauty. She wanted the
family to be happy and comfortable while living there. Happiness while growing up she considered of great importance
to her children, and what she thought about rearing them

properly she summed up in her belief that "whatever else you do, unless you raise your children well, I think you have failed."

Caroline and John-John were "good" children and usually easy to manage, and Caroline especially was. Once when a family friend was taking her and some other children to a circus the friend had to keep telling her own children to stop bouncing around and sit quietly in the car. "You cause your mother a lot of trouble," Caroline said disapprovingly.

But the Kennedy two were not the complete angels of good behavior which the legends made them. They were much too normal, lively, outgoing, and full of curiosity to be considered angelic. Their mother said, after reading a book on child behavior, "It's a relief to know that other people's children are as bad . . . at the same age." Caroline at times ate forbidden candy before supper and refused to admit it.

John-John as he grew to the little-boy stage was quite a handful. He one morning inserted himself into a staff conference and refused to leave, despite Daddy's best efforts. Deciding to ignore him, the President asked, "What have we got today?" "I've got a glass of water," was the first answer— from his son. Daddy sent for the nurse, who persuaded the tot that he should join his sister. "Marvelous," said the President. "There would have been a storm of tears if I had tried that."

The youngest Kennedy's tears provided great photographs; a camera first caught them when John-John could not go with Daddy in the helicopter which landed on the White House lawn. On numerous occasions he was pictured rapidly climbing the helicopter steps and being pulled down them again—in tears. Before then he had slight public identity, his sister being the child in focus. The public, noting that he was a most attractive child, noted also that he had a bushy-banged haircut which his mother called European. The President decreed that it was time to change to a more boylike cut for his all-boy son.

John-John liked to be asked his name so that he could strut a bit before replying, "John F. Kennedy, Jr."

The children had as many pets as the Teddy Roosevelt children had, but there were no snakes and rats among them. They had five dogs of various sizes, one named Pushinka and sent to Caroline by Russia's Premier Khrushchev and one, a dignified Welsh terrier called Charlie, which was their favorite. John Jr. rarely wanted to leave the grounds without going by to "talk to Charlie."

Tom Kitten was a gray cat. Robin and Bluebell were canaries. Debbie and Billie were hamsters, and Caroline had three ponies: Tex, a gift from Vice-President Lyndon B. Johnson, then Leprechaun and Macaroni. She, like her mother, loved to ride and learned to do so before she was three. John did not enjoy horses of any kind. To his mother's disappointment, his comment on his first ride was, "I wanna get off."

The two met more heads of state than most Cabinet members did. John made a very nice bow when introduced and Caroline curtsied perfectly. They also watched the red-carpet arrivals of state guests on the south lawn, Caroline and her schoolmates from her third floor school and John usually from the second floor balcony. The President was irritated by Caroline and group when Ben Bela, the president of Algeria, arrived and they began going "Boom-Boom" in unison with the 21-gun salute, and kept it up while the visitor was making his speech. Marshal Tito of Yugoslavia was arriving two days later and the President warned the teacher and nurse that he wanted no childish disturbance. Caroline's school remained quiet but John chose this time to drop one of his toy pistols through the balcony onto the head of a soldier. Its descent and the ensuing commotion showed on a television newsreel.

A baby brother for Caroline and John was born in August,

1963, and named Patrick Bouvier—but was destined to live only two days. After Patrick's death the First Lady took a recuperative Grecian cruise and John F. Kennedy again had the pleasure of becoming chief baby-sitter. He began to take the children for late afternoon swims in the White House pool —delightful times for all three. During this time also he became more closely acquainted with his son, who was nearing the age of three.

The President began to take John with him to some public events. One of their last appearances together was on Armistice Day of that year at ceremonies honoring the Unknown Soldiers in Arlington Cemetery. John saluted the colors and the soldiers, and became the star in most of the pictures. Eleven days later the President was dead in Dallas, Texas.

In the harrowing days after his assassination, the behavior of his children, their rapport with their mother, as television audiences glimpsed the three of them going to the Capitol where the President's body lay in state and next day at the Cathedral for the funeral, provided a touch of solace. Mixed with overwhelming sympathy for the mourning First Lady was the thought that she assuredly was not failing in the rearing of her children.

Nurse Shaw acquainted Caroline with the sorrowful news and little Buttons, as her Daddy often called her, sobbed herself to sleep before Mommy came home. John was too young to sense his full loss, but more-sensitive Caroline did not smile again for some time.

The shattered family hastened from the White House to live in a borrowed home until one could be purchased in Georgetown near where they had lived previously. This home on N Street became such a target for sightseers, who would loiter and peer, that normal privacy was impossible. Rear exits for coming and going made the life an unnatural one for the children. Mrs. Kennedy decided to move them to New York, hoping that in the larger and more impersonal city she could work out a new mode of living. What a relief it was to her to be able to take the children boating in Central Park without causing a traffic jam.

Caroline entered her first real school as a day pupil at the Convent of the Sacred Heart. She loved her school's gray uniform with its white blouse and pretty red beret, and she made excellent grades.

John was full of boyish energy and was the life of the family. He learned to mimic the Beatles, was interested in Indians, cowboys and swords. When the family went to England for ceremonies dedicating an acre of ground at Runnymede to the late President's memory he captured British hearts with his freewheeling and self-assured enjoyment of the trip. At the Tower of London he crawled into the mouth of a World War I cannon. When shown the crown jewels he said, "Tell me, who owns these?" Told that the Queen did he replied, "Very good." He had met the Queen and she was all right!

For years to come and perhaps all their lives Caroline and John will continue to hold the interest of the public in whatever they do. The spotlight always will be searching for them because of the affection America felt for them and because of the tragedy which cut their White House days to less than three years.

The Johnson Sisters

TWO DARK-EYED CHARMERS

THE youngest, most talkative and, at the time, the least known LBJ—sixteen-year-old Luci (née Lucy) Baines Johnson—moved into the White House on December 7, 1963, believing that it would rob her of her youth and thinking that now she never would be able to find an identity of her own.

"Let's face it," she said. "I'll never be just Luci Johnson. I'll always be the President's younger daughter."

Finding the "real me" and being recognized as herself were of paramount importance to Luci. With an adolescent's logic, she doubted that her parents understood her, and she was concerned that the public seemed to consider her merely a smaller version of her tall (5 feet, 9½ inches), dimpled and beautiful sister, nineteen-year-old Lynda Bird, who was an honor roll sophomore at the University of Texas.

"We're like oil and water," Luci kept saying. "Lynda's smart. What she can't do well she won't do at all. She never risks making a fool of herself. The more I see her with a book in her hand the worse I feel. My problem is I'm irresponsible."

Her mother, the new First Lady, described her as "a blue and white, lace and ruffles, very feminine little girl." Luci, however, did not consider herself to be a little girl and, she confided to friends, "I'm more the tailored type. The thing is I'm a blue-eyed child in a brown-eyed family. I don't belong. I have to call dibs to get anything at all. Everything's by priority in my family: Daddy first, then my mother and my sister. I'm last."

In truth, Luci had grown up very quickly. Her very busy parents had been away from home so often during her father's three years as Vice-President that perhaps they had not grasped the depth of her longing to be a young lady and "to express the real me." And in the hectic, sorrow-filled days following the death of President Kennedy hurried reporters did confuse her with Lynda.

It particularly irked her that Lynda's collections of stuffed animals and dolls should be attributed to her. "I don't mind what is written about me," she said. "I truly don't, just so it shows the real me. But I don't collect stuffed things!" She felt that anyone who knew her at all should know that she was a *live* animal fan and always had preferred baby-sitting to playing with dolls.

In fact, she had started the beagle trend in her family by begging for one when she was three years of age. Lady Bird Johnson, thinking of her new rugs, tried to delay the inevitable but Luci's sympathetic father had braved a snowstorm to search several kennels in Virginia for just the right dog. It was immediately named Little Beagle. "It's cheaper if we all have the same monogram," he explained. "That way we can share the same suitcase."

Little Beagle became the most noted dog in Washington, not only because dynamic Senator Lyndon B. Johnson and his frisky daughter talked about him so much but also because when he was lost, J. Edgar Hoover, a Johnson neighbor, put him on the FBI's Most Wanted list. By the time the oldest LBJ became President, however, the canine LBJ was dead and replaced by two of his offspring: "Him" and "Her." Luci had these two puppies as passengers when she drove up to the White House in the white convertible her father had given her on her sixteenth birthday.

It was not long until Luci's efforts to reveal "the real me" came through loud and clear, and people began to keep a "Luci file" for the sheer fun of checking what she said one day against the day before. She detested being classified with teen-agers, but she seemed to be all of them rolled into one and was as full of contradictions as she was of words. The image she created was of a bubbly and freewheeling adolescent who would tackle any subject. She loved to receive and give surprises, was completely irrepressible and, at times, she was irresistible.

There was more than a touch of Southern belle in some of her strategy. Her father once said, "Luci could walk down the street with her clothes off and everyone would say, 'How cute!'" "I get along best with Daddy," Luci lilted, as if in reply. Her mother, who had dreaded the teen years of her daughters and then dismissed the fear because in Lynda they made no change, admitted that she never had any idea what Luci would say next. "I find this both frightening and interesting," she said.

At times Luci probed her soul with agonizing honesty and worried out loud about her mother and sister because "They hold things in too much." "I believe in expressing your feelings," she said. "If I'm angry I express it. If I'm happy I show it. I cry more." At other times she danced the Watusi with abandon while maintaining, "Youth is the time for irresponsibility. I like to just goof."

It developed that she had boy friends all over the country. She had accumulated an impressive file of them while her father was Senate Majority Leader by taking a proprietary interest in Capitol Hill pages and student interns. She invited them to parties and, when they were ill, took them food she had cooked herself. One who lived in New Orleans wrote of being her escort when she went to that city to visit Head Start programs and speak at a meeting of optometrists. "Luci has a great many friends," he said, "and likes to contact them as she goes about the country."

One of her first trips as the President's daughter was to the Interlochen Music Camp in Michigan to narrate "Peter and the Wolf," with Van Cliburn at the piano and directing. She did a fine job and was offered a movie role in *I'll Take Sweden*. "I've got to take school," Luci said. "I'm very conscientious about school, but not about things that are optional. Some day I'm going to be sorry. I know I don't read enough. It's a sad, sad part of my life, but reading I can do without. My trouble is I don't like stuff that's good for me."

Luci was doing well as a junior in high school after two years of low grades due to visual defects which Dr. Robert Kraskin, an optometrist, discovered and corrected. She worked for Dr. Kraskin during two of her three White House summers and became voluntary chairman of Volunteers for Vision, which was organized to test eyes of children enrolled in the Head Start program.

During the second summer she was seeking a more serious image for herself than that of a dancing teen-ager. When it was reported that she and Lynda planned to make a grand tour of Europe she was irate. "I must admit that I have never been so shocked," she said. "This takes the plaid rabbit. I have called my employer that I will be there. I love working and it gives me a chance to get an education on the side."

Lynda's story was different. She was studious, reserved and shy, secretive about her personal life, an introvert who watched what she said and how she said it, and she DID mind what was written about her. If she worried about "the real me," she kept it to herself. She could be both silent and aloof. Also, she could be warm and gay.

The President says, "I have the best two daughters in this world," and he long ago stated that he never need worry about either of them. "Lynda is so smart she always can take care of herself and Luci's so feminine some man always will want to make a living for her."

Part of Lynda's philosophy about her life in the White House is in her comment that "children of men in public life —somewhat like the children of preachers—learn early in life that people expect them to be adults before they are even adolescents."

She has been called "the royalty" in the family because at an early age she began being Duchess and Queen of so many festivals. At one time conscious of her height, she came to appreciate its worth and said, "It makes me feel like a queen."

When her father became President she was engaged to a Navy lieutenant whose Annapolis pin she began wearing at age seventeen, and it was expected that they would be married the following summer. This was one reason the First Lady wished her to leave Texas University at midyear and enter George Washington University in Washington. She wanted Lynda to have a taste of White House living before the big event, and also she wanted her older daughter near her. Lynda came home, bringing her roommate, Warrie Lynn Smith, with her—but talk of a wedding began to evaporate and the engagement was broken by mutual consent.

During vacation Lynda worked without pay in a White House office and helped in her father's campaign for election in his own right. She and Luci appeared at innumerable barbecues staged by the Youth for Johnson group. Lynda spoke first and then presented her sister with, "And now here's Watusi—I mean Luci."

As the older daughter she had accompanied Vice-President and Mrs. Johnson on several goodwill trips abroad and enjoyed them thoroughly. She hoped that after her junior year at GW she could spend the whole summer in Europe, and she worked toward it. Her grades at GW were good but not always the invariable "A's" to which she had been accustomed, nor did she participate in campus activities. She was too busy at the White House helping receive groups and entertaining visitors, among them some European princesses.

Her father's battle to cut American spending abroad stopped her European travel plans and, after deciding to return to Texas for her final college year, she set out to "See America" instead. Mixing business with pleasure, she contracted to write articles for two magazines and headed for Arizona to live in a trailer on the reservation of White River Apache Indians. There she joined in the archaeological "dig" sponsored by the University of Arizona.

"Velvet" was the Secret Service code name for Lynda. (Mother was Victoria and Luci was Venus.) But the hands of the amateur archaeologist lost their velvet in learning to use the shovel, pickax, trowels and scalpels needed to excavate the skeleton she found. In her new boots, her heels were skinned from field trips, her muscles sore from evening volley ball and wheelbarrow loads. Life at camp was not life at the White House, but Lynda enjoyed it.

To get the trailer over the mountain and into Grasshopper, an address so remote that a letter sent to her by Arizona's governor was returned to him, road crews had to widen dirt roads and fill ravines. An especially bad place near the Indian commissary was renamed Lynda Dip. The Apaches gave a barbecue and dance in her honor, and a tribal name meaning "pretty little yellow bird."

Before she came home again her tour included the Grand Canyon, Yellowstone, the West Coast, and a canoe trip near the Canadian border. Then she joined her mother in the

Grand Tetons and they tackled the Snake River rapids on a raft, and she met a handsome summer woodsman named Brent Eastman, who became one of her beaux. That summer she also met George Hamilton, the movie star who was to change her image from outdoor girl into that of a glamorous beauty. (Her most constant escort before this was David Le Feve, a White House Marine aide who became a stockbroker.)

Lynda claims she has a dating handicap because the publicity she receives scares men away and makes it almost impossible to have more than one boy friend at a time, and she cannot know for sure whether the date is interested in her for herself. After her engagement to Bernard Rosenbach was broken she said, "I hoped I'd get a lot of—you know—contestants."

Meantime, that summer also was a momentous one for Luci. On her eighteenth birthday she became a Roman Catholic and began to realize that she was in love with Patrick Nugent, who had attended a surprise party given for her when she graduated from high school in June.

Changing her religion was not a new idea with Luci nor did her parents try to prevent it. All they asked, when she requested their permission in her sixteenth year, was that she consider it carefully and wait until she was sure.

She had waited and was sure. She also was sure that she wished to be a nurse despite the hard study involved. In the autumn she entered Georgetown University's School of Nursing, and Lynda began her final college year.

In their less than two years at the White House both girls had changed considerably, Luci growing more serious and Lynda more relaxed. At the University of Texas, Lynda participated more often than formerly in student affairs. She lived in the Zeta Tau Alpha sorority house, worked on the committee which brought noted speakers to the campus, and had some blind dates. Luci had more homework at night, her father said, than he had.

Lynda's romance with George Hamilton burgeoned into constant headlines. They had Thanksgiving together in Acapulco and Mardi Gras in New Orleans. He was at the White House dinner honoring Princess Margaret. She went to Hollywood for the Academy Awards dinner and in her new free-flowing hairdo was a sensation. "The most glamorous person there," some said. Speculation about an engagement and marriage filled many a column. George called her "one of the most interesting and very nicest girls" he ever knew. Lynda kept silent.

Luci's wedding to her Patrick on August 6 was the major romantic news of 1966. The seventh daughter of a President to be married while living in the White House and the first in 52 years, she chose to have the noontime ceremony in the Shrine of the Immaculate Conception, the largest Roman Catholic Church in the United States, and the reception at the White House. There were 700 guests and 42 participants, including Lynda as maid of honor. The large and beautiful event consumed most of a hot summer Saturday, matched in splendor and ritual the wedding of any other Presidential daughter in American history. In the shrine was eighty-two-year-old Alice Roosevelt Longworth, who had married in the White House 60 years before with the same number of guests but no attendants except her father.

The young Nugents went to live in Austin so that Pat could get a master's degree in business administration at Texas U. Surrounded by wedding gifts and furniture mostly borrowed from the family, Luci began to keep house in earnest, enrolled for a home economics course in the university and did her own grocery shopping.

Lynda, the wedding over, had a brief trip to Europe with a

friend and pondered her future. Teaching, once her goal, was abandoned as unfeasible as long as the White House was her home and Secret Service agents her constant guards. From among several job offers she selected to work for *McCall's* Magazine as consultant and writer, on a part-time basis, so that she could be on call to help her mother and to support projects connected with her father's Great Society.

Bibliography

ADAMS, CHARLES FRANCIS, *Diary*. Harvard University Press, 1964.

ADAMS, JAMES TRUSLOW, *The Adams Family*. Little Brown & Co., 1930.

ADAMS, JOHN QUINCY, *Diary, 1794-1845*. Longmans, Green & Co., 1929.

AMES, MARY CLEMMER, *Ten Years in Washington*. A. D. Worthington & Co., 1878.

BEALE, MARIE. *Decatur House and Its Inhabitants*. National Trust for Historic Preservation, 1954.

BEMIS, SAMUEL FLAGG, *John Quincy Adams and the Union*. Alfred A. Knopf, 1956.

BISHOP, JIM, *A Day in the Life of President Kennedy*. Random House, 1964.

BISHOP, JOSEPH BUCHLIN, *Theodore Roosevelt's Letters To His Children*. Charles Scribner's Sons, 1919.

BRANDT, IRVING, *James Madison*. The Bobbs Merrill Co., 1941-61.

BROOKS, NOAH, *Washington in Lincoln's Time*. Rinehart & Co., Inc., 1958.

BURKE, PAULINE WILCOX, *Emily Donelson of Tennessee*. Garrett and Massie, 1941.

BUTT, ARCHIBALD, *Taft and Roosevelt*. Doubleday, Doran & Co., 1930.

CARPENTER, FRANCIS, *Carp's Washington*. McGraw-Hill Book Company, 1960.

CANTACUZENE, PRINCESS. (NÉE JULIA GRANT) *My Life Here and There*. Charles Scribner's Sons, 1921.

CAVANAUGH, FRANCES, *Children of the White House*. Rand McNally and Company, 1955.

CLAY-CLOPTON, VIRGINIA, *Memoirs*. Doubleday, Page & Co., 1902.

COLEMAN, ELIZABETH TYLER, *Priscilla Cooper Tyler*. U. of Ala. Press, 1955.

COMER, LUCRETIA G., *Strands From the Weaving*. (Garfield's Granddaughter) Vantage Press, 1959.

CUTTS, L. B., *Memoirs and Letters of Dolley Madison*. Houghton, Mifflin and Co., 1887.

DESMOND, ALICE CURTIS, *Martha Washington*. Dodd Mead & Co., 1951.

FEIS, RUTH STANLEY-BROWN, *Molly Garfield in the White House*. Rand McNally & Co., 1963.

FORD, WORTHINGTON CHAUNCEY, *Letters of Henry Adams 1858-1891*. Houghton Mifflin Co., 1930.

FREEMAN, DOUGLAS SOUTHALL, *George Washington. Charles Scribner's* Sons, 1948-1957.

FURMAN, BESS, *White House Profile*. The Bobbs Merrill Co., 1951.

GOUVERNEUR, MARIAN (CAMPBELL), *As I Remember*. D. Appleton & Co., 1911.

GREEN, CONSTANCE McLAUGHLIN, *Washington-Village and Capital, 1800-1878*. Princeton U. Press, 1962.

HAMILTON, HOLMAN, *Zachary Taylor, Soldier of the Republic*. The Bobbs Merrill Co., 1941.

———, *Zachary Taylor, Soldier in the White House*. The Bobbs Merrill Co., 1951.

HAGEDORN, HERMANN, *The Roosevelt Family of Sagamore Hill*. The Macmillan Co., 1955.

HATCH, ALDEN, *Edith Bolling Wilson*. Dodd, Mead & Co., 1961.

HELM, EDITH BENHAM, *The Captains and the Kings*. G. P. Putnam's Sons, 1954.

HESS, STEPHEN, *America's Political Dynasties*. Doubleday & Co., Inc., 1966.

HOLLOWAY, LAURA C., *The Ladies of the White House*. Bradley & Co., 1881.

HOOVER, IRWIN HOOD (IKE), *Forty-two Years in the White House*. Houghton-Mifflin Co., 1934.

HUBBARD, C. V. D. & H. D. EBERLEIN, *Historic Homes of Georgetown and Washington City*. The Dietz Press, 1958.

JAMES, MARQUIS, *Andrew Jackson*. The Bobbs Merrill Co., 1933-1938.

JEFFRIES, ONA GRIFFIN, *In and Out of the White House*. Wilfred Funk Inc., 1960.

JENSEN, AMY LaFOLLETTE, *The White House and Its Thirty-two Families*. McGraw-Hill Book Co., Inc., 1958.

JONES, GRANSTON, *Homes of the American Presidents*. Bonanza Books, 1962.

KECKLEY, ELIZABETH HOBBS, *Behind the Scenes*. G. W. Carleton & Co., 1868.

KLAPTHOR, MARGARET B., *Dresses of the First Ladies of the White House*. Smithsonian Institution, 1952.

LOGAN, MRS. JOHN A., *Thirty Years in Washington*. A. D. Worthington & Co., 1901.

LONGWORTH, ALICE ROOSEVELT, *Crowded Hours*. Charles Scribner's Sons, 1933.

MAYO, LIDA, *Miss Adams in Love*. American Heritage, Feb. 1965.

McADOO, ELEANOR WILSON, *The Woodrow Wilsons*. The MacMillan Co., 1937.

MITCHELL, STEWART, *New Letters of Abigail Adams*. Houghton-Mifflin Co., 1947.

NELLIGAN, MURRAY H., *Old Arlington*. National Park Service, 1953.

NICHOLS, ROY FRANKLIN, *Franklin Pierce*. U. of Pa. Press, 1931—Revised 1958.

MONTGOMERY, RUTH, *Mrs. L. B. J.*, Holt, Rinehart and Winston, 1964.

PARKS, LILLIAN ROGERS, *My 30 Years Backstairs at the White House*. Fleet Publishing Co., 1961.

PERLING, J. J., *Presidents' Sons*. The Odyssey Press, 1947.

POORE, BEN:PERLEY, *Reminiscences*. Hubbard Bros., 1886.

RANDALL, RUTH PAINTER, *Mary Lincoln, Biography of a Marriage*. Little Brown & Co., 1953.

RANDOLPH, SARAH N., *The Domestic Life of Thomas Jefferson*. Harper & Bros., 1871.

ROOF, KATHARINE METCALF, *Colonel Wm. Smith and Lady*. Houghton-Mifflin Co., 1929.

ROOSEVELT, ELEANOR, *Autobiography*. Harper & Bros., 1961.

ROOSEVELT, ELLIOTT, *As He Saw It*. Duell, Sloan and Pearce, 1946.

ROSS, ISHBEL, *An American Family: The Tafts—1678 to 1964*. The World Publishing Co., 1964.

———, *Grace Coolidge & Her Era*. Dodd, Mead & Co., 1962.

———, *First Lady of the South*. Harper & Brothers, 1958.

SAMSON, WM. H., Letters of Zachary Taylor from the Battle Fields of the Mexican War. Genesee Press, 1908.

SAYRE, FRANCIS BOWES, *Glad Adventure*. The Macmillan Co., 1957.

SEAGER II, ROBERT, *And Tyler, Too*. McGraw-Hill Book Co., 1963.

SEATON, WILLIAM WINSTON, *A Biographical Sketch*. James R. Osgood & Co., 1871.

SIEVERS, HARRY, *Benjamin Harrison*. University Publishers, Inc., 1952-59.

SINGLETON, ESTHER, *The Story of the White House* (2 vols.). The McClure Co., 1907.

SMITH, MARGARET BAYARD, *First Forty Years of Washington Society*. Charles Scribner's Sons, 1906.

SMITH, MARIE, *The President's Lady*, Random House, 1964.

SMITH, PAGE, *John Adams*. Doubleday & Co., 1962.

SMITH, THEODORE CLARKE, *The Life and Letters of James A. Garfield*. Yale U. Press, 1925.

SORENSEN, THEODORE C., *Kennedy*. Harper & Row, 1965.

STONE, IRVING, *Love Is Eternal*. Doubleday & Co., 1954.

TAFT, MRS. WILLIAM HOWARD, *Recollections of Full Years*. Dodd, Mead & Co., 1914.

TAYLOR, RICHARD, *Destruction and Reconstruction*. Longmans, Green & Co., 1879.

THAYER, MARY VAN RENSSELAER, *Jacqueline Bouvier Kennedy*. Doubleday & Co., Inc., 1961.

TORBERT, ALICE COYLE, *Eleanor Calvert and Her Circle*. National Society of Colonial Dames, 1950.

TRUMAN, MARGARET, *Souvenir*. McGraw-Hill Book Co., 1956.

TYLER, LYON G., *Letters and Times of the Tylers* (vol. II). Whittet & Shepperson, 1885.

WEBSTER, SIDNEY, *Franklin Pierce and His Administration*. D. Appleton & Co., 1892.

WHARTON, ANNE HOLLINGSWORTH, *Social Life in the Early Republic*. J. B. Lippincott Co., 1902.

WHITE, WM. ALLEN, *A Puritan in Babylon*. The Macmillan Co., 1939.

WHITTEN, MARY ORMSBEE, *First First Ladies (1789-1865)*. Hastings House, 1948.

WILSON, EDITH BOLLING, *My Memoir*. The Bobbs Merrill Co., 1936.

YOUNG, J. RUSSELL, *Around the World with General Grant* (2 vols). The American News Co., 1879.